MANUFACTURING TALES

MANUFACTURING TALES
Sex and Money in Contemporary Legends

Publications of the American Folklore Society, New Series
General Editor, Patrick B. Mullen

Gary Alan Fine

THE UNIVERSITY OF TENNESSEE PRESS / KNOXVILLE

Copyright © 1992 by The University of Tennessee Press / Knoxville.
All Rights Reserved. Manufactured in the United States of America.
Cloth: 1st printing, 1992.
Paper: 1st printing, 1992; 2nd printing, 1994.

The paper in this book meets the minimum requirements of the American National
Standard for Permanence of Paper for Printed Library Materials. ⊖ The binding
materials have been chosen for strength and durability.

Library of Congress Cataloging in Publication Data

Fine, Gary Alan.
      Manufacturing tales: sex and money in contemporary legends /
      Gary Alan Fine.—1st ed.
      p.   cm.—(Publications of the American Folklore Society.
      New series)
      Includes bibliographical references and index.
      ISBN 0-87049-754-5 (cloth: alk. paper)
      ISBN 0-87049-755-3 (pbk.: alk. paper)
      1. Sex—Folklore. 2. Money—Folklore. I. Title. II. Series:
Publications of the American Folklore Society. New series (Unnumbered)
GR462.F56 1992
398.27—dc20   91-46237
                                                                        CIP

To Sue Samuelson (1956–1991)
A Legend in Her Own Time

Contents

Tables

Figures

Introduction: Toward a Framework for Contemporary Legends

If the ballad and the *Märchen* were the archetypal forms of folklore of an earlier age, I exaggerate little to claim that in the late twentieth century the contemporary legend is the genre of narrative preference.[1] The change is in part ecological. Folklorists' interpretations of the ballad and the *Märchen* were based on the fact that these narratives were performed in semi-isolated folk communities and diffused through trade and migration routes; in contrast, contemporary legends thrive in societies crosscut by multiple communication channels and relatively open networks.[2] These modern texts are less confined to sub (folk)-communities and have passed into national (mass) culture, often through the mass media (Mullen 1972; Bird 1972).

But what are these "legends"? Robert Georges (1981:18) once playfully, but significantly, suggested that for most folklorists: "A legend is a story or narrative that may not be a story or narrative at all; it is set in a recent or historical past that may be conceived to be remote or antihistorical or not really past at all; it is believed to be true by some, false by others, and both or neither by most." Bill Ellis (1989b) claims that legends are chameleonlike and, pointing to the situated qualities of this genre, suggests that the proper question is "when is a legend?" Ellis emphasizes how a legend names, translates, polishes, and reports a claimed happening.

Within the subgenre, contemporary legend, the problem is even more complex. The label "contemporary legend" is a compromise of convenience. What routinely was, and still frequently is, called "urban legend," and sometimes "modern legend," is now often labeled "contemporary legend"—as exemplified by the recently organized International Society for Contemporary Legend Research.[3] The question of whether we should define our genres geographically ("urban") or temporally ("contemporary") has not been solved adequately, but the creation and naming of a scholarly organization has solved the issue for the moment. And, indeed, my own preference is for a temporal base for this term that refers to narratives transmitted beyond city boundaries. Within the introduction, then, I shall refer to these phenomena as "contemporary legends." These legends are not always urban, often are transmitted in suburbs and are about suburban life, and sometimes are about rural areas and small towns. Neither are they always contemporary, in the sense of being found only in the late twentieth century. Texts currently being transmitted can be traced back centuries (e.g., Simpson 1983, Ellis 1983), but at least, when told, they typically refer to contemporary events. These texts hold a mirror—a distorted one—to the social and economic conditions of modern, Western, industrial society. By this I mean that they depict topics of public concern—allegations about "real" happenings and metaphors that include "symbolic truths." Some legends, classified as "mercantile legends," deal explicitly with the consequences of mass marketing and the strictures of industrial enterprises; others report sexual mores, alienation, or the rise in public violence. In their ability to borrow from and to transcend the traditional and the current, contemporary legends are a variety of what is now frequently termed "postmodern" discourse. Contemporary legends represent an attempt to use traditional themes in a post-industrial context, in which "late capitalism" and "sexual license" are seen as contending with the anchors of morality. These legends, using techniques of "bricolage," borrow traditional themes, placing them in current contexts.

Recognizing the impossibility of presenting a fully acceptable definition, and hoping for a plausible one, I propose that a "contemporary legend" is a narrative that a teller presents to an audience in the context of their relationship. The text is an account of a happening in which the narrator or an immediate personal contact was not directly involved,[4] and is presented as a *proposition for belief;* it is not always believed by speaker or audience, but it is presented as something that *could* have occurred and is told *as if* it happened. These occurrences are notable happenings of the kind that are allegedly "strange but true." The content of the narrative involves events that happened in contemporary society and depicts persons, relations, organizations, and institutions that are recognized by narrator and audience to characterize the modern world.

While the definition of this genre, like most definitions, only captures "family resemblances," it serves as an operational definition, with a certain penumbra of ambiguity. Contemporary legends, as is true for legends generally (Dégh and Vázsonyi 1976), tend to be relatively formless, and, as a consequence, definitions that examine formal characteristics of the text have little descriptive power. Like so many genres, we know them when we hear them, and we know that other verbal discourses fall outside the definition.

My preference is for an inclusive definition—a choice that is particularly salient when surveying the connection between the related concepts of rumor and legend. Although some scholars sharply differentiate rumor and legend, I sense that the boundary between the two is hazy. Rumor, too, presents a proposition for belief. Like legends, rumors may be traditional and may respond to the immediate social situation of the performers. Rumors typically are defined (e.g., Rosnow and Fine 1976) as truth claims that lack secure standards of evidence, i.e., they are unauthenticated information. Needless to say what constitutes such standards is a matter of debate. However, a key feature of the definition involves "the structure of credibility." Legends typically are known by virtue of their more extensive narrative structure, coupled with their traditional content (see Allport and Postman 1947, Mullen 1972). Often one finds the same text presented in an elaborated or restricted fashion—the same material can be conveyed through different styles of discourse. One wonders whether the competence of the teller or the constraints of the situation should be the *sine qua non* of rumor or legend. Admittedly some texts demand a detailed narrative structure ("The Hookman"), while others are easily summarized in a statement ("the president will resign tomorrow"). But sometimes rumor and legend do overlap, and some texts fit into both categories. I refer to those texts that have some longevity and the possibility of narrative expansion as legends, but I am less fanatical than some in dividing these two genres, and often refer to rumors when making my point.

For the construct "contemporary legend" to be usable it must be grounded in a shared understanding of the domain. That is, we need to know the approximate dimensions of the definition before we use it. Definitions wilt when they are created *de novo*. So, we understand the central features of contemporary legends, if not all of their boundaries, by considering some of the more common examples of the genre.[5] "The Vanishing Hitchhiker" is among the best studied of all contemporary legends (e.g., Beardsley and Hankey 1942, Jones 1944, George 1972, Montell 1974, Wilson 1975, Fish 1976, Brunvand 1981:24–40) and one of the few contemporary legends with a motif number assigned to it in Baughman's motif index of Anglo-American folktales (Motif E332.3.3.1 in Baughman 1966).

In most versions a girl is hitchhiking along a lonely road. After being picked up, she directs the driver to a local address. When the drivers arrives, the girl is no longer in the car, and, upon inquiring at the house, he learns that the girl had died some time previously, but her revenant appears regularly along the same deserted stretch of road. The hundreds of variants differ in detail, but collectively they place traditional ghostlore in a contemporary context. The girl is hitchhiking and is said to have been killed in a automobile accident, suggesting that even though this narrative had roots in earlier ghostlore, narrators transformed the text to fit modern transportation. Recent versions suggest that the hitchhiker is malevolent and will try to cause a car wreck, perhaps speaking to the current fear of murderous hitchhikers, as reflected in contemporary legends such as "The Hairy-Handed Hitchhiker" (Brunvand 1984:52–55). Contemporary legends rely on traditional themes, while placing them in new material and moral contexts. The tale, as typically narrated, does not compel the audience to accept it as "fact," but it does demand an attitude of credulity, a suspension of disbelief.[6] The event is reported as a "notable happening" (see Garfinkel 1967:37) that deserves attention, although audiences can choose the "meaning" of the text.

Another contemporary legend, one describing the acquiring of an extremely expensive recipe, reflects other basic themes commonly found in these narratives. According to this account, a consumer requests a recipe from a restaurant, hotel, or food manufacturer—many versions target either the Waldorf-Astoria Hotel in New York, which allegedly served "Red Velvet Cake" (Brunvand 1981:154–60), or Mrs. Fields Cookies (Brunvand 1989:219–26). Along with the recipe the consumer receives an outrageous bill. The consumer gains revenge by duplicating the recipe and distributing it widely. This story reflects a theme encountered frequently in this volume: hostility by the public toward large corporations which are depicted as uncaring, manipulative, hostile, greedy, and/or incompetent.

While hundreds of examples could be presented, these two synopses provide a sense of the type of narrative to which the label "contemporary legend" refers. Jan Harold Brunvand has collected files on 450 different texts of this sort, although he suggests that only a few dozen reflect clearly distinct themes and topics (Brunvand, personal communication, 1990). In order to systematize this material, scholars have begun to sort through texts, developing a classification of contemporary legend types, primarily based on the content of the major action or characters in the text (Brunvand 1987, Glazer, 1988). This classification will help to sort out the tales and permit a comparative analysis of parallel and related motifs.

Arguably the most significant gap in the scholarly treatment of urban legends involves the emphasis on legends transmitted by urban, middle-class, white Americans, often college students or the ubiquitous mass media. The diffusion of stories among people of color in the United States or among foreign nationals has generally been ignored in legend research. The examination of contemporary legends shared by minority group members has only recently begun (see, for instance, George 1972, Fry 1975, Glazer 1984, 1987, Turner 1987, Cunningham 1988, Herrera-Sobek 1988) and there is now increasing interest by scholars in continental Europe, the Pacific Rim, and the Third World (Klintberg 1986, Schmidt 1987, Simonides 1987, Virtanen 1988, Campion-Vincent 1989). Given that most researchers collect texts from those sources with whom they are most comfortable and to whom access is easiest, a bias creeps into data, as most researchers have been American white males, housed in university bureaucracies. This limits the conclusions that can be drawn, even if we believe in principle that these processes can be generalized beyond the groups examined. In presenting the outlines of a perspective on contemporary legends, I recognize the limitations of the data from which the arguments derive.

A Framework for Contemporary Legends

Four classes of variables are critical in the analysis of the dynamics of contemporary legends: 1) Social Structure: the larger societal, institutional, or communal context in which the narrative is set (see Fine 1988); 2) Personal Imperatives: the internal or intrapsychic state of the narrator (this includes memory, self-image, mood, and personality); 3) Situated Dynamics: the immediate, interactional setting or behavioral context in which the narrative is transmitted ("the performance"), and the expectations and standards of the group in which that transmission occurs; and 4) Narrative Content: the text of the narrative, as selected, altered, or ignored. A comprehensive framework must incorporate all four sets of variables: Social Structure, Personal Imperatives, Situated Dynamics, and Narrative Content.

I propose a simple model of the interconnection among these elements (see Figure I.1): a Folklore Diamond.[7] Although one can hardly deny that everything eventually affects everything else, some connections are more robust than others. Rather than draw arrows running madly in all directions, I emphasize the strongest connections: a perspective that links the external world to the content of the text, through the mediation of the person and the situation. My *primary* goal is to explain the existence, meaning, and significance of contemporary legends. Consequently the content of the contemporary legend is my "dependent variable." I ask: why do stories take the form that they do and have the content that they have?

Contemporary legends have—at least in theory—some power to influence social structure and the ordering of society, although such subtle effects typ-

Figure 1.1

The Folklore Diamond

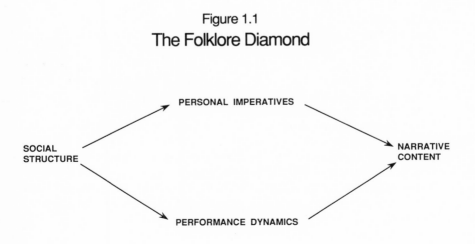

ically take an extended time to become manifest and operate in conjunction with an array of social forces, making a definitive analysis of the effects of folklore on social structure challenging. Variables do not inevitably have specific effects, but they do direct and channel behavior. People have numerous behavioral options, but most options are disregarded because of real or imagined costs, or because making that choice never seems to be an option.[8]

In the Folklore Diamond, Social Structural forces are the bedrock, "external variables," which provide a grounding for the rest of the model. Although structural forces are altered by interaction, personal characteristics, and content, these changes seem less dramatic and consequential, and I treat them as of secondary import.

Structural conditions do not directly alter or select the content and form of contemporary legends; rather they must be *mediated*. The two primary ways in which this mediation operates are through individual perception, cognition, and memory, and through public performance and audience response (Georges 1969). Both personal imperatives and situated dynamics *rely upon* the content of contemporary legends, in that individual variants are not created *de novo,* but are reconstructions of known, yet only partially remembered, texts (Bartlett, 1932). Performances are based upon these reconstructions, given the conditions of the interactional setting (Kirschenblatt-Gimblett 1975). The content of a legend does not *cause* personality, other than in the partial, occasional, and indirect way in which it affects a social system. The content of a particularly dramatic legend may make a dramatic impression on an audience member (ghost stories on frightened children, for instance), but it is a minor influence on personality and memory.

Likewise, the situated performance has a more profound influence on content than do the effects of the content of a contemporary legend on interaction, although a humorous text may set the tone of a gathering and narrative content surely influences the style of presentation. Ghost legends are told differently from humorous sexual legends (see Ellis 1981). The selection of narrative style is a consequence of content. Still, it is awkward to allege that content causes the performance. Performance skills exist prior to the learned content, and the content is fitted into a pre-existing style. Styles permit certain contents to be played in public arenas. Types of social gatherings provide venues for the performance of particular texts, whereas texts do not create venues.[9]

Although to some degree everything is linked to everything else, this insight is theoretically distracting. A parsimonious model must select a set of crucial linkages among concepts. Having provided an overview of the Folklore Diamond, I examine nodes within that framework in depth. In presenting the four major components in turn, I explore the dynamic process through which each—separately and together—creates, spreads, and maintains contemporary legends.

Social Structure

Narratives reside in a structural surround. The primary shaping forces of narrative are structural. I do not suggest that individual creativity is unimportant, and creativity will be discussed when we consider personal imperatives. Yet, individual creativity also is shaped through social structure. Social structure sets the ground for personal action.

While there are many social structural forces that might be named,[10] a few seem particularly central. Variations in any of these reverberate through the model, ultimately altering the narratives that are told. These features of structure represent the broad reality in which individuals live their lives and tell their tales.

Specifically I address four structural themes, each transcending individual action: 1) class structure; 2) demographic divisions, including race, gender, ethnicity, and age; 3) institutional structures, including state, economic, religious, educational, and familial institutions; and 4) the organization of social networks. Ultimately my concern revolves around the question: What makes our culture of such a character that these legends are so prevalent?[11]

Class Structure. Folklorists have traditionally paid little attention to the niceties of class divisions (but see Zipes 1979), despite the self-evident impact that class position has on social organization and group resources. It is the rare folklorist who struggles with the implications of economic strata and the political economy. Although the understanding of class has typically been assigned a relatively minor position within folkloristics, its influence on other social sciences has been profound. The definition of class is hotly controversial, though generally the term refers to the position, in a society, of individuals. But ultimately a social class is consequential even if it is not recognized (i.e., as a *Klasse an sich*—a class in itself), but this power is magnified when a collective consciousness flourishes (i.e., as a *Klasse für sich*—a class for itself[12]).

The recognition of class-consciousness is most evident among those who examine political folklore (Fine 1985), such as political epics (Wilson 1976), ballads and songs (Reuss 1971), or tales of outlaw heroes (Hobsbawm 1981). Contemporary legends are set in a less explicitly political discourse, but they do develop from orientations to the political order. Legends and rumors about extremely wealthy and well-known citizens reflect an indirect, if unconscious, political critique. Consider narratives that a certain celebrity (often Johnny Carson or Burt Reynolds) announced on "The Tonight Show" that the public could use his telephone credit card number to make unlimited calls (Brunvand 1984:205–208), that Paul McCartney is dead (Suczek 1972, Rosnow and Fine 1976), that a children's television celebrity (often Bozo the Clown) uttered an obscenity on the air (Brunvand 1986:184–85), that numerous political leaders have had affairs with numerous starlets, or that a black sports star frightened several old ladies in a hotel elevator when ordering his huge dog to sit ("The Elevator Incident," Brunvand 1984:18–28). One of the fascinations of gossip about celebrities (see Levin and Arluke 1987) is that this discourse reflects divisions in social class and status.

This concern with class is also evident in texts depicting the other end of the class continuum. The majority of Americans, up to 80 percent in some surveys, define themselves as middle class. They wish they were richer, but know they could be poorer. They're set in the great, bulging middle—the core of the community. Their attitude toward the wealthy, the class to which they aspire, is a stew of envy, admiration, and condescending pity. Their attitude toward the poor, the level to which they fear they may slip, blends anxiety, revulsion, charity, and condescending pity. Narratives about the "Welfare Cadillac" implicitly reflect the frustration that the middle class have with their own stultifying work life and pose the question whether they might do better striving less and being sharper. The persistent fear of the middle class is that both the upper and lower class are happier than they are and have an easier life. The protagonist of the Welfare Cadillac legend—the person who picks up a welfare check in a Cadillac—melds upper and lower class in a figure who lives off the sweat of others. This narrative is complex in the way its themes reflect social order. That the car is a Cadillac suggests to some tellers and audiences that the welfare cheat is black—perhaps an entrepreneur in the underground economy, such as a pimp or drug dealer. The meaning of the legend can be that eligibility for welfare is not checked sufficiently or that benefits are set too high. In either case there is an implicit criticism of government programs. Accounts of wordy government memos on trivial subjects (Hall 1965) or of government errors in providing VA benefits or social security also arise from and fuel the mistrust of government. Such narratives constitute a conservative, sometimes racist, critique of the welfare state. If this is false consciousness, it is quite real in the emotions that audiences feel.

The depiction of class and status differences is a regular feature of contemporary American legends, appearing within the content of the texts. The texts are structured as "realist tales," and in their implicit claims to truth they reflect the class structure—both the way that it is and, implicitly, the way that it *should be*. These texts are fragmented reflections of social and historical circumstances.

Demographic Divisions. Any large, heterogeneous society is segmented along lines that connect to the salient characteristics of actors within the society. Gender, race, and, to some degree, ethnicity, are often unthinkingly defined as how society "ought" to be divided.[13] Individuals are born into these statuses, and they have little or no control over them; such statuses are relatively impermeable, and are "ascribed," rather than "achieved." Ascribed positions are constantly referred to and they are used by society members as the basis for differential responses. Achieved statuses, positions attained by virtue of personal action, also play a critical role, but, as they are a function of decisions of social actors, I discuss them under personal imperatives.

Divisions based on ascribed statuses affect the content and performance of contemporary legends. Through the power of socialization, demographic categories shape the identity and personality of the person so categorized. Socialization shapes interests, which, in turn, has direct effects in determining who is likely to transmit which genres of folklore with which content. Not everyone will choose to tell dirty jokes or legends about an "evil" corporation.

Perhaps the demographic divisions that most dramatically affect contemporary legends are racial divisions. Patricia Turner, a pioneer in the study of contemporary legends in African-American communities, notes that what black Americans find credible differs markedly from white Americans. Few white Americans would accept as plausible that the AIDS epidemic was linked to a U.S. government experiment in biological warfare in Africa or Haiti that got out of control (Turner 1988) or that the Ku Klux Klan owns Church's Fried Chicken (Turner 1987), TROOP sportswear, or Marlboro cigarettes (see chapter 9). Such conspiracy beliefs seem paranoid to white Americans who have not experienced racial oppression and malevolent social control, but among segments of the black community the possibility seems only too real. These stories can be traced to folk beliefs about threats to blacks in previous generations (e.g., Fry 1975).

Stories that reflect racial fears are by no means limited to blacks, as the Elevator Incident, cited above, in which whites are fearful of a black celebrity, attests. Whites are willing to believe almost anything about black individuals, whereas blacks tend to focus on white-dominated institutions.

Women's folklore, now emerging as a central research domain, equally demonstrates the importance of demographic divisions. While "feminist" legends are perhaps not as thematically different from white male culture as those of blacks, they speak to concerns and fears of women. Discourse and beliefs about menstruation (Tampax stories) and sexual practices (the "Superglue Revenge" [Brunvand 1984:146–47]) are part of a rich body of traditions that are known largely by women (Johnston 1973; Fish 1972; Kalčik 1975). Men and women have distinct perspectives on the content or thematic significance of narratives that involve raw sexuality. The legend of the "Promiscuous Cheerleader"—an account of a young woman who engages in oral intercourse with the members of the team for which she is cheering and then must have her stomach pumped (see chapter 2)—is told largely among males, and relates to their fantasies about unlimited female sexuality. Gulzow and Mitchell (1980) demonstrate male fears inherent in the "Vagina Dentata" and "Incurable VD" stories, told by servicemen during the War in Vietnam. As I have demonstrated, the legend about the deliberate spread of the AIDS virus (see chapter 3, and Brunvand 1989:195–202) can be linked to fantasies of female revenge by both males and females, but with different implications. These stories can change over time, as the AIDS story originally was told about a female infecting a male, but now is known with male protagonists (AIDS Murray as well as AIDS Mary).

Perhaps the arena in which gender differences are most dramatically evident are horror stories, such as "The Hookman" (Dégh 1968, Dundes 1971) or "The Boyfriend's Death" (Dégh 1969), which reflect the threatened position of women. These stories, often narrated in the slumber parties of preadolescent or early adolescent girls (Simons 1980), remind us of the importance of age boundaries as well as those of gender. The narratives can be variously interpreted, but the fears of adult male malevolence and adolescent sexuality are central. Adolescent horror stories such as "The Man Upstairs," "The Roommate's Death," or "The Hookman" are part of this tradition (see Baker 1982:201–10, Brunvand 1981:47–69). Given that these horror stories are typically narrated by teenage girls and have females as the victims, the gendered reality of the social order and the possibilities of violence toward women are plausible themes. These texts serve as protofeminist narratives.

When one is considering ethnicity with regard to contemporary legends, the analysis becomes more complex. In contemporary American society, most forms of ethnicity[14] are shunted aside in the quest for an ethic of tolerance. Ethnic identity is bracketed and displayed in muted form on quasi-public holidays—Columbus Day, Cinque de Mayo, or St. Patrick's Day. Relatively few contemporary legends reveal dramatic ethnic effects of tellers or audiences. Responses to modernism and contemporary life are not generally mediated in ethnically based texts, although a patina of customs, holiday celebrations, foodways, naming practices, and other folklore genres lingers. Some ethnic groups, because of their recent immigrant status, hereditary characteristics, or language choices may maintain a more robust or continuous tradition than others.

One arena in which ethnicity occasionally plays a potent role, is the labeling of target figures in contemporary legends. Italian Americans suffer ethnic attack because of the popular assumption that a wealthy Italian American must be a member of the mafia, as in stories about the Mafia neighbor (Brunvand 1986:147). Texts depicting Indochinese immigrants stealing and eating pet cats and dogs (Mitchell 1987) reveal residual ethnic misunderstanding and prejudice and attempts to deal with ethnic "strangeness" in our culture. This is particularly evident with regard to recent immigrants, who have not been fully assimilated. Earlier accounts of the "inappropriate" food served in Chinese and Indian restaurants (e.g., Domowitz 1979) demonstrate that such ethnic themes are not new. Similar texts, picturing other ethnic groups, collected in Europe

(Smith 1983, Klintberg 1986), remind Americans that ethnocentrism is not limited to our own shores.

Demographic realities and, in particular, demographic changes demand attention by students of contemporary legends, both in terms of the performances of such groups and in terms of the depiction of these groups in the texts. While the virulence of *blaison populaire* has decreased, such beliefs are unlikely to vanish in a mass, heterogeneous society in which competition exists for scarce resources, and in which some groups are viewed as gaining resources that belong to others.

Institutional Structures. All complex social systems require the existence of powerful institutions that compel and constrain behavior. Institutions comprise a linked set of organizations, supported explicitly or implicitly by state structures, which strive for communally sanctioned goals. These institutions constitute the building blocks of society, the means by which things get done. Defined sociologically, an institution is a "social arrangement that channels behavior in prescribed ways in the important areas of societal life" (Eitzen with Baca Zinn 1988:592). Examples of institutions include the economy, religion, universities and other educational systems, and the family. Although institutions are defined and labeled in terms of the content of their goals, they have power because they operate through organizations, translating socially held values and norms into behaviors through techniques of socialization and social control. Organizations can be of great size (a large corporation) or be small (a family). Layers of organizations operate within an institution. The institution of religion is composed of church denominations (the United Methodist Church) as well as particular churches (Wesley Methodist Church of St. Paul, Minnesota). Norms and values are made "visible" and are given power by the presence of these recognizable groupings. With such power, it is no surprise that they should affect legend content and performance.

Organizations influence contemporary legends by affecting individuals, situations, and narrative content. In short, humans are socialized through institutions—notably the school, family, and church. These institutions help to determine the values of individuals, alter their personality, shape their interests, and teach them to communicate, by establishing the "proper" and expected ways of doing things. This socialization process inevitably influences the types of narratives people select, present, and treasure. We tell what we tell because of the institutional nexus.

Given the amount of time we spend as agents or clients of organizations, performance settings are often located within an institutional ambit. Many contemporary legends and rumors are communicated in work places (Davis 1969) or schools. Institutional agoras provide a hospitable environment for the spread of topical narratives, as social niches are made available for chats. These narratives—particularly brief rumors—frequently deal directly with the actions and plans of the organization, but even if the topic is an external one, a compelling demand for sociability promotes diffusion.

The connection between the institutional structure and the legend, mediated though it is, is particularly evident in the narrative's topic. Many legends refer directly to institutions and their foibles. The "Welfare Cadillac" legend described above has as one theme the failure of the welfare bureaucracy. The legend of the college student who received straight As (a 4.0) if his or her roommate commits suicide underlines the stress that another institution can produce. Accounts of incompetent lawyers and doctors similarly speak to the perceived dangers from social institutions, even those that ostensibly mean well.

The mercantile legends discussed throughout the volume challenge American society by criticizing the shift to anonymous, mass capitalist enterprises and state-directed bureaucracies. The diversity of narratives about McDonald's and the longevity of those about Procter & Gamble reveal the central place of economic organizations in our culture. The political economy inevitably influences the issues that narrators feel are tellable.

Narratives about religious denominations or cults (e.g., Catholics, Jews, Mormons, or Unification Church members) testify to the significance of sacred institutions; indeed, the legends seem to attribute to such institutions a greater conspiratorial power than they actually have. We spread rumors and legends about the societal institutions that are most symbolically central—just as we gossip about those who mean the most to us (Spacks 1985, Levin and Arluke 1988). Both rumor and gossip are mechanisms of social control (Lumley 1925, Merry 1984) that punish those persons or institutions that stray too far from the community's expectations.

One last institution demands special attention: the mass media. The contemporary legend is a distinctive folklore genre because of the role of the mass media in its diffusion (Bird 1972, Koenig 1985). Although the media do not create these legends, they provide a forum in which diverse audiences are exposed. Texts are placed on the public agenda. The competition among media outlets encourages the presentation of particularly dramatic texts. The mass media have significant effects on performance and presentation but are less directly relevant to the personal imperatives of narrators, although even here individual selections are given voice by media organizations.[15]

Networks. Every social system is characterized by interconnections of relationships. These connections are based not only on personal choice or random happenstance but on the structure of the system. Co-presence in an institutional environment, demographic and class similarity, and the life-world effects of one's social location, such as on residential choices, constrain and channel social networks.

We can conceive of networks in terms of individual personal relationships and on a more "macro" level as links among groups (Granovetter 1973, Fine and Kleinman 1979, 1983). The diffusion of contemporary legends depends on the structure of both personal and societal networks (Greenberg 1973, Dégh and Vázsonyi 1975, Fine 1980, 1987). People narrate material to acquaintances whom they believe will be receptive. Once narrated, a contemporary legend can spread rapidly within a tight-knit group or in an organization in which there is sustained interaction among members. One's placement within a social network affects the likelihood of one's knowing or spreading a text (Caplow 1947, Rosnow and Fine 1976). In analyzing the diffusion of a contemporary legend about a death from Pop Rocks candy and a rumor about the breaking of a school window, I discovered that social standing and popularity affected the likelihood of an individual's having heard the story (see chapter 5). While outsiders may be early narrators, once diffusion begins, high-status individuals are more likely to be narrators. Narrating a contemporary legend is a means of gaining audience attention, of capturing the floor and receiving esteem.

But how are contemporary legends spread so widely and rapidly? Some "juicy" texts that are both dramatic and symbolically important can spread nationally in days or weeks without benefit of the mass media. What "interlocks" exist among tightly knit groups? Some individuals are members of several groups simultaneously or sequentially. Legends move with their narrators. Other individuals move from group to group because of a structural role in which they are embedded, such as invited speakers who address many groups or those entrepreneurs who sell Tupperware under the auspices of local housewives. Finally, there are acquaintance relations or "weak ties" (Granovetter 1973). While not as strong as the intimate ties of a small group, these ties may be sufficient to generate verbal entertainment. Penpals, distant cousins, business contacts, or friends living apart spread legends. Mark Granovetter suggests that these "weak ties" are of particular importance for social action and information transfer. With the advent of information technologies, including copier machines (e.g., Barrick 1972, Dundes and Pagter 1975, Preston and Preston 1981, Smith 1987), computer networks, long-distance telephones and, most recently, FAX machines,[16] adults have a powerful diffusion network. Computer "bulletin boards" with their informal, chatty, and humorous notes are particularly efficient in transmitting legends; indeed, one network specializes in folklore communication. For children, the network is less extensive, but because of residential mobility, phone calls, vacations, and national and regional gatherings, such as sports tournaments, church retreats, summer camps, or scout jamborees, diffusion may be rapid.

The form of diffusion affects narrative style. Xeroxlore requires that the text be written or drawn; computer transmissions are accessible to a wide group of strangers and also involves a written or designed text; telephones are based on aural communication; brief face-to-face encounters among those who rarely see each other demand rapid updating (Yerkovich 1977); and close friends should be told "everything" in dramatic detail. The circumstance of the relationship and the channel affect performance.

A central way in which individuals are woven together in a social network is through the division of labor. Occupational structures may be simple in pastoral or peasant farming communities, where class structures are rudimentary, but in complex societies work possibilities explode. According to the United States Department of Labor, there are now over twenty thousand job specialties. We depend on numerous other people for our welfare. This dependence provides for interaction and, consequently, the spread of information. Contemporary legends allow acquaintances to communicate in a way that is dramatic, involving, and entertaining. The contemporary legend is a *lingua franca* for those who because of their backgrounds might otherwise have little in common. All that is required is a spark for narration, as one reference leads to the next. The links between occupational workers provide a path for rapid diffusion.

The mass media are the most dramatic "specialized" networks, operating as independent sources of diffusion and in conjunction with interpersonal communication through "media-enhanced conduits" (Bill Ellis, personal communication, 1990). In media transmission the connection between narrator and audience is assumed, and the style of narration may differ considerably from interpersonal transactions. Media—especially the truly mass media, such as television, radio, and mass circulation magazines—can be conceived as the nodes, or central actors, of an enormous network. They are undiscriminating in selecting who learns what. As a result of open access, much of the mass media attempts to avoid offending, particularly avoiding explicit sexual legends or treading gently with texts that attack corporate advertisers, emphasizing the falsity of the claims. More specialized media may revel in sexual material or may give prominence to those tales that attack large, mistrusted institutions. They know their audience, and like all narrators pitch their discourse so it will be seen as entertaining, informative, and appropriate.

Taken together, class effects, demographic divisions, institutional structures, and social networks suggest how the supra-individual structure of society channels the performance and content of contemporary legends. This background, often ignored by folklorists, is the bedrock for the choices and options available to narrators and audiences.

Personal Imperatives

Folklore and psychology have traditionally had a prickly relationship. While twentieth-century folklorists recognize that the character ("personality") of the narrator is an important determinant of narrative style and content (e.g., Azadovski 1926, Dégh 1969), they resist reducing texts to impulses of the self. Yet, the centrality of the self is salient when one examines those genres (folktales, epics, ballads) that few community members perform. Thomas Burns (1976) has demonstrated that even variations from a core text, such as a smutty joke, may be understood through the personal equations of the performers. Still, for texts known widely and performed by individuals who are not genre specialists, the characteristics of tellers are of diminished significance when compared to those who perform lengthy poetic epics.

Perhaps the root of the objections to a psychological or psychoanalytic approach to folklore has stemmed from resistance to "placing society on the couch" or looking for strands of "national character." Although this approach is intriguing, it implies, for some, a whiff of racism and national chauvinism. Conclusions are singularly difficult to prove to a skeptical reader. The work of psychological anthropologists of mid-century such as Kardiner (1945) and Roheim (1952) are barely read today: their claims are too broad for most folkloristic analysis, particularly the metaphor of society as a person writ large and the notion of dreams as origins of traditional texts.

That there are objections to psychologizing does not eliminate the possibility that the internal states of actors play a critical role in their narrative constructions. Personal characteristics, personality, and drives should not be ignored. The "who" is as important as the "how" and the "what." I discuss four components of internal states, recognizing the lack of research; much of my analysis is a research agenda, rather than a literature review. I consider: 1) the personal self, 2) unconscious motives, 3) mood states, and 4) rational choice.

The Personal Self. Perhaps no area of social psychology has been studied with as much fervor as the self. The self represents a nexus between social forces and individual principles. As sociological social psychologists have emphasized from the writing of Charles Horton Cooley (1902) onward, the self is shaped through social interaction. Through the responses of others we learn who and what we are. From our earliest years we find ourselves mirrored in others. Personality is, from this perspective, part of socialization. Instead of conceiving of personality as something that is mystifyingly internal, we can understand personality traits as standard modes of responding to external stimuli. Personality is known through public behavior. For instance, we know some people as "outgoing," others as "shy," still others as "aggressive." We know this not because of how they feel, but how we see them respond.

The personal self also incorporates the individual's reaction to his or her social placement. Here demographic divisions affect the self. A person's choices are not free, but are affected by the groups to which he or she belongs. In other words, a self is a demographic self. The public consequences of race, gender, and ethnicity helps to define *who* a person is, through patterns of social-ization, experiences with institutions, and placements in social networks. These experiences shape individuals.

Both the feeling self (or personality) and the demographic self channel in-terests, and these interests, such as leisure pursuits or work skills, affect one's orientation to contemporary legends. We gravitate to things that fascinate us and stray from those with little charm.

Folklorists strive to determine whether personality, attitudes, self-concept, or identity affect the likelihood of knowing or spreading particular contempo-rary legends. Although these effects are typically modest, some orientations to folklore may be tethered to political attitudes. Does one's stance toward capital-ism correspond to the likelihood of accepting stories that corporations engage in nefarious behavior? Are mercantile legends swayed by attitudes? I have already suggested that key demographic divisions, such as gender and race, affect the diffusion and credibility of legends, but whether features of the self or person-ality play a mediating role in this process remains unexplored.

Unconscious Motives. Freudian psychoanalysis (and other branches of psychiatry, see Drake 1969, Hufford 1974) is a rich source of interpretations of contemporary legends, even though often scorned by nonanalytically trained folklorists (see chapter 1 and Oring 1975). From this perspective, legends are a technique of evading psychic repression. Like dreams and jokes, legends per-mit socially sanctioned projection. Even if one rejects Roheim's claim that folklore begins in dreamwork, dreams and narrative involve working through emotional stress. Psychological analyses are particularly compelling for leg-ends that deal directly or indirectly with sexual and aggressive themes, such as symbolic castration. Adolescent horror legends offer abundant opportunities for this kind of speculation. For instance, Alan Dundes relies on psychoanalytic theory to explain the Hookman legend. In this well-known tale, a maniac with a large metal hook on the stump of one arm attacks an adolescent couple parked in Lovers' Lane. When the alarmed boy revs his automobile in an attempt to get away, the hook is pulled from the maniac's arm and is later found attached to the door on the girl's side of the car. Dundes suggests that the legend reflects the teenaged audience's fear of its own imminent sexuality. Dundes (1971:30) writes:

> It . . . appears to be a narrative from a girl's point [of] view, a narrative that
> seems to summarize teen-age girls' fears about parking with their boyfriends. In
> the legend, we find an expression of the so-called double standard: the boy is ex-
> pected to try to make out, the girl is expected to resist. . . . The girl is frightened
> by the report of the hook that may have sexual overtones. Girls fear that boys out
> on dates will be "all hands," that is, the boy's hands will be constantly engaged in
> exploring various parts of the girl's body. . . . The typical fear of the girl might
> then be that a boy's hand, signifying relatively elementary necking, might sud-

denly become a hook (an erect, aggressive phallus). . . . If the hook were a phallic substitute, then it would make perfect sense for the hook to be severed as a
result of the girl instigating the sudden move to return home. . . . One way of
keeping a sexually aggressive boy at bay is to castrate him!

Michael Carroll (1987; see also Ridley 1967, Rosenthal 1971) describes a
rumor about a boy castrated in a shopping center restroom. A young boy goes
into the men's room by himself, and later is discovered castrated, lying in a pool
of blood. Carroll suggests that the child is usually about five years old, the age
at which a boy is not supposed to follow his mother to the toilet. Although this
text has often been characterized as revealing themes of racial or ethnic prejudice and elements of "blood libel" (e.g., Toelken 1979:176–78), Carroll suggests that the age of the child—the Oedipal age—and the fact that the legend is
frequently told by mothers is critical to the interpretation of this gruesome tale.
The narrative motivation of the tale is located in the unconscious wishes of the
female tellers: it is a female castration fantasy aimed at males:

> females repeat the story in all its gory details *not* because it reflects a desire to pro-
> tect children, but rather *because a story that emphasizes the castration of a young
> boy reflects the gratification of their unconscious desire to castrate a male.*
> [1987:219, emphasis in original]

Carroll asserts, but does not prove, that "a great many" adult females have such
an unconscious desire (Carroll 1987:230).

The fact that this text first emerged in the 1960s at precisely the time that
women were recognizing their positions of structural inequality suggests that
this legend, along with the dead baby jokes of the same period (Dundes 1979),
were narrative attempts to cope with the lived experience of gender bias. Carroll contends that the story will continue to be narrated "as long as there is a
public emphasis upon the social inequalities between males and females in our
society" (1987:223).

In judging the validity of the arguments put forth by Dundes, Carroll, and
others, we must accept the existence of unconscious urges. Such an acceptance
is not inevitable, although one could hardly deny the existence of unspoken beliefs and feelings that are only expressed after prodding. Whether this is the
uncovering of a deep "unconscious" or a shaded "pre-conscious" can be de-
bated. Jokes and legends are effective techniques of expression because they are
projected outward: jokes are defined as "not serious" and legends are defined as
events that "really happened." Both shield the self from the implications of the
narrative.

How can we judge an unconscious that we can only discover indirectly? In
"Evaluating Psychoanalytic Folklore: Are Freudians Ever Right?" (chapter 1) I
argue that folklorists should rely on two criteria to judge the adequacy of psychoanalytic interpretations of folklore texts: first, internal consistency—does

the explanation account for all or most of the core details in the story?; second, external validity—does the explanation account for the historical and situational contexts in which the narrative is spread? Using these criteria Dundes's explanation of the Hookman legend is persuasive. Carroll, in contrast, needs to present more information about who tells the story, where, and when. He does not analyze the "details" of the shopping center men's room or the pool of blood, focusing only on the castration. While Carroll's claims are provocative, the absence of texts and the lack of a more comprehensive explanation vitiates the power of his presentation.

External validity connects the understanding of unconscious motivation to performance and to social structure. Unconscious needs are shaped by networks in which a person is embedded and by demographic position (e.g., gender). The unconscious, while not controllable, is not random, and follows the same channels as conscious thought.

Mood States. Social psychologists frequently distinguish between *traits* and *states*. Traits are the relatively stable and autonomous components of the self (e.g., personality *traits*), whereas states are more situational and evanescent. Researchers debate the weight of these two components of self, but it should be evident that whatever its weight, the state of mind ("mood") of a narrator affects the performance of the legend.

This is one reason that alcohol and, in some circles, illicit drugs are found in intimate congress with narrations. Dirty jokes, for instance, are often told under the stimulus of liquid refreshment. Walle (1976) has demonstrated that dirty jokes are told by those aroused to gauge or increase the arousal of those with whom they share a space. Legends with erotic themes may be shared in similar circumstances. It is a reasonable, if unproven, surmise that some texts will be more likely to be narrated when one is expansively euphoric, and others will be shared under conditions of anger, frustration, or paranoia. Gossipy stories particularly have the reputation of being deployed to express hostile feelings.

Perhaps the most dramatic evidence of the effects of mood on narrative is found in rumors. Tamotsu Shibutani, working from the sociological approach to collective behavior known as "emergent norm theory," describes the case of a milling crowd, searching for information in a situation laced with fear and tension. Shibutani (1966:31) notes that: "In disasters one of the first things that men seek, after saving themselves, is news. Sometimes they become so desperate for such information that they get careless about its source." Such emotional conditions predispose persons and groups to accept whatever information fits their expectations. Under stress and with low critical ability (Chorus 1953) they are primed to believe, spread, and transform the rumors. A shared narrative community often forms in the aftermath of disasters and other traumatic events such as assassinations. Emotions channel narratives. Although the effect of mood is dramatic in "hot news," such as rumors, a similar process is likely, in attenuated form, in contemporary legends. Sharing a "newsworthy" story reveals a willingness to be sociable and to be part of a community. Depressed people are rarely effective narrators. Contemporary legends have similarities to rumors, but unlike those brief rumors spread in the midst of disaster and stress, legendary narratives are more often shared in tranquility, and are more associated with sociability than with strain.[17] These emotions connect to "good times"—the enjoyment of acquaintances, friends, lovers, and relatives.

Narration provides an outlet for the expression of felt emotion, and may be part of what Hochschild (1983) has termed "emotion work"—the public display of an emotional state as a function of one's role. For instance, comedians are committed to exhibiting certain emotions during a performance, whether or not these correspond to their internal states. Mood must bow to organizational demands (the comedy club, television show), and recursively this influences the performance. The organizational contingencies set by an organization shape the lived experience of the narrator, and this lived experience affects how the person is revealed through behavior.

Rational Choice. A fourth topic connected to individual action has rarely been linked to folkloric analysis, although in the past decade it has steadily expanded from its "home" in economics into political science, sociology, and psychology. This is the concept of "rational action." Rational actor theory proclaims that human behavior can be adequately, if incompletely, understood if we think of each actor—or each group of actors—as operating out of a desire to maximize rewards and minimize costs. This approach reminds one of neoclassical economics, although with more socially sophisticated models (e.g., Becker 1976, Hechter 1987, Coleman 1990). These theorists attempt to transcend the individual agent to demonstrate how social institutions and group behavior, such as marriage markets or communal solidarity, can be explained by seeing each agent operating as if he or she were a rational sharpie, aware of the full array of constraints and advantages. While there is disagreement on the extent to which these assumptions must hold, there is a core belief that a calculus of value is of explanatory use.

As noted, this approach has not been applied to folklore—the closest analyses are those few that are grounded in behaviorism (e.g., Bachrach 1962), a related, if less analytically developed, perspective. Whatever the final shape of rational actor theory, people often act in ways that they perceive, either explicitly or barely, are in line with their own interests. In all social situations there are costs and benefits. Is narration a cost or a benefit? For some, narrating is desirable: one gains the attention of an audience, and some individuals seek this. One may also gain esteem. Yet, there are costs as well: the energy involved in narration and the possibility of audience rejection. In addition, while narrating, one cannot be listening and gaining *those* benefits. In being an audience, one gains information, is entertained, and has an opportunity to compare one's experiences or knowledge with others. On the other hand, when listening, one is forced to remain in a certain location and is deprived of the possibility of finding more rewarding alternatives. Everyone has had the experience of being caught in a cocktail party conversation, heading nowhere, while other more scintillating conversations swirl around. Mechanisms of social control bind us in narrative traps, and demand that we participate as narrators ourselves. There is an informal rule in many performance settings, particularly of short forms, such as jokes, contemporary legends, gossipy anecdotes, or rumors, that everyone takes a turn—narrating, commenting on, or embroidering. This system of turn-taking does not distribute turns at talk equally, but it tends to assure that each speaker will both have an audience and be an audience. The more the production of a narrative is seen as a specialized task, as with ballad singing or the recital of epic poetry, the more the expectation of equal participation is abrogated. The more participants in the gathering, the less important is it that each one participate actively. A dyadic interaction would rapidly disintegrate if turn-taking did not occur, whereas the structure of larger groups permits that there be non-narrators.

The rational choice perspective emphasizes that the participation of each individual depends on a decision grounded on available options and choices. These options and choices are structured through processes of social control and group surveillance. The potential narrator who knew that he or she would be discredited by active participation would be unlikely to narrate. Likewise, some narrators are impelled to share tales by the evaluation of how others might define their silence.

Folklorists have not framed their research so as to be open to rational choice analysis. However, this model has the virtue of recognizing that performance is a service that is provided by a supplier to those who are, for the moment, placed into the role of clients. The rational choice perspective clarifies the connection between the structures in which individuals are embedded and how their performances are shaped. It also, by implication, recognizes that some content will prove more usable than other content.

In examining the personal imperatives involved in the narration of contemporary legends, I draw from models that suggest that the self is relatively stable and unchangeable, either as a result of emotional socialization (unconscious motivations) or because of structural position (demographic features), and, further, that the self is both calculating (rational choice) and controlled by local experiences of the moment (mood). These approaches emphasize the critical role that the social actor plays in the construction and performance of contemporary legends. To the extent that actors behave similarly, these factors have general applicability and permit us to predict the use of and response to legends without resorting to knowledge of idiosyncratic human beings.

Performance Dynamics

Consider the construction of contemporary legends: the nuances of performance. More than for many genres of folklore, performance dynamics matter in understanding contemporary legends. It is not that performances are typically artful, they are not; rather, they are presented within the context of interaction, and involve a "collaborative performance." In this section I discuss four components of performance situations: 1) setting, including the spatial and temporal aspects of performance, 2) style and "texture," 3) interactional purpose, and 4) audience response. Each has a direct bearing on the *doing* of contemporary legends.

Setting. Contemporary legends, like all folklore, are situated within a particular community. I have noted this when considering the structural features of background variables, but it also applies to where and how these narratives are performed. The structural conditions of community life produce the settings in which performances occur. The economic organization of the community, for instance, affects the existence of public spaces and whether these spaces encourage group interaction (see Jacobs 1961, Whyte 1988); some communities have malls, others have busy street corners, while still others have courtyard squares. The spatial arrangements in which individuals stand or sit determine the groups that are likely to form. Is the space conducive to loud narrating or raucous laughter? Must juicy stories be told in hushed voices because of concern over who else might overhear, as in schools or under brutal state regimes?

One way in which the setting channels the performance of a contemporary legend is through situational *monitoring* (Hechter 1987). Group members receive rewards or incur costs by virtue of the observations of their actions by agents of social control. An agent might be a parent, a teacher, a policeman, or even other children or adults who feel that they have rights and responsibilities to respond to the narrator's words. Because of the possibility of monitoring, it is not surprising that children will cautiously watch for adults when narrating dirty jokes or sexual legends (see Fine 1987). Settings defined as private and not susceptible to monitoring will be particularly amenable to transmission of this material. Monitors, of course, hope to gain access to these types of settings because of the likelihood of finding disreputable, sanctionable material.

Related to the setting is the connection between mood and location. Some places facilitate emotional response that, in turn, influence narratives. Workers in certain occupations are expected to engage in "emotion work" and so circumstances direct the kinds of possible talk (Hochschild 1983). Likewise, some places generate emotions. Police stations may produce fear among those who visit them; amusement parks are expected to generate amusement.

Analyses of contemporary legends suggest that the face-to-face narration often occurs when social control is mild—in informal settings. While the location itself may be formal, such as school or work, the particular occasion of the telling is not. These narrations occur within lightly monitored corners of the setting—on coffee breaks or at recess. Much photocopy lore is found within offices, in places that transcend the boundaries between the formal and informal, public and private, such as cubicle walls or employee bulletin boards (Dundes and Pagter 1975). Similarly urban legends may fill in sermons or lectures in slots reserved for frothy, attention-getting anecdotes (Brunvand 1989). Although media diffusion of legends may be authoritative and serious, and lead to the possibility of panic (accounts of child-snatching or vicious hitchhikers), personal narration rarely has this quality.

The temporal order of a social system also influences performance. Some settings have more free time built into them than others, and this unmonitored time permits the sharing of contemporary legends. Because rumors and legends can be compressed, they can be fitted into settings inaccessible to longer texts, but such transmission still requires the existence of a focused gathering that can maintain an audience. The time involved is not the time of a single individual, but the coordination of the schedules of several actors.

A setting provides a link between the structural features of the environment, including the institutional order and network coordination, and the actual production of the discourse. It is a funnel for narrative possibilities.

Style and Texture. The first thing that most audiences—academic and folk—listen for in a text is its content; yet, the aesthetic qualities of *how* the narrative is performed are crucial to analysis. The paraverbal, nonverbal, and word choices of narratives—their texture (Dundes 1964)—influence the meaning of texts to audiences, even if these effects flicker at the edges of awareness. As Bill Ellis has reminded students of contemporary legends, capturing the precise telling of an contemporary legend may be critical to analysis (Ellis 1987:31–32). Ellis presents a detailed transcription of a text of the Hookman demonstrating that the text suggests that the maniac is a moral custodian, an embodiment of society's injunction against adolescent sexuality. This claim can be seen in the text and in the paraverbal reactions to the text. Ultimately, the issue in data collection and in detailed presentation involves the purpose to which the material will be put. In some instances, presenting synopses may be more prudent, and certainly more efficient, than detailed textual analysis. Still, this textual approach is in line with "performance theory" and reminds us that the details of a narration may be at variance with our stereotypes.

Surrounding rules of presentation is narrative style, which connects to the formal and informal rules of those written and oral registers in which contemporary legends are transmitted. While "contemporary legend" is a shorthand "genre" label, it may be more precise to think of these narratives as abutting on other genres. Some of what we readily label contemporary legends have characteristics of jokes. They are told to amuse, to make an audience laugh.[18] Although by virtue of their designation as legend they are told as true, no narrator *really* expects the audience to accept them as fact. Some legends that are not believed are told explicitly as jokes, as when comedy shows, such as "Saturday Night Live," perform sketches that portray transformed versions of contemporary legends—for instance, the kitten in the microwave or the Kentucky Fried Rat. Other legends that play off "serious" legends, similar to the way that shaggy dog stories play off jokes, have been termed "humorous anti-legends" (Vlach 1971). Mildly risque legends, such as the "Nude Housewife" (Brunvand 1981:139–40) or the "Nude Surprise Party" (Brunvand 1981:140–46) can be transmitted in either way.

Some contemporary legends have the texture of rumors; they are told as propositions for belief, with an implicit request for additional information. Other contemporary legends may be told as personal experience narratives (Dégh and Vázsonyi 1983), with the narrator having a main, if not always factually accurate, role in the narrative (see Dégh and Vázsonyi 1978, Slotkin 1988). Two explanations arise: first, these may be false stories knowingly told for their entertainment (or other) value, or second, they may be actual lived experience, for which a traditional story provides a convenient and compelling explanation (Bill Ellis, personal communication, 1990). The cultural name for the experience provides a basis under which stories can be communicated. Finally, a few, such as ghost tales (Ellis 1981) may have characteristics of *Märchen* in their requirement for a willing suspension of disbelief. These genre constraints determine the form of the presentation.

The role of style is dramatic when contemporary legends are written, as in newspapers. Even here their presentation can take several forms. Some columnists treat these texts as sources for play, or as a falsehood ("myth") to debunk. In other instances, the contemporary legend may be presented as "news"—as something that "really happened" or as a widely held claim with public policy implications. Folklorists have learned to follow advice columns (Ann Landers, Dear Abby) for the data that these sources provide about public concerns. Indeed, some legends *emerge* directly from newspaper columns, before taking on a life of their own in public narrations (Brunvand 1990b).

A key component of the contemporary legend is the style and form of the narration. "Texture" can be connected to the characteristics of the narrator and to the structural demands of the location in which this narration occurs. A single contemporary legend may be told in varied forms and styles depending on circumstances (see Brunvand's [1989:26–36, 151–61] discussion of "Curses! Broiled Again" and "The Hare Drier") and the level of belief to which narrator and audience are willing to accord it.

Interactional Purpose. All intentional communication is motivated. Discourse is always purposeful. This constitutes what philosopher J. L. Austin (1975) terms the "illocutionary force" of an utterance—that is, what the speaker is attempting to do through that communication. From this perspective, narrative is linked to pragmatic philosophy, and folklorists have become increasingly sensitized to the "pragmatics of performance." Speech-act theory and pragmatics connect with the issues previously raised about the genre and texture of a performance; the purpose stands behind the form. Folkloristics is now intimately linked to discourse analysis.

In analyzing the purpose of a narration we are confronted by the model of interaction given substance by Erving Goffman (1959): the need for individuals to engage in strategies of "presentation of self" or "impression management." Goffman's model assumes that the fundamental purposes of interaction are the related goals of making the actor "look good"—morally and socially worthy in the light of collective values—in the eyes of those who are monitoring his actions, and to make the interaction in which he or she is embedded flow more smoothly. Each goal is rewarding for the actors.

Transmitting a contemporary legend can be a ritual of solidarity, and contributes to the establishment of the relationship. The telling connects those who are party to it within a common informational preserve.[19] They share information that may be valuable or entertaining, and this differentiates them from those outside their group. If knowledge or belief is power, than such communication provides power and reflects the consensus within the community. If one person narrates, the other is under pressure to do the same. An exchange relationship develops based on the pretense of mutual respect. In this way, the interactional purpose solidifies the structural form of the network relationship.

Ellis (1987) depicts how an erotic text, "The Hookman," is embedded within natural conversation and the role that it plays in defining the statuses and the standings of female college students in terms of suggesting the legitimate place of their own sexuality. Through examining the "verbatim" details of the text as it is played, Ellis argues that these speakers are challenging "conventional morality," while supporting the "conventional" morality of college women. Comments by the primary teller about the act of narration ("metanarrative"), demonstrating her competence and sophistication, enhance her ability to control the story while permitting her two listeners to contribute to the construction of the text (p. 50; see Fine 1986). These texts are sensitive to the dynamics of the event as a ribald gathering, and, as a result, will be contextualized to make them relevant to the interactional tone. A similar narrative told at a slumber party of junior high school girls (or by a girl's mother) would have dramatically different comments surrounding it. The process of contextualization is a common feature of narrative, although there are circumstances in which texts are decontextualized or recontextualized to separate them from the setting or to provide a basis for a new setting.

Particularly when legends are presented through collaboration (Georges

1981), tellers share a determination to make the scene work. Participants are often friends, a relationship history that makes telling easier, because they can rely on shared biographies and understandings, and also because they are less willing to see their positive relations destroyed through a gaffe. In longstanding relationships participants attempt to insure that the material is brought off without a hitch, because such smooth interaction gives testimony to the strength and vitality of the relationship.

One is struck by the association between positive affect and the desire to please, inform, and amuse through narrative. Narration is linked to consensus building. Even though contemporary legends may contain within them negative emotion, these feelings are limited by the framing of the story as the occasion for good fellowship and the presentation of interesting material. The horror of the content is placed within a performance setting in which there is no immediate danger. The only danger is that the narration will not be perceived as a success—an interpretation that may smear all who are party to it.

Audience Response. Whereas our understanding of contemporary legends as interaction is linked to the narrator, one cannot escape the related questions of how the intended audience responds: What sense do they make of what they have just been presented with? Such questions constitute a folkloric version of the currently fashionable reader-response theory in literary criticism in which scholars combine textual analysis with ethnographically based contextual analysis about the uses of the texts in the lives of readers (see Radway 1984). This approach involves asking questions about the structure of credibility and about the appropriate response of readers. The structure of credibility derives from the beliefs and values that individuals hold about their society.

Evaluating credibility is tricky. We constantly hear claims made about some corner of the world, and some of these claims appeal to us as plausible, while others seem outside the realm of possibility. There are no explicit or formal standards of judgment. The audience relies upon past experiences and collective "folk" theories of motivation. Thus, when we hear that it is common for strangers to poison children on Halloween, we consider what we know about our neighbors and about human nature, and many of us decide that this story might just be true. Particularly when the allegation comes from a source of authority, such as a newspaper columnist or television broadcaster, we may not ask for confirmation, even though there are no records of such Halloween sadism (Best and Horiuchi 1985). Likewise, we find it plausible that companies "give away" dialysis machines when can tabs are brought in or that Asian refugees eat pets or that children are horribly mutilated in restrooms of shopping centers.

Audience response is more complicated than the making of a simple judgment on the factual adequacy or credibility of the narrative. The performance itself is being evaluated. How well was the material presented? How entertaining was the narrative? How well liked is the speaker? Some speakers are given more leeway in the evaluation of their performance because of past satisfactions, friendship, or sympathy. They have a margin of idiosyncrasy credits (Hollander 1958). The audience evaluation may be communicated or announced in the form of explicit evaluations, involuntary paraverbal cues (laughter or groaning), nonverbal behavior (yawns, smiles, rolling one's eyes), or overt behavior (leaving the scene when the same narrator begins another story). Through the narrative, the narrator gains a reputation, and through the audience response that reputation is made visible.

Some narratives lead to action. Discourse can move people to alter their behavior—for instance, after having heard a contemporary legend defined as a "true story." When I was collecting texts of the "Kentucky Fried Rat" (chapter 6), several informants announced that, as a result of the story, they no longer patronized Kentucky Fried Chicken outlets. Others, hearing that firms exchange product proofs of purchase for medical technology, switch brand loyalty. However, the extent to which this happens is unclear: Procter & Gamble apparently suffered little despite the prevalence of rumors of their connection to Satanism. The credibility and significance of a given case determines the behavioral responses.

Rumors or legends that cause hysterical contagion are extreme instances of behavioral change. Actors may believe that they are being affected by insects (June bugs [Kerckhoff and Back 1968]), poison (radiation [Medalia and Larson 1954]), or criminals (the phantom anesthetist of Mattoon, Illinois [Johnson 1945]). More common is the case in which the public accepts the reality of a public danger, and then acts to avoid it, for example, by not sending one's children to school or staying home from work. Fears about children being tempted with LSD ("acid" on Mickey Mouse stickers [Brunvand 1984:162–69]) are common, as parents are concerned for their "innocent" children (see Best 1990). The recent case of the "Chelsea Smilers" in London seems to be such a mini-panic. The tale has the following core elements:

> A gang of youths called the Chelsea Smilers are going round schools attacking pupils on their way home. They question children about the Chelsea Football Club. They cut pupils' mouths at the sides in a grotesque smile (using knives/razors/credit cards). They do something else (e.g., punch in the stomach to make the victim scream), which splits their face even wider. They were at so-and-so local school on day X, and will be here on day Y. [Roud 1989:1]

On the day in question some mothers kept their children home, not because they believed the threat, but just to be on the safe side. Behavioral responses frequently have this element: doubt, but action *as if* the story might be true.[20]

One behavioral response to contemporary legends comes in the form of what semioticians term *ostension* (see chapter 11; Dégh and Vázsonyi 1983,

Ellis 1989). Individuals attempt to act out intriguing contemporary legends. Those who stick pins inside Halloween candy or poison treats, infrequent though that might be, seem to be "copying" a narration that they have heard or read, perhaps as a means of committing a mundane crime (Grider 1984). Likewise, as Ellis (1989a, 1990b) demonstrates, one effect of accounts of Satanism found in television talk shows, tabloid newspapers, and word of mouth, is to cause some youths to try it for themselves or to use these claims as a cover for nefarious doings that have no direct connection with Satanism. As Ellis notes, discussing a crime linked to Satanism:

> It is possible, however, that folklore came first, the crime second: unbalanced persons could have used existing legends as models for real-life actions. Certainly the case of Richard Kasso, a Long Island teenager and heavy-metal admirer, illustrates this model. In July 1984, angered over the theft of drugs, Kasso stabbed and mutilated a fellow teen during a mock satanic ritual. After forcing the victim to say "I love Satan," Kasso gouged out his eyes and announcing that "the devil had ordered him to kill," struck the fatal blow. . . . it is clear that Kasso's actions were guided by legendary accounts of devil-worship [Ellis 1989a:216]

These and other instances of ostension demonstrate the extreme way in which an audience can respond to legends. Whether this response takes slightly more benign forms, such as taking a "legend trip" to visit sites of local horrors (Ellis, 1982–1983, 1991), urinating on a hamburger grill, placing a mouse in a beer can (see Preston 1989), or actually frying a rat in a chicken vat, folklore can prod behavior, in accord with popularly held attitudes and in line with orientations to institutions and rules of conduct. Performance may not only be a part of the communication of the contemporary legend, but a consequence.

Elements of Content

I have discussed everything but the content of legends; now I must stop my little dance and focus on *what* is being said. It is in the content of contemporary legends that the previous analyses meld. Content is the product; the other issues represent the conditions and process of narration. No matter how much folklorists wish to examine the conditions or process of production, we cannot escape the necessity of confronting the text. In this section, I focus on four components of the content of contemporary legends: 1) the details of the legend, 2) the themes within the legend, 3) the moral structure of the legend, and 4) the functions of the legend in contemporary society.

   Details. All effective narratives are filled with details. Details load a narrative with spice and zest: specifics that are heavy with connotations for the audience; they should involve the listeners in the world within the text. On some level, the text must be appreciated from the inside. Whatever narrators intend, audiences appropriate the narration, and they may literally wrest control by sharing narrative responsibility. They share "facts," rather than leaving it to the authority of the speaker. More than is true for most literary productions, contemporary legends are decentered, unowned, poststructural, and continually transformed.

One way in which this process is evident is that the details of a narrative are changed, consciously or not, to refresh its relevance. As I describe when considering legends surrounding deaths caused by Pop Rocks candy (chapter 5), the locale in which the event was said to have occurred changed to bring it closer to the suburb in which it was told (see also Rudinger 1976). Narratives about happenings at fast food outlets are routinely linked to a specific local fast food outlet. The same process is evident in that contemporary legends "actually" happen to "a friend of a friend"—a "foaf" (Dale 1978): someone twice removed from the teller. This identity keeps changing as the tale is spread.

The role of details in contemporary legend texts is to keep the material fresh for retellings. It also aids memory (e.g., Bartlett 1932; Dégh and Vázsonyi 1975; chapter 7). Individuals do not recall texts verbatim, but restructure them. They may remember the story kernel (e.g., Kalčik 1975), and then elaborate on this kernel. An account of a rat found in a box of fried chicken is transformed, with appropriately gruesome details, into a story about a Kentucky Fried Chicken outlet in a particular community. The details that are chosen are those that "make sense" in the context of the text. Narratives are driven by the temporal demands of interaction. Speakers are rarely given time to remember details; rather, audiences assume that they will produce a flow of words that make sense in the setting in which they are embedded. The details that are selected connect the content of the legend to those other concepts discussed above: images of institutions, demography, unconscious needs, and features of personal identity. For instance, racial and gender stereotypes guide a narrator's memory in presenting the details of the story, and, to the extent that such stereotypes are culturally stable, the details that are presented are likely to be identical with or similar to details that had previously been part of the story, as told by others.

Following Sigmund Freud's analyses of dreams, parapraxes, and jokes, we expect the details that are selected for a telling of a contemporary legend to be personally and culturally symptomatic. The psychoanalytic approach emphasizes the centrality of details as tools for interpretation (e.g., Dundes 1971). For instance, Tom Burns's extensive analysis of multiple narrations of a single off-color joke (1976) demonstrates that a close reading of narrative details can provide insight to people and texts that a broad overview cannot do.[21]

While the examination of the details of texts might appear to be a rather casuistic analysis; in reality, the placement of details connects directly to the other levels of analysis. Details ultimately reflect the placement of the text in the social order, in a setting, and as an expression of the identity of narrator and audience.

   Themes. Perhaps more effort has been given to an exploration of the themes of contemporary legends than any other single aspect of the subject. What do these peculiar narratives *mean* and why do they occur where they do? Why, for instance, did rumors and legends about Satanism (Victor 1989) or missing children (Best 1990) flourish in the 1980s? Answering these questions always involves some presumption by the researcher. What empirical methods exist for testing whether an interpretation is adequate? How does one know when one discovers the truth? The truth is, of course, a precious and elusive commodity, and perhaps a better goal is simply to find an explanation that is plausible, and that makes sense given what we know now. Indeed, as Clements (1986) demonstrates for "The Hookman," multiple interpretations may provide useful and plausible interpretations in the context of particular tellings. Ultimately, theoretical integration may be a desirable analytic strategy. As described above, I argue that to understand the themes of folklore texts we must consider both the internal consistency of an explanation and its external validity. With regard to the former, we ask: Does it explain most of the relevant details? With regard to the latter, we ask: Does the explanation make sense in light of external circumstances—features of the tellers and audience members, social and political change, or other narratives that are told in the same groups? Combining internal consistency with external validity, we discover explanations that are credible, if not proven. Unconscious needs take form in the themes of a text.

   Thus, Victor suggests that the underlying theme of Satanist stories is that "the moral order of society, especially the family, is being threatened by mysterious evil forces, and we have lost faith in society's authorities to deal with the threat" (Victor 1989:42). When I discuss the legends relating to the Kentucky Fried Rat, I note that the text may arise in response to changes in sites of food preparation, particularly the reality that food is increasingly produced outside of the home, and that this anonymous preparation of sustenance causes anxiety. In discussing the themes of "Welcome to the World of AIDS" (chapter 3), I suggest that these stories reflect an otherwise inexpressible female desire for revenge against men for sexual violence perpetrated against them and male fears of female castration. Carroll (1987) suggests that the contemporary legend of the castrated boy in the shopping center reveals female penis envy. Every interpretation rests ultimately on what seems plausible to readers of these interpreters—to the audiences of these academic narrators.

   Thematic analysis has close connections with the social structural categories and personal imperatives discussed above. This view presupposes that narrators are trying to *make a point* in their narration—a point about the social order, and that sets of narrations address issues within the structure of the societies in which they are embedded. Each of the interpretations cited above can be linked to the demographic, economic, or institutional order. They are a means of making feelings and attitudes visible—feelings and attitudes that reflect and critique the social order. The themes of contemporary legends represent a transformation of society: the social environment exemplified through narrative.

Moral Order. Closely related to the themes of contemporary legends is the moral order that these themes depict. While themes can be found in all contemporary legends, some narratives are explicitly moral tales. They are designed to persuade or convince that some action should be performed or should be avoided. These texts depict good acts, or, more often, evil acts. This can be seen most concretely in contemporary legends that depict criminal activity. While the legend may seem on the surface to depict an "actual," real event, the rationale for its telling extends beyond: to editorialize about society. I discussed this process when considering, under performance, the reasons why people perform narratives (i.e., their illocutionary force).

Stories about a child who is castrated in a shopping center restroom (Rosenthal 1971) serve as direct warnings about leaving one's children alone in public places. The danger from the vicious behaviors of hooligan soccer fans (Roud 1989) carries an explicit moral condemnation of the decline of British civility and a warning about danger from improperly socialized strangers. In addition to a legend's covert messages, which may be unintended by the narrators or unrecognized by their audiences, some messages are intended and direct. These announcements are designed to persuade.

Certain contemporary legends have clear, direct, and narrow didactic functions. Consider those contemporary legends that address the dangers and proper uses of microwave ovens. In one example, a young man removes the door of a microwave in order to save time, and, eventually, discovers his stomach cooked. In another, kittens, puppies, and infants explode after being placed in the ovens to dry (Brunvand 1981:62–65). While the *theme* of these stories may be concern with a dangerous and barely understood technology, the moral is that microwaves should be used according to instructions and that the machine is potentially deadly when misused.

Although these warnings are less surprising to analysts, occurring as they do on the surface of the narration, they probably have more direct behavioral effects on audiences than covert persuasions do. Socialization has always been central to folklore, as it represents the creation of shared or communal standards and the ability of one member of a community to give advice to others. Discourse depicting the moral order is based upon knowledge of the world and of attempts to deal with it. As *advice* these messages are connected to the network in which the narration is embedded. They are designed to be spread to relevant others who care and who might face similar situations. For instance, narratives about childhood abductions are spread particularly among those who could potentially be at risk because they have offspring.

The setting and context in which the narrative occurs affects its moral and didactic tone. We continually strive to make others share our vision of the world, and feel comfortable when we succeed. This process presupposes a crucial role for the reflected social structure, our identity, and the circumstances in which we find ourselves.

Functions. Underlying the other elements of the content of a contemporary legend is the role that it plays for the society in which it is embedded. By this I mean something more general than the question of theme and message. Classical functional analysis assumes that texts are functional in that their existence implies that they serve some benefit for the larger social order—that they increase the likelihood that the community will survive. Such arguments are endlessly controversial in that they are circular—they assert that if a cultural form exists, it must be functional, with the goal for the researcher to discover that function, especially when it is not obvious. The nature of the argument provides little possibility for *proof:* How could one ever know the real reasons for a society's survival or success? How could one determine what the justifications for that survival might be?

Less extreme versions of functional analysis blend into thematic analysis, if they contend that these narratives serve as hidden voices or as means by which groups can express messages that *need* to be said. The functions served may be general for a corpus of legend texts, or there may be individual functions for each separate legend. In general, having a corpus of shared stories that reflects collective anxieties brings people together and fosters the recognition of community—the commonality of fears, knowledge, and attentional focus. These stories help to knit networks. A corpus of stories also provides a basis for social solidarity; these are stories that most individuals within the society have the ability to narrate successfully, and they are a basis for conversation. Although contemporary legends are not conversation starters, they do contribute to the smooth flow of dialogue and help to cement relationships.

Folklore, in general, and contemporary legends, in particular, can and do have political implications. In contrast to some of the conservative implications of functional theory, the politics of these narratives can be conservative, radical, or shades between (Fine 1985). A more subtle analysis suggests that some legends can serve both radical and conservative ends simultaneously. Consider a major theme that I present throughout this volume, the critique of the economic order inherent in mercantile folklore. On a surface level, this critique represents a radical view, suggesting that there is danger inherent in capital accumulation and pointing to the immorality within consumer capitalism. Yet, the nature of these narratives is to make these critiques of the system impotent.

They do not lead to action, because the instances are not combined to create a perspective that has an ideological basis. The horrible instances cited in the narratives, arising from events that are psychologically appalling, lead nowhere. And perhaps the very fact that these instances have been raised and explored but have led to no action may make it less likely that any action will be taken subsequently. To the extent that any political action emerges, as is occasionally the case surrounding food contamination beliefs,[22] the action attempts to deal with the symptom, rather than with the system that produced such industries. Thus, despite their surface reading as social criticism and the occasional legislative action that derives from them, contemporary legends have minimal effects on the fundamental economic or social structure of society.

Contemporary Legends and Folklore Theory

In this introduction I have presented a framework in which basic theoretical units can be fit together. I attempt to synthesize the arguments that are implicit in the articles that follow. Over the past dozen years I have attempted to understand the position and meaning of contemporary legends in American society. I have moved from the relatively narrow questions that characterize "Cokelore and Coke Law" to more general explorations as found in the "The Goliath Effect" and "Mercantile Legends and the World Economy." Yet, each of these essays developed from the same set of concerns: to understand how traditional material fits into contemporary social structure, both in terms of its content and its expression. Why do we find contemporary legends both appealing and appalling? What is the range of their meanings? Why, when, and where are they told? What do they tell us about the moral and social basis of society? What sense can be make of these odd strands from the tangle of talk and action that surround us?

   In this introduction I propose a framework for understanding contemporary legends. This perspective is not predictive in the sense that it can "predict" what legends will emerge at particular times and places. Rather, it is intended as a heuristic guide to the components of the contemporary legend that need to be studied. Admittedly this research agenda remains more of a wish list than an actual description of what we know about contemporary legends, but ultimately a framework such as the one that I have presented should underline that contemporary legends operate on several analytical planes. An adequate interpretation is one that views the situated character of these narratives: situated in society, in the narrator's sense of self, and in the context in which they are performed. Folklorists must not be satisfied with treating texts *only* as texts.

It is my hope that this volume with its fragments from a career of writing will suggest that as a group contemporary legends are worthy of continued examination; they matter for our understanding of ourselves. One of the glaring absences in research on contemporary legends is that there is no extended case study of a single legend, examining the text in terms of its context, text, and performance. The tradition in contemporary legend research has been to focus briefly on numerous legends, skipping from one to the next without reaching intellectual saturation. Few scholars spend more than an article or a chapter on the analysis of a single contemporary legend. The scholarly theoretical monograph that focuses on a single form of folklore, including "traditional" legends, with all related variants has been a staple of the discipline's past, and it deserves to be applied to these modern materials.

Human beings have many ways by which they construct community and share information about the world. Contemporary legends, which seem on their surface evanescent and unworthy of notice, serve critical roles in bolstering interaction. As dramatic, compelling, moving, comic, and involving texts, they build relationships among acquaintances and strangers; as depictions of the world that we must face each day, they provide perspective on potential challenges; and as shared information, they suggest a consensual understanding of reality. While these texts may be awkward shards, we use them as building blocks in our inexact social order.

I owe thanks to many colleagues for the shaping of ideas within this book. I particularly appreciate the willingness of Jan Harold Brunvand, Véronique Campion-Vincent, and Bill Ellis to comment on and critique an early draft of this first chapter. In addition, I wish to express my gratitude to Gillian Bennett, Donald Allport Bird, Simon Bronner, Linda Dégh, Alan Dundes, Mark Glazer, Sandy Hobbs, Marilyn Jorgensen, Janet Langlois, Jay Mechling, Patrick Mullen, W. F. Nicolaisen, Elliott Oring, Michael Preston, Paul Smith, Ellen Stekert, and Patricia Turner for ideas that have emerged in this chapter.

In order to preserve the "authenticity" of my own texts, I have refrained from significant revising or updating of the materials, other than making a few minor typographical or grammatical changes. I have divided the articles into four sections, which imperfectly reflect their contents. However, this organization permits the reader who chooses to consume the volume from cover to cover to follow the lines of my thought in particular areas. Specifically I have grouped the texts as follows: I. Sexual Fantasies, II. Dangerous Products, III. Dangerous Capitalism, and IV. Corporate Redemption. After dissecting a set of sexual legends, and analyzing methods of interpretation, I turn my attention to the images of material goods and the corporations that produce them. I begin with an examination of products that are said to have harmed people, and attempt to demonstrate that there are social-psychological components to these beliefs, social structural aspects to their diffusion, and some basis on which certain contemporary legends might reflect dangerous reality. In the third section, I examine broader themes about corporations—those that are large and prestigious, those that are foreign, and those that are mysterious. Finally, I conclude the volume with two articles that address the paradoxical contemporary legend of the "generous corporation" that provides medical technology for those who would redeem its products.

The articles have appeared in the following locations, and are reprinted with permission:

I Sexual Fantasies
1. "Evaluating Psychoanalytic Folklore: Are Freudians Ever Right?," *New York Folklore* 10 (1984):5–20.
2. "The Promiscuous Cheerleader: An Adolescent Male Legend," *Western Folklore* 39 (1980):120–29 (with Bruce N. Johnson).
3. "Welcome to the World of AIDS: Fantasies of Female Revenge," *Western Folklore* (1987) 46:192–97.

II Dangerous Products
4. "Cokelore and Coke Law: Urban Belief Tales and the Problem of Multiple Origins," *Journal of American Folklore* 92 (1979):478–82.
5. "Folklore Diffusion Through Interactive Social Networks: Conduits in a Preadolescent Community," *New York Folklore* 5 (1979):99–125.
6. "The Kentucky Fried Rat: Legends and Modern Society," *Journal of the Folklore Institute* 17 (1980):222–43.

III Dangerous Capitalism
7. "The Goliath Effect: Corporate Dominance and Mercantile Legends," *Journal of American Folklore* 98 (1985):63–84.
8. "Mercantile Legends and the World Economy: Dangerous Products from Abroad," *Western Folklore* 48 (1989):153–62.
9. Among Those Dark Satanic Mills: Rumors of Kooks, Cults, and Corporations," *Southern Folklore* 47 (1990):133–46.

IV Corporate Redemption
10. "Redemption Rumors: Mercantile Legends and Corporate Beneficence," *Journal of American Folklore* 99 (1986):208–22.
11. "Redemption Rumors and the Power of Ostension," *Journal of American Folklore* 104 (1991):179–81.

Notes

1. Other genres, such as jokes or humorous riddles, might also make a strong claim as to their popularity. Certainly these forms appear more rapidly in response to current events and reflect our current concerns (Jan Brunvand, personal communication, 1990). Contemporary legends are the most popular longer form of narration.

2. Contemporary legends emerged as a recognized folkloristic specialization in the late 1960s and 1970s in part because of the publication of contemporary legend texts and analyses in *Indiana Folklore,* under the editorship of Linda Dégh (see Dégh 1980), and the publication of Richard Dorson's *America in Legend,* which deals specifically with contemporary material (Dorson 1972). Richard Dorson had discussed such materials in his classroom lectures in the 1940s and referred to them in 1959 as "urban belief tales" (Dorson 1959). Since 1982, the annual International Conference on Contemporary Legend held at the Centre for English Cultural Tradition and Language at the University of Sheffield (and in 1989 at Texas A & M University) further solidified this intellectual concern, as did the establishment of the International Society for Contemporary Legend Research in 1987 (for more on the current state of contemporary legend research see Ellis 1990a).

3. Other terms for the same genre are "belief tales," "corporate legends," "foaftales" (friend of a friend tales), "asmuts" (apocryphal stories much told), "urban myths," "nasty legends," "monkey sandwiches," "ULs" (urban legends), "dead catters," "Mack Sennetts," or "red wagon stories" (Brunvand 1990a). The term "urban belief tales" can be traced back to Richard Dorson's interest in the topic in the late 1950s and the label "urban legend" is found in the writings of Brunvand and others. Each term has its defenders; none is perfect.

4. In the presentation of legends, some narrators attempt to make stories more immediate and compelling by claiming that they were involved in the events they narrate, even to the point of presenting material evidence and naming witnesses (Campion-Vincent, personal communication, 1990). However, if this were true, we would classify this text as a personal experience story, rather than a legend. Slotkin (1988) suggests that the form that a narrative takes (whether first or third person) is in part a function of its audience, and of the relationship between narrator and audience. The line separating memorates and legends can be quite fuzzy.

5. In this introduction, aimed at fellow scholars, I avoid presenting texts, instead choosing to refer to others who have presented this material. Because of the popularity of Jan Brunvand's four books on legends (1981, 1984, 1986, 1989), I frequently cite his works, since they provide clean texts that are easily accessible.

6. Ellis (personal communication, 1990) suggests that this story is not a contemporary legend at all, but a "scary story," claiming that the beliefs that this text demands are outside of those that most would accept. I question this, and argue that credibility is a function of audience and that many contemporary legends, even those that are secular, may require similar "leaps of faith" during narration.

7. In choosing this label, I recognize the similarity to Griswold's (1986) Cultural Diamond. While Griswold's writing has been influential in my thought, the two models are analytically separate, particularly as mine suggests causal connections.

8. A good example of this process is the fact that within our culture thirteen-year-olds never seriously conceive of marrying each other. They don't even *reject* the option because it is not seen as an option. At one time, such marriages were legitimate possibilities.

9. This is obviously not entirely accurate in that the existence of folk epics or ballads may

facilitate venues in which they can be performed. In the case of contemporary legends this venue construction is less significant.

10. For instance, I ignore the characteristics of the world economy, state formation, or centralized military control.

11. It is reasonable to assert that the global communications network and the world economy generally connects non-Western nations into the same structural web that is so characteristic of the West.

12. In a Marxian sense—which is from whence these terms derive—there need not be an inevitable psychological, individual recognition in class consciousness (*Klasse für sich*), but there is an activation of the class for its own ends.

13. The latter two, race and ethnicity, affect social class placement, and so demographic divisions affect social class.

14. This is particularly true of European ethnicity. It is said that Irish Americans are Irish only on St. Patrick's Day, when they symbolize their ethnicity by drinking green beer. While this argument has been, perhaps, pushed too far, given Irish-American attitudes towards The Troubles, much ethnicity in the United States has been blunted and ritualized.

15. The arguments that the media have an anti-business, liberal outlook (Stein 1979) or a centrist, establishment bias (Gitlin 1983) are well known, and studies of newspeople themselves suggest that they are not politically neutral. How this affects what gets written or broadcast is a matter of debate and acrimony.

16. Many of the appeals for postcards for Craig Shergold were spread from company to company by FAX messages (Brunvand, personal communication, 1990).

17. Brunvand notes (typescript, "Quake Rumblings Still Being Felt") that legends have emerged about the 1989 San Francisco earthquake. However, these apparently were told at some time after the aftershocks had ended.

18. Often when folklorists are interviewed in the mass media some of their texts are treated as occasions for merriments, transforming legends into jokes, as when Jan Harold Brunvand appeared on the "David Letterman Late Night Show" (Patrick Mullen, personal communication, 1991).

19. The analogic (e.g., nonverbal, paralinguistic) signals in a communication event may be particularly about the relationship among the parties to it. Trust, suspicion, interpersonal power emerge through the doing of relationship work (see Bateson 1972).

20. A similar phenomenon occurs in response to superstitions by some "sophisticates." They practice superstitions, while denying belief, just to be careful (Patrick Mullen, personal communication, 1991).

21. A similar argument is made by those who examine contemporary legends through sociolinguistic analysis, in which each lexeme or morpheme may be meaningful (Ellis 1987).

22. The responses surrounding Upton Sinclair's accounts of food contamination legends are a case in point. White slavery legends and legends of missing children also produce little structural change, but an occasional increase in monitoring by the forces of social control (Morin 1971, Best 1990).

References

Allport, Gordon, and Leo Postman. 1947. *The Psychology of Rumor*. New York: Holt.

Austin, J. L. 1975. *How to Do Things with Words*. Cambridge: Harvard University Press.

Azadovski, M. K. 1926. *Eine sibirische Märchenerzahlerin*. FFC68. Helsinki: Suomalainen Tiedeakatemia.

Bachrach, Arthur J. 1962. "An Experimental Approach to Superstitious Behavior." *Journal of American Folklore* 75:1–9.

Baker, Ronald. 1982. *Hoosier Folk Legends*. Bloomington: Indiana University Press.

Barrick, Mac. 1972. "Typescript Broadsides." *Keystone Folklore Quarterly* 17:27–38.

Bartlett, Frederick C. 1932. *Remembering*. Cambridge: Cambridge University Press.

Bateson, Gregory. 1972. *Steps to an Ecology of Mind*. San Francisco: Chandler.

Baughman, Ernest W. 1966. *Type and Motif-Index of the Folktales of England and North America*. Indiana University Folklore Series, no. 20. The Hague: Mouton.

Beardsley, Richard K., and Rosalie Hankey. 1942. "The Vanishing Hitchhiker." *California Folklore Quarterly* 1:303–35.

Becker, Gary. 1976. *The Economic Approach to Human Behavior*. Chicago: University of Chicago Press.

Best, Joel. 1990. *Threatened Innocents*. Chicago: University of Chicago Press.

Bird, Donald Allport. 1972. "A Theory For Folklore in Mass Media." *Southern Folklore Quarterly* 40:285–305.

Brunvand, Jan Harold. 1981. *The Vanishing Hitchhiker*. New York: Norton.

———. 1984. *The Choking Doberman*. New York: Norton.

———. 1986. *The Mexican Pet*. New York: Norton.

———. 1987. "Notes on my Working Classification of Urban Legends." manuscript, 8pp.

———. 1989. *Curses! Broiled Again!* New York: Norton.

———. 1990a. "An Urban Legend by Any Other Name Is an 'Asmut.'" *United Feature Syndicate* (May 18).

———. 1990b. "Some News from the Miscellaneous Legend Files." *Western Folklore* 49:111–20.

Burns, Thomas. 1976. *Doing the Wash: An Expressive Culture and Personality Study of a Joke and Its Tellers*. Norwood, Penn.: Norwood Editions.

Campion-Vincent, Véronique. 1989. "Complots et Avertissements: Les Légendes Urbaines dans la Ville." *Revue Française de Sociologie* 30:91–105.

Caplow, Theodore. 1947. "Rumors in War." *Social Forces* 25:298–302.

Carroll, Michael P. 1987. "The Castrated Boy: Another Contribution to the Psychoanalytic Study of Urban Legends." *Folklore* 98:216–25.

Chorus, A. 1953. "The Basic Law of Rumor." *Journal of Abnormal and Social Psychology* 48:313–14.

Clements, William M. 1986. "Mythography and the Modern Legend: Interpreting 'The Hook.'" *Journal of Popular Culture* 19:34–46.

Coleman, James. 1990. *Foundations of Social Theory*. Cambridge: Harvard University Press.

Cooley, Charles Horton. 1902. *Human Nature and Social Order*. New York: Schocken.

Cunningham, Keith. 1988. "Franklin was Witched by a Horse: Contemporary Zuni Narrative." In Gillian Bennett and Paul Smith, eds. *Monsters with Iron Teeth*, 183–99. Sheffield: Sheffield Academic Press.

Dale, Rodney. 1978. *The Tumour in the Whale: A Collection of Modern Myths*. London: Duckworth.

Davis, Keith. 1969. "Grapevine Communication Among Lower and Middle Managers." *Personnel Journal* 48:299–72.

Dégh, Linda. 1968. "The Hook." *Indiana Folklore* 1:92–100.

———. 1969. *Folktales and Society.* Bloomington: Indiana University Press.

———. 1980. *Indiana Folklore.* Bloomington: Indiana University Press.

Dégh, Linda, and Andrew Vázsonyi. 1975. "The Hypothesis of Multi-Conduit Transmission in Folklore." In Dan Ben-Amos and Kenneth Goldstein, eds. *Folklore: Performance and Communication,* 207–51. The Hague: Mouton.

———. 1976. "Legend and Belief." In Dan Ben-Amos, ed., *Folklore Genres,* 93–123. Austin: University of Texas Press.

———. 1978. "The Crack on the Red Goblet or Truth and Modern Legend." In Richard M. Dorson, ed., *Folklore in the Modern World,* 253–72. The Hague: Mouton.

———. 1983. "Does the Word "Dog" Bite?: Ostensive Action as Means of Legend Telling." *Journal of Folklore Research* 20:5–34.

Domowitz, Susan. 1979. "Foreign Matter in Food: A Legend Type." *Indiana Folklore* 12:86–95.

Dorson, Richard. 1959. *American Folklore.* Chicago: University of Chicago Press.

———. 1972. *American in Legend.* New York: Pantheon.

Drake, Carlos. 1969. "Jungian Psychology and Its Use in Folklore." *Journal of American Folklore* 82:122–31.

Dundes, Alan. 1964. "Texture, Text, and Context." *Southern Folklore Quarterly* 28:251–65.

———. 1971. "On the Psychology of Legend." In Wayland Hand, ed., *American Folk Legend,* 92–100. Berkeley: University of California Press.

———. 1979. "The Dead Baby Joke Cycle." *Western Folklore* 36:145–57.

Dundes, Alan, and Carl Pagter. 1975. *Urban Folklore from the Paperwork Empire.* Austin: American Folklore Society.

Eitzen, D. Stanley, with Maxine Baca Zinn. 1988. *Understanding Conflict and Order.* Fourth Edition. Boston: Allyn and Bacon.

Ellis, Bill. 1981. "The Camp Mock-Ordeal: Theatre as Life." *Journal of American Folklore* 94:486–505.

———. 1982–1983. "Legend-Tripping in Ohio: A Behavioral Study." *Papers in Comparative Studies* 2:52–69.

———. 1983. "De Legendis Urbis: Modern Legends in Ancient Rome." *Journal of American Folklore* 96:200–208.

———. 1987. "Why Are Verbatim Transcripts of Legends Necessary?" In Gillian Bennett, Paul Smith, and J. D. A. Widdowson, eds., *Perspectives on Contemporary Legend,* Volume III: 31–60 Sheffield: Sheffield Academic Press.

———. 1989a. "Death of Folklore: Ostension, Contemporary Legend, and Murder." *Western Folklore* 48:201–20.

———. 1989b. "When is a Legend?: An Essay in Legend Morphology." In Gillian Bennett and Paul Smith, eds., *The Questing Beast: Perspectives on Contemporary Legend,* 31–53. Sheffield: Sheffield Academic Press.

———. 1990a. "Introduction." *Western Folklore* 49:1–8.

———. 1990b. "The Devil-Worshipers at the Prom: Rumor-Panic as Therapeutic Magic." *Western Folklore* 49:27–49.

———. 1991. "Legend-Trips and Satanism: Adolescents Ostensive Traditions as "Cult" Activity." In James Richardson, Joel Best, and David Bromley, eds., *The Satanism Scare,* 279–95. New York: Aldine de Gruyter.

Fine, Gray Alan. 1980. "Multi-Conduit Transmission and Social Structure: Expanding a Folklore Classic." In Nikolai Burlakoff and Carl Lindahl, eds., *Folklore on Two Continents: Essays in Honor of Linda Dégh,* 300–309. Bloomington, Indiana: Trickster.
———. 1985. "Social Change and Folklore: The Interpretation of Social Structure and Culture." *ARV* 41:7–15.
———. 1986. "Adolescent Gossip as Social Interaction." In Jenny Cook-Gumperz, William A. Corsaro, and Jürgen Streeck, eds., *Children's Worlds and Children's Language,* 405–23. Berlin: Mouton de Gruyter.
———. 1987. *With the Boys: Little League Baseball and Preadolescent Culture.* Chicago: University of Chicago Press.
———. 1988. "The Third Force in American Folklore: Folk Narratives and Social Structures." *Fabula* 29:342–53.
Fine, Gary Alan and Sherryl Kleinman. 1979. "Rethinking Subculture." *American Journal of Sociology* 85:1–20.
———. 1983. "Network and Meaning: An Interactionist Approach to Structure." *Symbolic Interaction* 6:97–110.
Fish, Lydia. 1972. "The Old Wife in the Dormitory: Sexual Folklore and Magical Practices from State University College." *New York Folklore Quarterly* 28:30–36.
———. 1976. "Jesus on the Thruway: The Vanishing Hitchhiker Strikes Again." *Indiana Folklore* 9:5–13.
Form, William. 1985. *Divided We Stand.* Urbana: University of Illinois Press.
Fry, Gladys Marie. 1975. *Night Riders in Black Folk History.* Knoxville: University of Tennessee Press.
Garfinkel, Harold. 1967. *Studies in Ethnomethodology.* New York: Prentice-Hall.
Geertz, Clifford. 1983. *Local Knowledge.* New York: Basic Books.
George, Phillip B. 1972. "The Ghost of Cline Avenue." *Indiana Folklore* 5:56–91.
Georges, Robert. 1969. "Toward an Understanding of Storytelling Events." *Journal of American Folklore* 82:313–28.
———. 1981. "Do Narrators Really Digress?" *Western Folklore* 40:245–52.
Gitlin, Todd. 1983. *Inside Prime Time.* New York: Pantheon.
Glazer, Mark. 1984. "Continuity and Change in Legendry: Two Mexican-American Examples." In Paul Smith, ed., *Perspectives on Contemporary Legends,* 108–27. CECTAL Conference Papers Series No. 4. Sheffield: Centre for English Cultural Tradition and Language.
———. 1987. "The Cultural Adaptation of a Rumor Legend: The Boyfriend's Death in South Texas." In Gillian Bennett, Paul Smith, and J. D. A. Widdowson, eds., *Perspectives on Contemporary Legend.* Volume II, 93–108. Sheffield: Sheffield Academic Press.
———. 1988. "Classification of Urban Legends." Manuscript, 10pp.
Goffman, Erving. 1959. *Presentation of Self in Everyday Life.* New York: Doubleday, Anchor.
Granovetter, Mark. 1973. "The Strength of Weak Ties." *American Journal of Sociology* 78:1360–80.
Greenberg, Andrea. 1973. "Drugged and Seduced: A Contemporary Legend." *New York Folklore Quarterly* 29:131–58.
Grider, Sylvia. 1984. "The Razor Blades in Apples Syndrome." In Paul Smith, ed., *Perspectives on Contemporary Legend,* 128–40. CECTAL Conference Papers Series No. 4. Sheffield: Centre for English Cultural Tradition and Language.
Griswold, Wendy. 1986. *Renaissance Revivals.* Chicago: University of Chicago Press.
Gulzow, Monte, and Carol Mitchell. 1980. "'Vagina Dentata' and 'Incurable Venereal Disease' Legends from the Viet Nam War." *Western Folklore* 39:306–16.

Hall, Max. 1965. "The Great Cabbage Hoax: A Case Study." *Journal of Personality and Social Psychology* 2:563–69.

Hechter, Michael. 1987. *Principles of Group Solidarity.* Berkeley: University of California Press.

Herrera-Sobek, Maria. 1988. "The Devil in the Discotheque: A Semiotic Analysis of a Contemporary Legend." In Gillian Bennett and Paul Smith, eds., *Monsters with Iron Teeth,* 147–57. Sheffield: Sheffield Academic Press.

Hobsbawm, Eric. 1981. *Bandits.* Revised Edition. New York: Pantheon.

Hochschild, Arlie Russell. 1983. *The Managed Heart.* Berkeley: University of California Press.

Hollander, Edwin. 1958. "Conformity, Status, and Idiosyncrasy Credit." *Psychological Review* 65:117–27.

Hufford, David. 1974. "Psychology, Psychoanalysis, and Folklore." *Southern Folklore Quarterly* 38:187–97.

Jacobs, Jane. 1961. *The Life and Death of Great American Cities.* New York: Random House.

Johnson, D. M. 1945. "The Phantom Anesthetist of Mattoon: A Field Study of Mass Hysteria." *Journal of Abnormal and Social Psychology* 40:175–86.

Johnston, Robbie D. 1973. "Folklore and Women: A Social Interactional Analysis of the Folklore of a Texas Madam." *Journal of American Folklore* 86:211–24.

Jones, Louis C. 1944. "Hitchhiking Ghosts in New York." *California Folklore Quarterly* 3:284–92.

Kalčik, Susan. 1975. ". . . Like Ann's Gynecologist or the Time I Was Almost Raped: Personal Narratives in Women's Rap Groups." *Journal of American Folklore* 88:3–11.

Kardiner, Abram. 1945. *The Psychological Frontiers of Society.* New York: Columbia University Press.

Kerckhoff, Alan, and Kurt Back. 1968. *The June Bug: A Study of Hysterical Contagion.* New York: Appleton-Century-Crofts.

Kirschenblatt-Gimblett, Barbara. 1975. *Speech Play.* Philadelphia: University of Pennsylvania Press.

Klintberg, Bengt af. 1986. *Rattan I Pizzan.* Stockholm: Norstedts.

Koenig, Frederick. 1985. *Rumor in the Marketplace: The Social Psychology of Commercial Hearsay.* Dover, Mass.: Auburn House.

Levin, Jack, and Arnold Arluke. 1987. *Gossip: The Inside Scoop.* New York: Plenum.

Lumley, F. E. 1925. *Means of Social Control.* New York: Century.

Medalia, N. Z., and O. N. Larsen. 1954. "Diffusion and Belief in a Collective Delusion: The Seattle Windshield Pitting Epidemic." *American Sociological Review.* 23:180–86.

Merry, Sally Engle. 1984. "Rethinking Gossip and Scandal." In Donald Black, ed., *Toward a General Theory of Social Control.* Volume I, 271–302. Orlando: Academic Press.

Mitchell, Roger. 1987. "The Will to Believe and Anti-Refugee Rumors." *Midwestern Folklore* 13:5–15.

Montell, William Lynwood. 1975. *Ghosts Along the Cumberland: Deathlore in the Kentucky Foothills.* Knoxville: University of Tennessee Press.

Morin, Edgar. 1971. *Rumor in Orleans.* Translated by P. Green. New York: Pantheon.

Mullen, Patrick. 1972. "Modern Legend and Rumor Theory." *Journal of the Folklore Institute* 9:95–109.

Oring, Elliott. 1975. "Everything is a Shade of Elephant: An Alternative to a Psychoanalysis of Humor." *New York Folklore* 1:149–59.

Preston, Cathy, and Michael Preston. 1981. "Things Better Left Unsaid: Photocopy Humor." *Maledicta* 5:171–76.

Preston, Michael. 1989. "The Mouse in the Coors Beer Can: Goliath Strikes Back." *Foaftale News* 14 (June):1–3.

Radway, Janice. 1984. *Reading the Romance*. Chapel Hill: University of North Carolina Press.

Reuss, Richard A. 1971. "The Roots of American Left-Wing Interest in Folksong." *Labor History* 12:259–79.

Ridley, Florence H. 1967. "A Tale Told Too Often." *Western Folklore* 26:153–56.

Roheim, Geza. 1952. *The Gate of the Dream*. New York: International University Press.

Rosenthal, Marilyn. 1971. "Where Rumor Raged." *Trans-Action* 8(4):34–43.

Rosnow, Ralph L., and Gary Alan Fine. 1976. *Rumor and Gossip: The Social Psychology of Hearsay*. New York: Elsevier.

Roud, Steve. 1989. "Chelsea Smilers: Interim Report on a Gang-Violence Rumor." *Foaftale News* 15(September):1–2.

Rudinger, Joel D. 1976. "Folk Ogres of the Firelands: Narrative Variations of a North Central Ohio Community." *Indiana Folklore* 9:41–93.

Schmidt, Sigrid. 1987. "Contemporary Legends of Europeans in Namibia." In Gillian Bennett, Paul Smith, and J. D. A. Widdowson, eds., *Perspectives on Contemporary Legend*. Volume II, 117–29. Sheffield: Sheffield Academic Press.

Shibutani, Tamotsu. 1966. *Improvised News*. Indianapolis: Bobbs-Merrill.

Simonides, Dorota. 1987. "Moderne Sagenbildung in Polnischen Grosstadtmillieu." *Fabula* 28:269–78.

Simons, Elizabeth Radin. 1980. "The Slumber Party as Folk Ritual: An Analysis of the Informal Sex Education of Preadolescents." M. A. Thesis (Folklore) University of California, Berkeley.

Simpson, Jacqueline. 1983. "Urban Legends in *The Pickwick Papers*." *Journal of American Folklore* 96:462–70.

Slotkin, Edgar M. 1988. "Legend Genre as a Function of Audience." In Gillian Bennett and Paul Smith, eds., *Monsters With Iron Teeth*, 89–111. Sheffield: Sheffield Academic Press.

Smith, Paul. 1983. *The Book of Nasty Legends*. London: Routledge and Kegan Paul.

———. 1987. "Contemporary Legend and the Photocopy Revolution." In Gillian Bennett, Paul Smith, and J. D. A. Widdowson, eds., *Perspectives on Contemporary Legend*. Volume II, 177–202. Sheffield: Sheffield Academic Press.

Spacks, Patricia. 1985. *Gossip*. New Haven: Yale University Press.

Stein, Benjamin. 1979. *The View From Sunset Boulevard*. New York: Basic Books.

Suczek, Barbara. 1972. "The Curious Case of the "Death" of Paul McCartney." *Urban Life and Culture* 1:61–76.

Toelken, Barre. 1979. *The Dynamics of Folklore*. Boston: Houghton Mifflin.

Turner, Patricia. 1987. "Church's Fried Chicken and the Klan: A Rhetorical Analysis of Rumor in the Black Community." *Western Folklore* 46:294–306.

———. 1988. "See, They Didn't Care What Happened to Black Folks: An AIDS Urban Legend and Afro-American Worldview." Paper presented at the American Folklore Society Annual Meeting.

Victor, Jeffrey. 1989. "A Rumor-Panic about a Dangerous Satanic Cult in Western New York." *New York Folklore* 15:23–49.

Virtanen, Leaa. 1988. *Varastettu isoaiti*. Helsinki: Kustannusosakeyhtio Tammi.

Vlach, John. 1971. "One Black Eye and Other Horrors: A Case for the Humorous Anti-Legend." *Indiana Folklore* 4:95–140.

Walle, Alf. 1976. "Getting Picked Up without Being Put Down: Jokes and the Bar Rush. *Journal of the Folklore Institute* 13:201–17.

Whyte, William H. 1988. *City: Rediscovering the Center.* New York: Doubleday.
Wilson, William A. 1975. "The Vanishing Hitchhiker Among the Mormons." *Indiana Folklore* 8:80–97.
———. 1976. *Folklore and Nationalism in Modern Finland.* Bloomington: Indiana University Press.
Yerkovich, Sally. 1977. "Gossiping as a Way of Speaking." *Journal of Communication* 27:192–96.
Zipes, Jack. 1979. *Breaking the Magic Spell.* Austin: University of Texas Press.

I   SEXUAL FANTASIES

I

Evaluating Psychoanalytic Folklore:
Are Freudians Ever Right?

Folklore and psychoanalysis have had a lengthy, if not always intimate, relationship. Psychoanalysts have long believed that folklore reflects important collective psychological concerns. Sigmund Freud himself freely drew upon
folkloristic sources in his analyses of culture (e.g., Freud and Oppenheim 1958;
Freud 1961) and believed that the analysis of folklore could provide psychoanalytic insight (Freud 1957 233–35). Later, anthropologically oriented psychoanalysts such as Geza Roheim (e.g., 1969) and Abram Kardiner (1945) attempted to analyze the personality dynamics of the people of a society through
their folk beliefs, rituals, and traditions. Folklore was treated as a lens through
which the workings of the collective mind or "national character" could be
seen. Other psychoanalysts have demonstrated the connections between the
culture of a group and its child-rearing practices—often suggesting that the folk
traditions influence the patterns of upbringing, and, in turn, the personality of
the children (see Boyer 1979 on the Apache, and Erikson 1963 on the Sioux and
Yurok). Articles still regularly appear in psychoanalytic journals such as *American Imago,* which analyze narratives, tales, or other folk genres for what they
say about the human condition according to Freud. These studies supplement
and often expand on the base of knowledge provided by the many clinical studies of personal "traditions" and images. Recently the prestigious New York Psychoanalytic Institute (a classical Freudian group) sponsored a colloquium on
mythology for its members.

This extensive interest in folklore by psychoanalysts has not been much
acknowledged by most academically trained folklorists. For the most part,
those who have written about the relationship between psychoanalysis and
folklore have been, to paraphrase Richard Dorson's description of British
scholars in the 1890s, Freudian evening folklorists. For most of these analysts,
folklore is an avocational interest.

With a few exceptions, professionally trained folklorists have tended to describe psychoanalysis as an "interesting" approach, but one without much value
to their pursuits (Hufford 1974). Richard Dorson in his survey of folklore theories dismisses psychoanalysis:

> The most speculative body of current folklore theory belongs to the psychoanalytic school that memorializes Sigmund Freud. This is also the school of interpretation most abhorrent to orthodox folklorists. [Dorson 1972:25]

Although Dorson may be exaggerating folklorists' repugnance to this approach, it is certainly true that most folklorists do not attempt to disprove psychoanalytic interpretations as much as they ignore them or reject them *ex cathedra*. Recognizing that some psychoanalysts are well trained in folklore (such as L. Bryce Boyer 1979, 1980) and some folklorists have written sympathetic psychoanalytic analyses (e.g., Melville Jacobs, 1952, Tom Burns 1976, and Jay Mechling 1980), psychoanalysis is not much alive as a vigorous tradition in folklore scholarship in the 1980s.

This doleful conclusion is somewhat disappointing in light of the optimism that many had for the impact of this grand theory in its intellectual heyday during the 1930s and 1940s. With psychoanalysis currently in decline in therapeutic situations, it is not unexpected to find little psychoanalytic folklore in our leading journals. And, yet, such a situation is unfortunate, for the best psychoanalytic writing has produced considerable insight. For the most part the assumptions of Freudian theory have not been disproven (although they *could* be; see Wax 1983), as much as they have been set aside because of their proponents' inability to provide "proof" satisfactory to other sectors of the scientific community.

For example, the massive writings of folklorist-turned-analyst Geza Roheim on the traditional practices of Australian aborigines are widely ignored today because most folklorists (those few who have read them) have reached a scholarly consensus that the interpretations that Roheim presents (about dreams producing myths and tales, 1952, for example) are not theoretically plausible. I do not challenge the empirical validity of this scholarly consensus; however, I claim that the decision is primarily based on the fact that Roheim's theories are both speculative and "out of fashion." Such is the case in regard to psychoanalytic folklore today. By consensus it is not a major approach.

When contemporary folklorists think of psychoanalytic folklore they typically think first of the writings of Alan Dundes. Dundes's writing falls in several categories, one of which deals with psychoanalytic theory. He is also widely known for his structuralist writings, and in some articles, such as that on the hero pattern in the life of Jesus (1980:223–61), he attempts to integrate the two approaches. It is probably not much of an overstatement to claim that Alan Dundes is currently the only prominent academically trained folklorist who uses the psychoanalytic approach as his central theoretical reference point. In a real sense, Alan Dundes *is* psychoanalytic folklore, and, as a result, his writings will be my primary focus in this paper.

Throughout his distinguished career, Alan Dundes has attempted to persuade fellow folklorists of his claim that one must do more than simply describe folklore (Dundes 1971, 1980); one must also analyze the meaning that it has for its audience. Collecting is only a part of the folklorist's task; the specific traditions that people share *mean* something—both consciously and, more controversially, unconsciously. From this perspective folklore is an interpretive science.

Interpretation is tricky for adherents of most theoretical perspectives. The easiest way to discover the meaning of a folkloric item is simply to ask its creators,[1] tellers, or audiences: What does this mean to you? What do you do with this? Why do you do it? Folk (or ethnoscientific) explanations are valuable for understanding worldviews and folk-ideas. Yet, few argue that our interpretations should be limited to those rationalizations provided by respondents. Some patterns can be perceived only through a close examination of the data and the circumstances of the telling—recognition shared by such unlikely allies as psychoanalysts, structuralists, semioticians, Marxists, sociobiologists, and comparative ethnologists. Some of these theorists direct the locus of interpretation to the supra-individual level—to the realm of social relations, or macrosociology (e.g., the Marxists). For others, most notably the psychoanalysts, the interpretation is grounded in the unconscious. Only a very self-aware individual would be conscious of what his/her traditions "meant." The biological and developmental similarities of human beings permit us to analyze cultural traditions as reflecting the concerns of a society. Yet, meaning is ultimately grounded in the individual psyche.

Critics of psychoanalysis emphasize the hubris of this approach. Psychoanalytically inclined researchers feel that they know better than their subjects what these subjects' cultural traditions really mean. These outsiders provide the meaning of traditions—often traditions which are outside the analyst's own culture sphere. No wonder that some are offended, especially when the interpretations are offensive in light of the community's public mores (e.g., regarding homosexuality, masturbation, or incest). Yet, the audience's sense of outrage does not disprove the interpretation, but only denies its validity *ex cathedra*.

Folklore for psychoanalytic folklorists is the reflection of the concerns and anxieties of those who are its creators, performers, and also its audience, at least that segment of the audience that reacts to it—positively, in most cases, but negatively as well. For Dundes, the folk must be given (at least) equal weight with the lore (1977b, 1980: viii), because lore is not possible without a folk for whom it has meaning. Thus, the goal of folkloristics is not to understand the text, but to understand people. In the case of collective traditions (as opposed to dreams or individual fantasies) the analysis of folklore informs us about the anxieties of the group (Fine 1983), the "national character," or the human condition. Although these concerns are often repressed sexual themes, they need not be. Some involve power (e.g., the relations between men and women) (Dundes 1976); others involve racial or ethnic conflict (Dundes 1977a; Abrahams and Dundes 1969) or the Oedipal complex (Abrahams and Dundes 1969).

Because of Alan Dundes's status as a senior professional folklorist (a member of the tribe, and neither an outsider nor a marginal man), his writings are particularly apt as examples of psychoanalytic folklore. Among the topics Dundes has covered in his extensive and diverse folkloric writings are such folklore forms as elephant jokes, accounts of the life of Jesus, Jack and the Beanstalk, King Lear, legends about George Washington, couvade, potlatch, football, Turkish verbal duels, the Palio festival of Siena, and the German national character. For each of these diverse topics, Dundes has explained the unconscious symbolism of the text. It is unconscious, because in psychoanalytic theory that is how tendentious meaning is expressed. Folklore provides a socially acceptable outlet for meaning that cannot be displayed otherwise. If the meaning was overt, the text would have to be repressed.

Despite Dundes's position as a senior scholar, one must admit that many of his interpretations have been received by his folkloristic brethren with a certain coolness. This reaction was most extreme in the aftermath of Dundes's 1980 presidential address, which dealt with German folklore representing the anality of German national character (Dundes 1984). The evaluations after the presentation were almost uniformly negative, although typically there was no basis given for the disagreement. One explanation for a portion of this reaction is that Dundes's lively and amusing style of presentation makes some treat him more like an entertainer than a scholar—at least those who cannot separate his style from his substance. Even in some of his writings he is playful, which may distract from the serious message. Some suggest that Freudian theory doesn't need to be more ludicrous than it already is, even if this style does capture our attention—as it did in his presidential address. Yet, a psychoanalyst might suggest that the themes treated in that analysis were more anxiety-producing than the themes in other presentations. Perhaps anality in German national character is more manifest than latent. Much like some of the more explicit challenges by Roheim to the moral order of human nature, non-psychoanalysts arose to condemn the "preposterous" theory by simply defining the conclusions as illegitimate.

Yet, this condemnation of the critics is an easy means of defense, and the argument reflects a weakness of Freudian theory. Specifically, the theoretical argument is in danger of becoming circular or tautological (and, thus, the similarity between psychoanalysis and religion). If you accept the analyst's interpretation, it indicates that he or she is correct; if you reject it, you are denying your repressed feelings and, obviously, she or he is correct for having provoked that reaction. The audience member who disputes an interpretation cannot win.

This leads to a situation in which any interpretation which has been presented by an analyst is, by virtue of that fact alone, valid.

Obviously such a position is ludicrous, and even the most enthusiastic Freudian analyst would hesitate before accepting it. But what is the alternative? Part of the problem in evaluating psychoanalytic folklore is that the grounds for evaluation are not clear. We lack criteria to judge whether a psychoanalytic interpretation is adequate. Dundes suggests, for example:

> [W]hen one turns to the question "why" (rather than "what"), one enters the ever treacherous area of interpretation. Interpretations often tend to be subjective rather than objective. It is a legitimate question whether one can effectively "prove" the validity of one interpretation over another. . . . Some interpretations may be more plausible and convincing than others. [Dundes, 1980:ix]

Dundes, indeed, does not answer the question of whether one can ever prove an interpretation.

There have been attempts to "prove" psychoanalytic theories, and there need to be more (Wax 1983). Most relevant among these approaches for folklorists are attempts to examine psychoanalytic theories and hypotheses by means of a sample of societies such as can be generated through the Human Relations Area Files. Such works as Whiting and Child's *Child Training and Personality* (1953) attempt to test hypotheses by using each society as an individual case. Yet, such an approach is not helpful for the analysis of texts. Since most of these texts are not cross-cultural, they do not reflect the characteristics of different societies. Although it might be possible to take a common tale type and analyze its differences among cultures, the conclusions would likely be ambiguous because the societies in which a tale type is found are typically similar (i.e., largely Indo-European). In addition, one would have to ask whether the texts collected represent a fair sample of all variants. Although such a massive undertaking would be worthwhile, it is likely not to provide a definitive testing of a Freudian hypothesis, because of the difficulty of operationalizing variables.

More to the point perhaps would be an examination of the similarities between texts—as reflecting symbolic equivalence between motifemes (e.g., the symbolic equivalence of the nose, foot, and penis) (Dundes 1979). This approach allows us to claim confidently that one symbol stands for another, and this provides a key for the interpretation of texts. Yet, symbolic equivalence provides a limited, though useful, tool for interpretation. Such equivalences must be used with caution and in parallel texts, since otherwise it is easy for everything to be equivalent to everything else simply because it can be substituted somewhere.

Much psychoanalytic interpretation is based on analytic intuition, rather than a set procedure which can be easily duplicated by any scholar (Ketner

1973). As a result, psychoanalytic interpretations have been mystified—knowingly, or not; the analyst's interpretation has been made into an art and judgments of its theoretical adequacy have become a matter of personal taste. In order to begin to demystify psychoanalytic folklore, we must ask what kind of theory is psychoanalysis; what are the dynamics behind interpretation?

Psychoanalysis is a form of micro-functionalism. That is, it assumes that folklore is created, and becomes traditional, because it satisfies some need for the individuals who are a party to it. Specifically, cultural traditions allow people to deal with their concerns and anxieties in symbolic form. A second assumption of psychoanalytic methodology is that a close, theoretically informed analysis can enable one to uncover the meaning of a text, even though this meaning may not be realized by those who are its performers and audience. The third assumption is that the interpretation may be sufficiently well hidden, through layers of repression, projection, and other defense mechanisms, that the participants, when told by the analyst what the significance of the cultural form is, may refuse to accept that interpretation, and may even deny it vigorously. This rejection was dramatically evident in the aftermath of Dundes's interpretation of American football as ritual homosexuality. Scores of players and fans rose up as one to proclaim their innocence of such a charge; but did they protest too much? The rejection of an interpretation by its audience is not particularly troubling to the Freudian analyst in that the rejection is assumed to be symptomatic of the defense mechanism of denial.

Ultimately the crux of the dilemma of proving or disproving a Freudian interpretation is that the rejection of the theory on intuitive grounds is not tantamount to disproving it, but even supports the interpretation. In this way, psychoanalysis is in principle distinctively different from other qualitative approaches in which judgment is based on a consensus model. Those approaches assume that qualitative theory can be shown to be right or wrong, helpful or not, by the reaction of its audience. If numerous people find the assertion plausible, it is correct; if they reject it, one needs to find an alternative theory. In practice, this is what happens in psychoanalysis, in that if one's audience of *analysts* do not accept the interpretation it will not be widely used and cited but, in theory, this is an inadequate measure because it allows the psychodynamics of the audience of specialists to determine the subtextual meaning of the form. This makes theorizing into a popularity context dependent on the extent to which an individual has self-reflective insight. Of course, this does not address what happens when analysts disagree—presumably the cogency of the argument or the status of the analyst determines the outcome. Such an approach also raises the question of audiences of judgment. The adequacy of an interpretation may depend on which audience is responding or how the interpretation connects to their self-image. For example, connecting American sport to homosexuality is profoundly threatening to many young men who have enjoyed playing or watching the game. One would imagine that an audience of women would have less difficulty accepting the argument. Since one of the most important criteria for any interpretation is how well it connects with our own life experiences, different audiences may react differently, despite similar academic training. Just as the texts themselves have audiences, so do interpretations, and the dynamics of audience reactions apply to them as well.

Although we will never eliminate the subjective in judgments of analytic adequacy, I propose two criteria by which we can inject some order into the determination of a psychoanalytic interpretation's adequacy: Is the analysis internally consistent? And is the analysis externally valid? Although neither question removes subjective judgment, they at least provide a more explicit basis for evaluation.

Internal Consistency. Psychoanalytic folklore differs from much folkloric analysis in that it holds that *all* details of a text are potentially symptomatic. Thus, a psychoanalytic folklore essay typically concerns itself with the details of the text in a much more fine-grained way than is true for many other approaches. This methodological dictum leaves the researcher open to the charge that he or she has been selective in the details chosen for analysis. So, for an interpretation to be internally valid, the researchers must demonstrate that they have explained most, if not all, of the relevant details. If the details fit together, providing consistent latent content, then we are likely to have some confidence in the analysis. Anyone can create an interpretation of a few details in a text, but to show that all the diverse elements collectively contribute to a meaningful structure is much more challenging.

A related problem concerns how to treat variants. Although many psychoanalytic interpretations (e.g., Jacobs 1952) focus on a single text, ideally one needs a sample of texts to work with. Each of these texts will be different, and since every detail is significant, each difference will be equally significant. In order to develop an interpretation which applies to the folk group as a whole, one must determine what the "ideal text" is—which details are sufficiently central that the entire community shares them and which are idiosyncratic to particular tellers and settings. The internal consistency of the interpretation as it relates to the community should be based on this admittedly artificial "ideal text." The other details can be used to interpret the personality dynamics of the performer, or, in the case of performers and audiences, of the relationship between the two. Each narration by a performer will be different and these differences, like all details, can potentially be interpreted through the psychoanalytic method.

External Validity. External validity requires that the analysis makes sense in light of the text's location in space and time. Does the interpretation explain plausible conscious or unconscious concerns of the audience and the performer? For example, an argument that a folklore form deals with emerging sexuality (as does "The Hook") would be inaccurate if that form were found primarily among middle-aged men. Likewise, folklore that has strong anal components (German slang, perhaps) should be found primarily in those cultures in which toilet training is seen as important and/or problematic. The text is always grounded in a social setting, and this setting, populated with individuals who have interests and concerns, produces the text.

As in the case of internal consistency, there are complications. Few folklore items have such a limited diffusion that only the expected folk group will have heard it or will have performed it. Although "The Hook" legend is *primarily* told among young girls, it is spread among some older women and some boys. Again, one should see the primary narrators, audiences, and settings as reflecting the meaning of the text as applied to the community, with the less common locations and participants reflecting idiosyncratic meaning.

Applying the Criteria

The Hook. To demonstrate briefly how these criteria might be applied I shall use the writings of Alan Dundes as examples, since his writings represent the current state of psychoanalysis in folklore studies. I shall first consider a rather simple and straightforward analysis which I believe is quite convincing—Dundes's discussion of "The Hook" legend in his essay "On the Psychology of Legend" (1971:29–30). Dundes reports the text of the legend as follows:

> The essence of the plot involves a couple in a car parked in a local lovers' lane. . . . The boy hoping to make out (sexually) turns on the car radio to find some soft music to set the stage. After several minutes of "necking," the couple is startled by a news flash that interrupts the music to say that a sex maniac has just escaped from the state insane asylum. The announcement also mentions that the one distinguishing feature of this man is that he has a hook in place of one arm. The girl is upset "cause she's just sure this guy is going to come and try and get in their car." Finally, after much argument, she convinces the boy to leave the area, whereupon he suddenly starts the car and roars away. At the girl's home, she gets out of the car and sees "a hook hanging on the door." [Dundes 1971:29]

In his interpretation, Dundes manages to marshall all of the details in the story to support his argument that the legend's primary focus is the girl's anxiety about the sexuality of the boys that she dates, and how she will be able to control them. All of the details of the legend seem to fit this account. The setting is a sexualized one—a location in which one expects the boyfriend to be sexually active. The radio, which broadcasts the message of danger, interrupting the sexualized rhythm of the music, serves as the conscience or super-ego. The fact that the maniac has just escaped from institutional constraints puts him in the same symbolic category as the boy in the dark car—he, too, is removed from the institutional constraints of family and school. Also, the fact that the Hookman is insane suggests that he is out of control, just as is the boyfriend. The connection between the long metal hook and the phallus is plausible, even for those who choose not to accept the entire range of Freudian symbolism ("he wanted to get his hooks into her"). The worry of the girl about the Hookman getting inside the parked car door (the car door as vaginal symbol) and the boy's use of the car to "pull out" of Lovers' Lane (the car as a phallic symbol) can both be seen as symbolically relevant to the main theme of the account. Finally, the presence of the severed hook on the car door, which effectively stops the maniac, represents castration, particularly if we have already accepted the attempt to get into the girl's door as a sexual attack on her, and the hook as a symbolic phallus. In other words, in this short account, all the major details have been explained in a reasonable fashion which is consistent with the proffered interpretation. The interpretation is internally consistent.

In terms of external validity, the legend is typically found at precisely the stage in a girl's life where it should be found. If the danger was truly from *outside* the car in Lovers' Lane, we might expect to find the story narrated at any time after the girl has started to visit Lovers' Lane (from sixteen to her early twenties); indeed, if that were the case, boys might repeat it as frequently. However, the story appears to be narrated most frequently by girls in late preadolescence or early adolescence, prior to the period that the manifest content of the story would be relevant. Yet, this is precisely the time that the latent symbolic meaning of the story is relevant. Girls are just thinking about how they will be able to attract and then control their boyfriends—particularly as this issue emerges in the years around puberty. The location of the legend reveals the interpretation to be externally valid.

Because of the completeness of the internal consistency and the plausibility of the external validity, this is a valid interpretation of the legend. However, several points need to be raised. First, the interpretation is, on its surface, reasonable. We are much more prone to accept an interpretation that adolescent girls are worried about the advances of their boyfriends—we know that they do this consciously—than we are to accept other interpretations, such as that football players regularly engage in ritual homosexuality. The latter, if it exists at all, is much more deeply repressed than is the former. The former is morally acceptable; the latter is, for many, morally unacceptable.

It is important to remember that in his short analysis, included as a part of a more general interpretation of legends, Dundes doesn't analyze a real text, but his reconstruction of one (which is grounded on texts found in Dégh 1968). To increase our confidence in the analysis, a large and representative corpus of texts should be examined to learn the degree to which the details that Dundes analyzes are actually present. Further, folklorists can conduct systematic surveys to learn if the story is actually told by the group that is claimed to tell the story and whether other groups tell the story as well. *Psychoanalytic interpretations must ultimately be based on empirical data.*

American Football. I now wish to discuss one of Dundes's analyses which I feel is less convincing as a psychoanalytic interpretation: that of American football. Dundes summarizes his approach toward the end of the article:

> . . . American football [is] a ritual combat between groups of males attempting to assert their masculinity by penetrating the endzones of their rivals. . . . I think it is highly likely that the ritual aspect of football, providing as it does a socially sanctioned framework for male body contact—football, after all, is a so-called "body contact" sport—is a form of homosexual behavior. . . . Sexual acts carried out in thinly disguised symbolic form by, and directed toward, males and males only, would seem to constitute ritual homosexuality. [Dundes 1978:86–87]

In criticizing Dundes's interpretation, I do not mean to imply that there is no truth to his argument—many aspects of social life have some sexual implications, and football is, by virtue of its all-male camaraderie, at least *homosocial*, if not homosexual.

In terms of internal consistency, one must be impressed by the array of sexual double entendres that Dundes discovered: endzone, making a pass, sacking, going in the pocket, tight end, penetrating, and scoring. However, there are other football terms which have less clear sexual referents: guard, punt, hashmarks, red-dogging, off-sides, safety, smashing through the line, kick-off, and field goal. Some football terminology has possible homosexual implications; other terminology does not. Likewise, although spiking the ball might have homosexual implications, does kicking the ball have the same implications? Does calling for a fair catch? Of course, one can strain to make all the details fit; but, as Dundes remarks about the psychoanalytic method: "the interpretations should be read out of the data rather than being read into the data!" (1980:ix).

What about the implications of external validity? Here, I think, the interpretation is particularly weak. Dundes correctly notes certain similar themes (e.g., verbal duels) in other cultures, but he does not address the non-universal character of football in our own culture. First, children start to play (and enjoy) football at a very early age. Why should this be? What need does preadolescent football serve for its participants? Is it merely imitation without any psychodynamic relevance until after puberty, or does ritual homosexuality begin as early as age eight? Second, Americans have many games of which they are fond: baseball, basketball, hockey, golf, tennis. Do all have homosexual implications? Presumably not, since the analysis of football is based on the details of its folk speech and behavior. Indeed, in a passing reference to the "crease" in hockey, Dundes casually puts forth a heterosexual interpretation of that sport. This, then, raises the question of what psychodynamically is the difference between football players and those who choose to participate in other sports? Are football players more "homosexual," or at least do they have a greater need to express their homosexual drives in symbolic form—through ritual homosexuality? Most Americans do not play football, and even in college the percentage of male students who play football is small. Are there group differences between football players and non-players? This, of course, is an empirical question—one that I have not seen addressed, and one that Dundes doesn't answer. Finally, football is seasonal, confined to the autumn. Why? Aren't these drives present to be expressed throughout the calendar year; are they repressed the other nine months? Why is football played in the fall (the new United States Football League not to the contrary)? Are there other male activities in American culture which function in the same way?

Finally, have the changes in football been related to psychodynamic needs? Is the increase in safety protection related to a change in sexual attitudes? Are the new rules preventing pass receivers from being jostled symptomatic of a change of sexual functioning? All of these questions raise doubt as to the interpretation of football as ritual homosexuality. Although it would be premature to assert that the analysis has no value, more evidence needs to be presented more systematically for the argument to be convincing to the majority of folklorists.

The weakness in this analysis of football (and, indeed, in the more successful analysis of The Hook legend) points to a weakness in Dundes's general method of analysis and implicitly to a direction for psychoanalytic research. Although past research is carefully, one might almost say lovingly, reported and, then, dissected, often no corpus of data is presented. So, when Abrahams and Dundes (1969) discuss elephant jokes, they collect jokes from nowhere— no information about the collection is given. Likewise, readers are presented with a string of facts about the Hookman, George Washington, football, the Easter bunny, and the German national character. The issue of the representativeness of the material is not adequately addressed. With few exceptions Freudian analyses are marred by a lack of interest in collecting. A more complete collection and a systematic analysis of that collection would provide a basis for a stronger psychoanalytic interpretation that truly comes from the data and not from the analyst (La Barre 1948:390).

Conclusion

From one perspective it appears that psychoanalysis was made for folkloric interpretation. With its concern for symbolism, Freudian theory can provide a key by which textual meaning can be unlocked. In the same way that the psychoanalyst will interpret a dream as symptomatic of the concerns of the dreamer, the folk narrative can provide a clue to the concerns of the society. The hidden grammar of folk symbolism can be understood by reaching into the sub-conscious of the folk.

Yet, this grammar is by no means definitive. Too often the meaning of a text is dependent on the insight of the analyst. Two analysts may (and have) provide widely divergent interpretations of the same material. As a result the resistance that many non-psychoanalytically oriented scholars have towards accepting these interpretations is not because of the defense mechanism of denial, but, rather, stems from the fact that to prove an interpretation that is, on prima facie grounds, implausible, one must do more than construct a good story. One must demonstrate that there are compelling reasons for the interpretation: that it ex-plains the material without room for alternate interpretations of the same mate-rial and that the psychodynamic functions of the material could be found only in those settings and among those persons where the material actually has been found. Too often analysts have been content to provide engaging and entertain-ing theories, rather than to subject them to harsh scrutiny. This, of course, doesn't imply that the analyses have been wrong, but only that they are un-proven, and, subject to rejection by those who have a prejudice against explana-tions of this type.

It should be evident from this discussion that I believe that there is con-siderable merit in certain psychoanalytic interpretations—more than most folklorists are prepared to admit. Thus, it is distressing that psychoanalytic scholars sometimes do not provide the empirical or ethnographic base for con-vincing their critics, and often do not make explicit the bases by which they know what they know.

Notes

A version of this paper was presented at the annual meeting of the American Folklore Society, October 1983, Nashville, Tennessee. I would like to thank Lydia Fish, Lee Haring, Jay Mechling, Elliott Oring, and Michael Preston for comments on this paper.

1.   In the remainder of this paper, for reasons of linguistic parsimony I shall refer only to narrators and texts, ignoring material culture and events. The analysis I present is, I believe, with few alterations equally applicable to folklore which is not oral.

References Cited

Abrahams, Roger D. and Alan Dundes. 1969. "On Elephantasy and Elephanticide." *Psycho-analytic Review* 56:225–41.

Boyer, L. Bryce. 1979. *Childhood and Folklore: A Psychoanalytic Study of Apache Personality.* New York: Library of Psychoanalytic Anthropology.

———. 1980. "Folklore, Anthropology, and Psychoanalysis." *Journal of Psychoanalytical Anthropology* 3:259–79.

Burns, Tom. 1976. *Doing the Wash: An Expressive Culture and Personality Study of a Joke and its Tellers.* Norwood, Penn.: Norwood Editions.

Dégh, Linda. 1968. "The Hook." *Indiana Folklore* 1:92–100.

Dorson, Richard M. 1972. "Introduction: Concepts of Folklore and Folklife Studies." In *Folklore and Folklife: An Introduction,* ed. Richard M. Dorson. Chicago: University of Chicago Press.

Dundes, Alan. 1971. "On the Psychology of Legend." In *American Folk Legend,* ed. Wayland D. Hand. Los Angeles: University of California Press.

———. 1976. "The Crowning Hen and the Easter Bunny: Male Chauvinism in American Folklore." In *Folklore Today: A Festschrift for Richard M. Dorson,* eds., Linda Dégh, Henry Glassie, and Felix J. Oinas. Bloomington: Research Center for Language and Semiotic Studies, Indiana University.

———. 1977a. "The Curious Case of the Wide-mouth Frog." *Language in Society* 6:141–47.

———. 1977b. "Who are the Folk?" In *Frontiers of Folklore,* ed. William Bascom. Boulder: Westview Press.

———. 1978. "Into the Endzone for a Touchdown: A Psychoanalytic Consideration of American Football." *Western Folklore* 37:75–88.

———. 1979. "The Symbolic Equivalence of Allomotifs in "The Rabbit Herd' " (AT 570). Paper presented at the Seventh Congress of the International Society for Folk-Narrative Research, Edinburgh, Scotland.

———. 1980. *Interpreting Folklore.* Bloomington: Indiana University Press.

———. 1984. *Life is Like a Chicken Coop Ladder.* New York: Columbia University Press.

Erickson, Erik. 1963. *Childhood and Society.* Second Edition. New York: Norton.

Fine, Gary Alan. 1983. *Shared Fantasy: Role Playing Games as Social Worlds.* Chicago: University of Chicago Press.

Freud, Sigmund. 1957. Letter to Dr. Friedrich S. Krauss on *Anthropophyteia.* In *The Standard Edition of the Complete Psychological Works of Sigmund Freud.* Volume XI, ed. James Strachey. London: Hogarth Press (orig. 1910).

———. 1961. "Introductory Lectures on Psycho-Analysis." In *The Standard Edition of the Complete Psychological Works of Sigmund Freud.* Volume XV, ed. James Strachey. London: Hogarth Press (orig. 1916).

Freud, Sigmund and Ernst Oppenheim. 1958. "Dreams of Folklore." In *The Standard Edition of the Complete Psychological Works of Sigmund Freud.* Volume XII, ed. James Strachey. London: Hogarth Press (orig. 1911).

Hufford, David. 1974. "Psychology, Psychoanalysis, and Folklore." *Southern Folklore Quarterly* 38:187–97.

Jacobs, Melville. 1952. "Psychological Inferences from a Chinook Myth." *Journal of American Folklore* 65:121–37.

Kardiner, Abram. 1945. *The Psychological Frontiers of Society.* New York: Columbia University Press.

Ketner, Kenneth L. 1973. "The Role of Hypotheses in Folkloristics." *Journal of American Folklore* 86:114–30.

La Barre, Weston. 1948. "Folklore and Psychology." *Journal of American Folklore* 61:382–90.

Mechling, Jay. 1980. "High Kybo Floater: Folk Speech and Naming at a Boy Scout Camp."

Unpublished paper delivered at annual meeting of the American Folklore Society, Pittsburgh, Penn.

Roheim, Geza. 1969. *Psychoanalysis and Anthropology: Culture, Personality and the Unconscious.* New York: International Universities Press.

———. 1952. *The Gates of the Dream.* New York: International Universities Press.

Wax, Murray L. 1983. "How Oeidpus Falsifies Popper: Psychoanalysis as a Normative Science." *Psychiatry* 46:95–105.

Whiting, John W. and I. L. Child. 1953. *Child Training and Personality: A Cross-Cultural Study.* New Haven: Yale University Press.

2

The Promiscuous Cheerleader:
An Adolescent Male Belief Legend

With Bruce Noel Johnson

Although most folkloric research has been conducted with male informants, the bulk of research on adolescent legend telling has been done with females. While legends of adolescent girls may have sexual overtones,[1] they are not clinical in detail—at least among middle-class teenagers. Typically sexuality in the legends of adolescent girls is symbolic rather than overt.[2] Even a memorate-belief story about being drugged and seduced[3] is told in such a way that the sexual content of the story is secondary to the situational and emotional involvements of the participants. Further, most of these female stories emphasize the negative consequences of sexual activity; they are cautionary tales rather than tales involving wish-fulfillment. Because different standards of appropriate sexual conduct and motivation for men and women exist in our culture, legends spread by males have quite distinct themes, often focusing more on wish fulfillment than on personal caution. As Toelken notes, sexually-oriented folk stories represent the feelings of a society and particularly of the group in society which tells them.[4]

Whatever the sexual implications of the folklore of adolescent girls coming of age in a sexualized society, there can be little debate that the few adolescent male legends collected have phallic implications. The grossness tales published anonymously in the *Journal of American Folklore* in 1962 provide an indication of the explicitness of male legendary stories.[5] Likewise, legends involving trading beer bottle labels for "a piece of ass" include little symbolic sublimation.[6] Because of the explicitness of male stories, psychosexual interpretations seem inevitable.

The following analysis presents a corpus of legend texts dealing with a high school or college cheerleader who has sex with the members of the team for which she is cheering. It is a theme that is not uncommon in the American popular arts—as perhaps most recently represented in a series of racy films entitled "The Cheerleaders," "The Revenge of the Cheerleaders," etc.[7] The cheerleader is generally seen both as a symbol of virtuous young womanhood and, because of her position, as a highly desirable sexual possession, who wears sexy clothing and dances in an enticing fashion. When female high school students were asked in a 1972–73 survey what they would most like to be, 81 percent answered "a Cheerleader."[8] The "rights" to cheerleaders are believed, in the main, to belong to members of a school's athletic teams—the "big" men on campus. Within this context, the legend of "The Promiscuous Cheerleader" has developed, transmitted primarily by males in all-male situations. It addresses, from a male perspective, the position of the adolescent woman, represented by the cheerleader, in contemporary society.

The legend tells of a girl who has sexual relations (often fellatio) with members of an athletic team. She becomes ill, sometimes while cheering at a game, and must be rushed to the hospital. There doctors pump her stomach, removing a miraculous amount of semen. We have collected twenty-nine variants of the basic legend text in Minnesota, enough to convince us that the story is traditional.[9]

The following version is typical:

> The story I remember from high school was of a University [of Minnesota] cheerleader who got her kicks by giving blow jobs to the basketball team, the players and that. And that she snuck down somehow, or I don't know if it was . . . I think it was before a game, or the night before a game or something. Ah, got it on with almost the entire team, gettin' off given' 'em all suck jobs. And uh she got sick, during the game she fainted, and they had to take her away and she got a quart of cum in her.
>
> Q. Where was the story told?
>
> I was at the basketball practice the first time I heard it.
>
> Q. Where else did you hear it?
>
> In the locker room [laugh]. We talked about it, that was the thing to talk about. The first time we were watching the girls gymnastics and we got talking about it. We all had hard ons.[10]

Content Issues

Despite a debate over subconscious sexual symbolism in legends of adolescent girls, the legend of the promiscuous cheerleader can only be interpreted sexually. Teen legends often indicate different ways for adolescents to deal with their emergent sexuality. For example, legends collected from both males and females stigmatize excessive behavior by a member of the opposite sex. In the popular legend "The Hook," according to Alan Dundes, sexuality merges with aggression, and *direct* sexual content is sublimated. Although "The Promiscuous Cheerleader" does not involve sublimation, psychiatric projection does take place. Unacceptable sexual desires are projected to the cheerleader, and are thus simultaneously expressed and controlled. In the legend, the cheerleader does not control her desires and therefore suffers negative consequences.

"The Promiscuous Cheerleader" expresses a collective male fantasy of the innocent, yet sexually avaricious, woman. She is the girl-next-door who will succumb to the expression of male prowess. This motif appeals to the male athlete, and many of the versions collected were transmitted by athletes and their friends. The athlete feels a growing sense of physical confidence in himself in the sports arena, and this confidence is bolstered by social esteem in his peer group[11]; however, as an adolescent, he still experiences uncertainty in his heterosexual relationships. Three versions of the legend deal directly with this conflict by having the cheerleader promise herself to the team *only* if they win the game. Thus the male's athletic prowess replaces the awkwardness felt in boy-girl encounters:

> All I remember is that uh, is that this girl made a bet with a high school hockey team in Edina East up when Edina was one school. . . . Back in about '71 . . . '70 that if they won the state tournament she'd blow everyone on the hockey team, and they won the tournament, and she blew all the guys on the hockey team at some party.[12]

In order to comprehend the social meaning of the legend it is necessary to examine the twenty-nine versions collected from mid-February to mid-June of 1977. These versions were collected from twenty-six individuals. Twenty-one of the twenty-six were males; all were white and between eighteen and twenty-five years of age; twenty-three were college students. We cannot deduce from these figures that the story is found primarily among white male adolescents and young adults, since this distribution represents our selective interviews; however, while some young women do know this story and tell it with similar details, our questioning suggests that women do not know it as well as men. We shall treat it in this analysis as a male legend.

Reports from informants indicate that the legend may have been particularly widely spread in Minnesota during the period 1971 through 1975. The fact that the story is said to have occurred in the early 1970s may have two implications. First, it suggests that the narrative is characteristic of the high school period: we collected our versions from college-age students, but they learned them during their high school years. Second, the early 1970s were characterized by the beginning of a change in the role and behavior of women. Women throughout America were demanding equal rights—economically and sexually —and the fact that these legend variants were transmitted during this period suggests that they were addressing important psychodynamic issues which may have become salient as a result of feminism.

Ten informants mentioned that the cheerleader and the players were associated with a football team, eight named a hockey team, nine mentioned a basketball team, and two others suggested that it was a girl and several guys. The three sports referred to are the major sports in Minnesota. In addition, they are team sports, sports that are characterized by a high degree of male-male cohesive bonding. Finally, all three involve considerable male-male bodily contact and thus include situations in which strong emotional ties to a member of the same sex are combined with physical contact. While it would be premature to suggest a homosexual implication[13] (though oral sex is characteristic of homosexual encounters), the communal sharing of a salient cultural object is characteristic of homosociality. The team serves as a sexual brotherhood, and this male narrative is a mechanism of dealing with the problem of limited female availability for sexual intimacy—a problem posed by Freud[14] as being at the core of human society. If all the brothers have equal access to the female, then the ideal brotherhood is protected.

Sexual Content

The core of the story involves an agreement by the cheerleader to have sexual relations with the team. She performs this action and subsequently becomes ill, requires hospitalization, and has her stomach pumped.

In twenty-two of the twenty-nine versions, the cheerleader is said to have performed oral sex on the members of the team. This is a central element of the narrative and would appear to be a logical necessity if the girl's stomach is to be pumped. In two versions both oral and genital sexual acts are performed, and in one case intercourse alone is specified. In the last instance the semen is believed to enter the stomach as a result of intercourse, a misconception akin to the traditional belief that babies grow within the mother's stomach.[15] Mentioning oral sex seems significant, because fellatio is typically considered a degrading sexual act for the woman. In addition, oral sex seems a symbolically appropriate act for a *cheer*leader. Cheerleading is primarily an oral activity, supplemented by erotic bodily contortions, conducted in a state of physical excitement.

An additional core element of the legend is the cheerleader's becoming ill and being taken to a hospital; this detail occurs in twenty-four versions—while only two explicitly deny it. In all cases in which the cheerleader is brought to the hospital, she is taken there to have her stomach pumped. The illness is natural, a result of her moral transgression. However, when taken to the hospital, she is placed under the supervision of adult authorities and, by following their prescriptions, recovers. Thus, "The Promiscuous Cheerleader," like "The Hook," can have an adult, middle-class perspective.

The amount of semen removed from the cheerleader's stomach varies, with estimates ranging from a pint to "up to four to six quarts." The average amount of semen contained in a male ejaculation is four to five cubic centimeters, or approximately one-half teaspoon; thus the figures given are psychologically significant exaggerations. The mistaken amount of seminal fluid indicates exaggeration of the male's sexual prowess—perhaps serving a wish-fulfillment function. Further, since semen is largely protein, there is no medical rationale for pumping the girls' stomach. The stomach-pumping serves as a symbolic punishment.

In only two versions are there negative consequences for the male players. In one case, they lose the game; in another they, along with the cheerleader, are suspended. However these are exceptions; most respondents mention no negative outcomes for the athletes beyond a few unsuccessful attempts to identify them:

> There was some . . . evidently there was supposed to be administrative um not investigation, but um evidently that somebody squealed or something, and wanted to start kind an investigation, and most everybody clammed up.
>
> Q. So there was an investigation?
>
> Not that was pursued, no.[16]

In terms of the psychological function of the narrative it is important for the cheerleader to be punished biologically, but not by the adult power structure, and for the players involved not to be punished at all. Because the girl's violation is supposedly against the natural order, her punishment is physical. The players on the other hand, are thought not to violate their proper sexual roles and thus receive no punishment. This legend exemplifies the traditional sexual order that American male adolescents have held to in the 1970s.

The legend also serves a social-political purpose by reinforcing the traditional roles of men and women in American society. As noted above, the early 1970s marked the emergence of the women's movement in the United States—a movement that threatened men in both their sexual and economic roles. Particularly affected were adolescent males just in the process of learning American adult sexual roles and sexual mores. This socialization process is anxiety-producing for the adolescent male because he often finds young women performing better academically.[17] Previously he could be assured that his female competitors would drop out of the job market; in addition, he could be sure that he was sexually dominant. The women's movement threatened to change his position of dominance. Under these conditions of social stress folklore can be expected to reflect the salient issues in narrative forms. By picturing the previously submissive young woman as a victim of her own liberated sexual

desires—a change from the traditional role of the sexually passive female—
this adolescent male legend argues for the legitimacy of the status quo while
simultaneously expressing a desire for the sexually open female.

Transmission Setting

Men hear these narratives from members of their all-male group, often in circumstances in which male peer bonding is emphasized. Of the twenty-four versions told by males, only one was told with women present. Transmission often
occurs in locker rooms, at practices, or while fellows are hanging around with
friends:

> Well, I was at a wrestling camp a couple of years ago and uh . . . I heard a few
> guys talk from out of state about an experience, you know, they've gone through.
> Some girl was giving them blow jobs [laugh], the whole football team, she got
> sick afterwards and had to get her stomach pumped, and came up with about 2 ¹/₂
> quarts of sperm. [18]

The legend is also transmitted in typical high school bull sessions. "The Promiscuous Cheerleader" is a stimulating narrative which high school boys respond to with a mixture of shock, surprise, voyeuristic interest, and perhaps
envy (at least publicly expressed envy):

> Q. What were the reactions [to the story]?
>
> Most of us believed it and were envious of that team. [19]

Eighteen versions were believed, while only two were definitely disbelieved.
Few doubted that the story as told *could* occur, despite its physical impossibility. The credibility given to the legend emphasizes its psychological impact
on those who hear it and indicates the extent of sexual ignorance that characterizes contemporary adolescents and young adults.

The reaction to the legend combines a degrading of the girl with an envy of
the team for which she cheers—an indication of the function of the story as
wish-fulfillment. Thus, the double standard in sexual relations is reinforced.
Several male informants have commented (humorously) that they would like to
get to know this cheerleader:

> My story as I hear it from alias B—— S——, ex-wrestler for the University of
> Minnesota told me that, on set given date, after the University basketball team
> won their 1972 championship that this cheerleader gave set players on the varsity
> squad set many blow jobs, uh . . . thereby filling up her belly with sperm and
> having to get it pumped out. Um, that's the story as I know it today. I don't know
> the girl's name, address, or phone number, but would like to get it. [Laugh]

Q. B——, do you know why she did it?

Hell, no! [Laugh][20]

Although the teller of this variant thought the story "crude" and could not understand why the cheerleader would engage in such behavior, he did express envy for the fortunate players. The dichotomy between "the good girl" and "the easy girl" is the emotional crux of the story. The cheerleader is the image of the good girl—sexually virtuous and highly desirable. She is the object her male contemporaries fantasize about and lust after. By projecting their desires onto her, they relieve themselves of the admission of unfulfilled sexual longing. In addition, since the cheerleader becomes involved with the members of the team she is cheering for, an element of incestuous fantasy is involved. In many of the stories, the event occurs at a party after the game—a party to which cheerleaders are invited because their role is structurally a part of the team. While one should not press the incest imagery, the fact that the cheerleader has a special relationship to the team "family" is a central element of these stories.

Social Content

Seven versions involve an additional projection. In these cases the locale of the story is set in the high school with which the informant's school has a long-standing rivalry. In this collection two rivalry relationships are involved— Burnsville vs. Prior Lake, and Edina (East) vs. Richfield. In both cases the schools have a long tradition of athletic competition. Although versions were collected from former students at all four high schools, only in Prior Lake and in Richfield were stories collected about the rival school. This is significant because Edina and Burnsville enjoy more social prestige than their rivals, and their sports teams have had a tradition of success. One former Edina student did claim to have heard the story about Edina, but from a former Richfield high school student, and had not heard the inverse story at Edina East High School.

> People who told it were sure that it happened in Edina. Richfield and Edina used to be big rivals back in that time [Spring 1973].[21]

> All I know is that she was a Burnsville cheerleader and at the time we heard about it, we were always big enemies with Burnsville and they always had cute looking cheerleaders, so . . . [22]

While not all of the stories concern rival schools, a sufficiently large number do to suggest that inter-school competition influences the localization of the legend—deviance is located in one's rival school. Yet, with the male's fantasized desire for sexual contact, the story also intensifies the envy by the less successful school of the more successful one.

The naming in twelve versions of Edina as the locale or possible locale indicates that this legend has attached itself to more than just any rivalry. Edina is the wealthiest major suburb in the Twin Cities metropolitan area and is stereotyped as the Scarsdale, Shaker Heights, Newton, or Grosse Pointe of Minneapolis. This envy is projected into the story—perhaps symbolizing the breakdown of moral values in this suburban community and/or the jealousy felt against those who have "everything." Part of the localization is due not only to economic interests but also to Edina East High School's reputation as one of the most successful high schools in Minnesota sports.

Conclusion

We have suggested that the legend of "The Promiscuous Cheerleader" serves social and psychological functions for those who transmit it. First, it denigrates the position of women by suggesting the dangers of their taking sexually aggressive roles. The legend reinforces the dominant position of the male by having a women perform what is seen as a "degrading" sexual act. Males, however, respond to this legend with a mixture of emotions—apparently they are projecting their fantasies to others. Further, for male athletes the legend signifies the importance of team unity—they are involved as a team rather than as individuals; the fact that the fellatio is often performed on the entire team stresses the brotherhood of these young men.

Second, the legend is popular among young men at a time in their lives when they must come to terms with their masculinity and their relations with the opposite sex. The promiscuous cheerleader effectively saves them from embarrassment about sexual maneuvering by offering herself to them. The risk of making a sexual advance and having it rejected is eliminated in this fantasy.

Third, the legend spread during the early 1970s, a period characterized by an increased emphasis on sexuality and on women's assertiveness. The response in the legend was ambivalent—a warning to sexually aggressive women and the implication that it was perfectly acceptable for members of the team to take advantage of the cheerleader's sexual proposition.

Finally, tellers of the legend seem to use it to belittle (while secretly envying) their rivals. The promiscuity of the rivals' cheerleaders provides further evidence of their moral turpitude but simultaneously provokes envy towards a school located in a better suburb and a school more successful athletically. The projection of these stories, then, is twofold—to the cheerleader and to the rival school. It thus serves both psychological and social ends.

Notes

The authors would like to acknowledge the help of Harry Foreman, Frank Hoffmann, James Leary, Ira Reiss, and Ellen Stekert in the preparation of this paper.

1. Sylvia Grider, "Dormitory Legend-Telling in Progress: Fall, 1971–Winter 1973," *Indiana Folklore* 6 (1973):1–32.

2. Alan Dundes, "On the Psychology of Legend," in *American Folk Legend: A Symposium,* ed. Wayland Hand (Berkeley, 1971), 21–36.

3. Andrea Greenberg, "Drugged and Seduced: A Contemporary Legend," *New York Folklore Quarterly* 29 (1973):131–58.

4. Barre Toelken, *The Dynamics of Folklore* (Boston, 1979), 272.

5. Anonymous, "Scatological Lore on Campus," *Journal of American Folklore* 75 (1962):260–62.

6. Michael J. Preston, "Olympia Beer Comes to Colorado: The Spread of a Tradition," *Western Folklore* 32 (1973):281–83.

7. More generally, the image of the female who is sexually accessible to star athletes is well known in fact and fancy. Frank Hoffmann (personal communication, 1978) suggests that this legend may have derived from the stereotype of the "college widow." He also notes "the widely circulated story about the 1920s actress Clara Bow, who reportedly took on the entire Southern Cal. team."

8. Randy Neil, *The Encyclopedia of Cheerleading* (Shawnee-Mission, Kansas, 1975), 26. Neil claims the survey sampled "10th, 11th and 12th grade students in 16 states coast to coast." As head of the International Cheerleading Foundation, Neil may be biased, and since the specifics of the study are not provided, they may over-state the desire to be a cheerleader. Whatever the actual figure, the cheerleader holds a highly esteemed status in American life.

9. James Leary (personal communication, 1978) claims that male informants from Waseca, Minnesota, the Catskill area of New York, and Reading, Pennsylvania, recognized the story as being attached to high school basketball teams in the late 1960s and early 1970s.

10. Collected by Bruce Johnson, 4/16/77. Male, truck driver and vocational student, age nineteen, from Prior Lake, Minnesota.

11. Alan A. Stone, "Football," in *Motivation in Play, Games and Sports,* ed. Ralph Slovenko and James A. Knight (Springfield, Illinois, 1967), 425.

12. Collected by Gary Alan Fine, 2/77. Male, University of Minnesota senior, age 22, from south Minneapolis (St. Thomas High School).

13. Alan Dundes, "Into the Endzone for a Touchdown: A Psychoanalytic Consideration of American Football," *Western Folklore* 37 (1978):75–88.

14. Sigmund Freud, *Totem and Taboo* (New York, 1918), 160.

15. Ellen Stekert has suggested (personal communication) that there is a connection between a woman's having her belly filled with sperm and pregnancy; if so, this would provide another significant example of male psychological needs being met by this legend, by emphasizing male progeny-producing potency. This theme corresponds to Aarne-Thompson Motif T512.6: Conception from drinking sperm.

16. Collected by Gray Alan Fine, 3/11/77. Male, senior, University of Minnesota, from St. Louis Park, Minnesota.

17. Eleanor E. Maccoby and Carol N. Jacklin, *The Psychology of Sex Differences* (Stanford, 1974), 135.

18. Collected by Bruce Johnson, 6/1/77. Male, Prior Lake High School senior, age 19, from Prior Lake, Minnesota.
19. Collected by Bruce Johnson, 4/8/77. Male, Mankato State University sophomore, age 19, from Prior Lake, Minnesota.
20. Collected by Bruce Johnson, 4/13/77. Male, gas station attendant, age 20, from Prior Lake, Minnesota.
21. Collected by Gary Alan Fine, 2/25/77. Male, University of Minnesota freshman, age 21, from Richfield, Minnesota.
22. Collected by Bruce Johnson, 4/19/77. Male, University of Minnesota sophomore, age 20, former cheerleader from Prior Lake, Minnesota.

3

Welcome to the World of AIDS:
Fantasies of Female Revenge

That folklore responds to current events is widely acknowledged. A fundamental problem for folklorists is to determine how it responds and what are the overt and covert meanings of that response. Folklorists must strive to present interpretations that make sense in light of the detailed content of the texts collected and the social environment in which they are embedded.[1]

Major epidemics have always provided a rich vein of folklore—particularly the creation of rumors, legends, folk beliefs, and even humor. Accounts of cholera, polio and the Black Plague[2] have demonstrated the connection of folklore to the popular understanding of disease. As a result, the existence of folklore surrounding the epidemic (or pandemic) of Acquired Immune Deficiency Syndrome is not surprising. Some of the earliest texts consisted of folk beliefs about the epidemiology of the disease. People discussed the possibility of the disease being spread by mosquitoes, sneezes, or toilet seats—each an actual or presumed vector for the dissemination of other diseases. At the same time, as AIDS spread widely within the homosexual community, a series of jokes linked homosexual male behavior with the disease.[3] While these jokes mined a new topic, the structure of the jokes was traditional:

> What do you get from listening to San Francisco gays?
> Hearing AIDS.

> How do you know that your garden has AIDS?
> When you find your pansies are dying.[4]

The AIDS epidemic has a dynamic of its own. As it has spread outside the homosexual male community, the folklore has changed. While jokes still focus on gays, urban legends dealing with heterosexual activity have recently been communicated, reflecting new levels of concern. Specifically, I focus on stories in which an individual deliberately and knowingly transmits the AIDS virus to another person.

This analysis is based upon a corpus of texts collected in the Twin Cities metropolitan area, primarily from students at the University of Minnesota in February 1987. I do not claim that these texts are representative of what is occurring elsewhere or among other populations, although texts have been reported from California, Connecticut, Florida, Illinois, Indiana, Missouri, New York, Texas, Washington, and Sweden. A public affairs specialist at the Centers for Disease Control in Atlanta had heard the story, but knew of no evidence that it was true. It has been reported as being spread on the "Joan Rivers Show" and in the *Chicago Sun-Times, Seattle Times,* and *San Francisco Examiner.*[5]

The corpus of Minnesota texts consists of sixteen full (if brief) rumor/legends, and seventeen partial accounts that indicate that students have heard something about the rumor/legend although few (or no) details were supplied. Of the sample of thirty-three informants, fifteen (45 percent) were male. The story is known widely by both young men and women. It should be emphasized that, given that the data collection was not based on random sampling, other demographic conclusions are not warranted. I shall focus on the sixteen full texts, but start with a lengthy text collected from a south Florida man:

This guy was a young single dude with everything going for him. He had his own house, brand new car and a real good job. This guy was no dummy. He just got a promotion and he had the chance to really go places. Well, anyway, he was downtown at a nice nightclub and he met this chick, nice looking, young . . . beautiful. So, he takes her home to his house and she spends the night with him. They have a good time and in the morning he goes to take her home. She tells him to drop her off downtown near where he picked her up and she'll walk home from there. He says "Why can't I take you home? Have you got a husband?" She says "No. I'm not married, it's just that I don't know what kind of guy you are. There are a lot of weirdos around, you know. I'd rather you didn't know where I live." So, he thinks, well, I can see that but . . . maybe she's trying to get rid of him, so he asks if he can see her again. She says, "Sure," and they make a date to meet at the same nightclub. So they meet and she goes home with him again and they get it on, but when he goes to take her home the same thing happens. This time she has him drop her off in another part of town. This goes on for about a month. She'll stay the night but she won't let him take her home. So he's thinking, OK, she wants to have sex but she doesn't want to get involved with him. Maybe she just got divorced or something, but she acts like she likes him, so he'll go along with that. Anyway, one morning, after they fucked all night, he wakes up and she's already gone. So he takes a shower and goes in the other room to get dressed and he sees where she wrote on the mirror with her lipstick—WELCOME TO THE WORLD OF AIDS. (At this point everyone is staring open-mouthed, some mutter: Gaw-dam. I'd kill that bitch. Sheeit . . . AIDS! What happened to him? Did he die?) No . . . he isn't dead . . . yet! But he checked it out with a couple of doctors and he's *definitely* got it. (Damn!) So now he spends all his time looking for that bitch. They told him he's only got about a year to live, so he drives around town looking to find her. He went back to the nightclub where he met her, but nobody knows her there and she hasn't been back. [Personal communication to Jan Harold Brunvand, from male plumber, Miami, Florida, area]

This guy picked up a girl at a bar and took her to his apartment, and the next morning she was gone. He went into his bathroom and written in red lipstick on his mirror was "Welcome to the world of AIDS." At first he thought it was a prank, but he called the police who told him, "We didn't want to worry people, but that's the seventh time that happened this year, and one of them tested positively." [Collected from male, twenties]

In my hometown of Cottage Grove [a suburb of St. Paul] there is a new bar called After the Gold Rush. Specifically a young lady lured a man to the Travel Host "local motel" and left a message in lipstick on the bathroom mirror. [Collected from male, eighteen]

A friend of [my roommate] picked up a woman in a bar, took her home. She was gone in the morning when he woke up and written on the bathroom mirror was "Welcome to the Wacky World of AIDS." Then he went to the doctor, asked for an AIDS test, and tested positive. [Collected from female, early twenties]

The first thing to note is that the virus is passed from the woman to the man. In fifteen of the sixteen accounts I collected and in eleven texts collected by Jan Harold Brunvand, it is the woman who transmits the virus.[6] This detail should be put in context; at the time this article is written (April 1987) there are apparently only three cases of AIDS in Minnesota that can be attributed to heterosexual transmission of the virus: all from men to women. While there are some cases of transmission from women to men nationally, the reverse is common. I shall return to this issue in my discussion of the meaning of the story. This is significant in that there was a controversy in the Twin Cities (reported nationally) two years before when one of the local TV stations did a report on a gay male prostitute who, knowing that he had AIDS (the disease, not just the infection), continued to engage in sexual relations for money. The television station paid this man to gain his permission to record his behavior and did not inform the public health authorities while filming the story. Thus, the Twin Cities public was aware that some individuals do continue to have sexual relations after knowing they are contagious—even though this was a gay man, not a heterosexual woman.

In thirteen cases (81 percent) the message that the woman has AIDS is left on the bathroom mirror. In one case a note is attached to the pillow, in one text an unspecified note is left, and the final case provides no information. Seven (54 percent) of the thirteen messages on the mirror are written in lipstick. Three informants specified that the message was written in red lipstick. This detail may have several explanations. First, it makes for an aesthetically pleasing story by introducing the movement of the man from the bedroom to the bathroom, and the implicit change from puzzlement (at not finding his lover) to horror when he reads the note. Second, such a detail corresponds to a recent magazine advertisement for Bill Blass men's underwear in which a handsome man in bikini briefs finds a note from his lover written in red lipstick on the bathroom mirror (*Playboy,* January 1986:211). Further, a woman wearing lipstick, and particularly red lipstick, has traditionally conveyed an image of sexuality, mystery, and, possibly, danger—as in the idea of a "scarlet" woman.

Eight of the sixteen suggest that the man and woman meet at a bar; of these, four name the popular suburban St. Paul dating bar, After the Gold Rush (supplying such identifying and confirming details are common in urban belief legends).[7] Such a setting emphasizes the anonymous quality of the relationship. Another variant claims that, as a rite of passage to male adulthood, the woman is hired:

> A brother buys a hooker for his younger brother's nineteenth birthday. In the morning the younger brother wakes up; the hooker is gone and on the bathroom mirror is written "Welcome to the World of AIDS." [Collected from female, twenty-one]

Again, the anonymous nature of the sexual relationship is emphasized in this text.

The message is consistently reported. Eleven of the sixteen accounts report a message. In nine of these cases (82 percent) the woman writes "Welcome to the World of AIDS." In one she writes "Welcome to the Wacky World of AIDS" and in one "Welcome to the AIDS family." Brunvand (personal communication) reports that in one instance the message was "Welcome to the AIDS club." They suggest that having AIDS (testing positively for the virus) cements the person into a social (or folk) community, from which one can never escape and which will expand.

As is typical in legend analysis, informants are divided over whether the story is to be believed. Of the twelve who provide information, five believe that the event happened, three claim disbelief, and four are unsure. All but one informant heard the legend through interpersonal channels—typically from friends or co-workers. Only one informant claimed to have heard the information from the mass media (this was the only informant who claimed that the victim was a female). Three of the informants insisted that the victim was "a friend of a friend."

What do these texts mean? Why do so many young Americans feel these urban legends are worthy of communication and belief? One answer is that in this age of sexually transmitted diseases, people are wary of impersonal sexual contact. While such an explanation is not wholly false, neither does it explain why this story is told.

If one considers the story as something that might have occurred, one might be surprises that the perpetrator is a woman and the victim is a male. Current medical evidence, as reported by the Centers for Diseases Control, suggests that it is easier for the AIDS virus to spread from man to woman than from woman to man. In addition, the likely heterosexual spread of most cases at the present time is from bisexual men or drug-using men to heterosexual women. The spread from women to men (with the possible exception of prostitutes) is still rare. Thus, one needs to explain why this story involves infection from woman to man.

First, we should note that this legend may have different functions for men and for women—although both represent attempts to come to terms with the relationships between men and women in the 1980s. I wish to suggest that the underlying meaning of these legends may not be about AIDS so much as it is about rape. During the last decade there has been increased attention and resources given to the problem of rape (although perhaps still modest considering the need). Many women feel that they are vulnerable to the attacks of males, particularly in the kind of anonymous "dates" described in these texts. The women have little control because accusations of forced sexual intercourse can easily be countered as engaged in by "mutual consent." What is called "date rape" is only now being recognized as a serious social problem. Many women note that living through a rape permanently changes them; sometimes this change involves losing the ability to enjoy sexual relations. The man vanishes from her life with no penalty.

Stories such as those cited here are, for women, a subtle revenge against men, a revenge, perhaps, in which they are not aware that they are engaged. The rape is turned on its head. The woman permanently changes the life of the male, removing the possibility of sexual satisfaction from him. She is in full control during the evening (whatever he might think), and he is unaware of what is in store for him. His shock the following morning and the humiliation of having the AIDS test are further indications of the power of the woman. The fact that the story is told to indicate that he will now join "the world of AIDS," "the AIDS club," or "the AIDS family" indicates that the woman is doing to the man what men have been doing to women for years, stigmatizing them as "damaged"—both sexes are now in the same moral community.

For men the story plays on their collective paranoia toward women. Although feminists have argued that men have patriarchal control over women, many men mistrust women. The image of the evil woman, the castrator, has a long history in folklore and literature. Here the story is brought up to the present. Women are able to tell personal experience stories that indicate their fear of men (stories of sexual assault and harassment). Men have no equivalent body of texts; and so to express similar fears (if less well-founded ones) they must rely on fantasy. The woman with her red lipstick, who disappears after intercourse, is such a fantasy figure—a modern succubus. The story indicates for men that their illusion of control may be just "an illusion."

Neither males nor females wish to admit the reality and depth of their fears, and so they purge the stories of drama and hatred. The woman might write a message expressing her undying hatred of men and her reasons for revenge. Instead, she crayons a *bon mot:* "welcome to the world of AIDS." The unacceptable impulses that lie behind this story remain discretely hidden, so hidden that it could reasonably be claimed that this is only a story about sexual promiscuity, rather than about sexual violence.

The analysis presented here provides for an explanation of the major details of the urban legend (its internal consistency) and the contexts in which the story is found (its external validity).[8] While any socio-psychological analysis must ultimately be tentative, we can feel some confidence in that the meaning of these texts goes beyond the simple fear of contracting this fatal disease. They are responsive to other social forces currently prevalent.

The sour truth is that we all now reside in "the world of AIDS." While medical researchers will attempt to develop cures, other virulent viruses will be spread in folklore. We must be as vigilant in decoding our texts as virologists are in decoding theirs.

Notes

I wish to thank Jan Harold Brunvand, Pack Carnes, and Bruce Jackson for their comments on an earlier version of this paper.

1. Alan Dundes, "The Psychology of the Legend," in *American Folk Legend,* ed. Wayland D. Hand (Berkeley, 1971), 21–36. Gary Alan Fine, "Evaluating Psychoanalytic Folklore: Are Freudians Ever Right?" *New York Folklore* 10 (1984):5–20.
2. Charles E. Rosenberg, *The Cholera Years* (Chicago, 1962); John R. Paul, *History of Poliomyelitis* (New Haven, 1971); Philip Ziegler, *The Black Death* (New York, 1969).
3. See Alan Dundes, "At Ease, Disease—AIDS Jokes as Sick Humor," *American Behavioral Scientist* 30 (1987):72–81; Casper G. Schmidt, "AIDS Jokes, or, Schadenfreude Around an Epidemic," *Maledicta* 8 (1984–85):69–75.
4. Reinhold Aman, "Kakologia: A Chronicle of Nasty Riddles and Naughty Wordplays," *Maledicta* 8 (1984–85):215–16.
5. Personal communication, Jan Harold Brunvand. Three texts (collected by Pack Carnes in Berkeley) recently came to my attention in which a woman infects an American serviceman in Southeast Asia with the AIDS virus. One of the texts is as follows:

    > This guy in the navy went to port, I don't know, somewhere in Southeast Asia. He went to a whorehouse and found this girl. He went to bed with her, but she was gone when he woke up and he couldn't find her. Instead he found on the mirror, written in lipstick: "Now *you've* got AIDS, sucker!" He tried to find her, but he couldn't. It turned out that she wasn't one of the regular girls in the whorehouse.

    This text, collected in January 1987, was allegedly heard by this male informant "a year or two ago" from his brother in the Navy. The raw hostility of the text, coupled with the exotic locale, and the lack of the now traditional tag line ("Welcome to the World of AIDS") suggests the possibility that this was an earlier version of the text now being collected widely in America. Armed forces personnel coping with their casual sexual encounters might have been the first group for which this theme was psychologically relevant.

6. In one newspaper account she is known as "AIDS Mary."
7. The manager confirms that he has heard the legend, but doesn't know how it started, and he has no evidence that it is true. (Steven McCarthy, personal communication).
8. Fine, 5–20.

II DANGEROUS PRODUCTS

4

Cokelore and Coke Law: Urban Belief Tales and the Problem of Multiple Origins

With the wide acceptance of the principle of diffusion as the key to understanding the existence of folklore variation, the theory of multiple origins (polygenesis) has drifted into academic antiquity. Folklorists admit that for local legends, simple forms, or motifs, polygenesis may have occurred, but that complex tales typically are spread through diffusion.[1] Thus, the scholarly *presumption* is that diffusion alone is sufficient to explain the wide knowledge of traditional forms, and is disproved only rarely and with some difficulty.

Such a belief in the power of diffusion applies to the examination of urban belief tales, with folklorists hoping (and sometimes searching) to find either the Ur-form[2] or actual event behind the narrative. Thus, Dorson claims to have discovered the actual automotive responsible for the "Death Car" legend:

> Did this modern big-city legend originate with an actual incident in a hamlet of two hundred people in a rural Negro community and by the devious ways of folklore spread to Michigan's metropolises, and then to other states? Unlikely as it seems, the evidence from many variants, compared through the historical-geographical method of tracing folktales, calls for an affirmative answer.[3]

While there is no reason (other than scepticism) to challenge this conclusion, it seems to rest on the diffusionist assumption that such tales *must* be derived from a single origin. Thus, a legend is assumed to be generated from a memorate or a personal experience story.[4] A problem arises when similar events are repeated frequently. In such cases a simple diffusion model is inadequate.

Multiple origin and diffusion theories, of course, refer to the creation of folklore forms, and not to the events on which these forms are based. However, neither approach has a *necessary* assumption that folklore forms are a function of imagination alone, although this view may have been promulgated by individual folklorists. Both recognize that folklore may originate as a fictional account or as a rendition of actual events. Thus, the issue of *number* of origins is structurally distinct from the issue of the *nature* of the creation. Legend researchers are prone to emphasize the kernel of truth in legend formation, and this applies to multiple origins as well as diffusion. If numerous similar events occur (of the type that potentially provokes legends), then it follows that parallel legends may develop independently.

Soft Drinks and Decomposed Mice

The account of a mouse found in a soft drink bottle is a common urban belief tale,[5] which is said to "reflect some of the basic anxieties of our time."[6] One characteristic example alleges:

> Two old ladies stopped into a restaurant to have a little lunch and they both sat down and made their orders and ordered Seven-Up. It came in the old green bottles. And they were sitting there and each poured themselves a glass, and they were chatting away as usual like old ladies do, and uh . . . they finished their first glass and one of them was pouring a second glass of Seven-Up, and all of a sudden she noticed something kinda toward the bottom of the bottle, and she just couldn't quite make out what it was, so they started looking at it, trying to figure out what this thing was at the bottom of the Seven-Up bottle, and finally they tried to pour it out and it came out and it was a decomposed mouse, and they both fainted and they were both revived later on, and after they got home they sued the Seven-Up company, and they made thousands of dollars on the lawsuit. [Tape transcription collected from L. H., 11/15/76, white male, mid-twenties, in Minneapolis; heard from male friends in Davenport, Iowa, circa 1960–65, believed as true]

Primarily, this story differs from other accounts only in its narrative strength, and in that the soft drink is Seven-Up, rather than one of the national colas. Similar stories have been collected in Massachusetts, California, Colorado, and Michigan. Clearly it has national distribution with perhaps 20–30 percent of college student informants having heard of the story. The factual basis of the story should have been apparent, as some versions were told as personal experience narratives:

> This is a true story but I am including it because of what was said in class about foreign objects dissolving in coca cola. It was mid-night when me and a buddy of mine had just gotten off of watch. We went down to the mess hall where we had a coke machine and got 2 cokes. This buddy of mine had his just about half gone when he noticed something in the bottle. We looked and seen this small mouse. We ran up to sick bay to get the doctor and he gave him some white stuff to drink to make him heave. He did, and was sick for the next three days. [Written account, collected by Dan Owens from himself, n.d. for collection, event occurred in Norfolk, Virginia, 1948. From Michigan State University file in Indiana University Folklore Archives]

And:

> Twenty-five years age several friends and I were having a tea party out in the backyard of our house, and one of them found a decomposed mouse in the bottom of a can of Pepsi, and they came in with it, and my mother went haywire. Pepsi came out and gave us a free case, and recalled the whole batch. [Collected by

Gary Alan Fine, 1979, from women, early thirties, who lived in Quincy, Massachusetts at the time of the incident]

Before the assumption is made that these individuals were the original victims and diffusion originated in Norfolk and Quincy, legal documentation should be checked. Unfortunately, records are not kept of the decisions of trial courts (district courts and county courts) in which state liability trials would be held. However, a complete record of the decisions of state appellate courts is available. These records consist of the trial verdicts of the court as well as all decisions written by appellate judges. The decisions typically consist of a summary of the important evidence of the case as well as the legal rationale for affirming or overruling the trial court's decision. Thus, they provide a legalese version of the facts of the case. A search of these documents indicates that in 1914 a case was appealed in Mississippi in which a man named Harry Chapman had brought suit against the Jackson Coca-Cola Bottling Co., won his case, and the local franchise of Coca-Cola appealed. As Justice Reed of the Supreme Court of Mississippi described the situation, heavily influenced by the spirit of Robert Burns: "A 'sma' mousie' caused the trouble in this case. The 'wee, sleekit, cow'rin', tim'rous beastie' drowned in a bottle of coca-cola." (64 So. 791)[7] The appeal was denied and the lower court ruling affirmed for Mr. Chapman. Although this was the first recorded case of this type, it was not to be the last. A total of forty-five cases can be cited in which mice were found in soft-drink bottles—from 1914 to as recently as 1976 (Coca-Cola Bottling Company of Plainview [Texas] v. N. C. White, 545 S.W. 2d 279). As Chief Justice Russell of the Georgia Court of Appeals commented in 1916, there is a "mental aversion which the Aryan race instinctively entertains to ratty nourishment" (Martin v. Waycross Coca-Cola Bottling Co., 89 S.E. 495). It should be emphasized that this figure of forty-five cases does not include cases settled out of court, cases that were not appealed, and of course instances in which no suit was brought. An appeal is brought on the claim of some legal error made in the trial, but in all cases the fact that a mouse was found in a soft drink bottle was not at issue.

The cases occurred regularly from 1914 to 1976 with the 1950s having a particularly large number of cases[8]—whether this was due to increasingly unsanitary bottling conditions, a greater feeling of entitlement of recompense by the victims ("the sue syndrome"), the growth of the soft-drink industry, or a greater legal pugnacity on the part of the industry is not clear from the data available. Victims included twenty-five males (55.5 percent) and twenty females; forty-one adults (91.1 percent) and four minors. Geographically cases can be found in twenty-three states and the District of Columbia,[9] with twenty-one instances (46.6 percent) in the eleven southern states—a function of market penetration and, possibly, relatively unsanitary conditions.

Of these forty-five cases, thirty were decided on appeal for the original plaintiff, eight required a new trial, and seven involved a directed verdict for the defendant. However, as mentioned above, even in these last two circumstances, it was not denied that a mouse was found in the bottle—how it got there and whether it caused any damage was the basis of the appeals. In thirty-five cases records of the trial court's monetary award to the plaintiff are available. Damages range from $50 (a 1953 case) to $20,000 (a 1969 case), with a median award of $1,000, and a mean award of $1,772. The majority of the cases were brought against one of Coca-Cola's franchises. Thirty-nine cases (86.7 percent) were against Coca-Cola, two were against Pepsi-Cola, and one each against Dad's Root Beer, Royal Crown Cola, Sundrop Cola, and Squirt. Before we assume that Coca-Cola is comparatively unsanitary, we should remember that it is the largest company, and for this reason may be more willing to have its lawyers contest trial court decisions. Thus, cases against Royal Crown and Coca-Cola on the trial or pretrial level may be proportional to sales, but Royal Crown may settle more rapidly.

Mice are not the only objects found in the bottles. In appeal court cases unsuspecting customers have discovered roaches, maggots, worms, putrid peanuts, cigarette butts, kerosene, concrete, glass slivers, hairpins, safety pins, paint, and even a condom. Similarly mice are not only discovered in soft-drink bottled but in milk cartons, beer bottles, pies, and dishes served at Chinese restaurants.

The legal accounts of the events bear similarity (as one would expect) to the urban belief tales. Two examples will be cited. The first from Chicago is similar to those cited above:

> On the night of July 24, 1943, plaintiff and her sister went into the Spa Sweet Shop, sat at the counter and each ordered a bottle of Coca-Cola. The waitress took two bottles of Coca-Cola from the cooler, removed the caps therefrom with a bottle opener and placed one bottle in front of plaintiff and one in front of her sister. Plaintiff placed a straw in each bottle and without looking particularly at the contents of her bottle she proceeded to drink same through the straw. According to plaintiff, the following then occurred: "When I got half way down, I remarked to my sister, 'It had an awful taste to it.' She said hers was all right. I kept on drinking, and when I came to the bottom of the bottle, the straw hit something. I picked up the bottle and looked at it, and there was a mouse in it. . . . I let out a scream, and the owner came up and told me to keep quiet, not to attract too much attention on account he had a few customers in the store. . . . I got nauseated, and I went on out and threw up." [Patargias v. Coca-Cola Bottling Co. of Chicago, Inc., 74 N.E. 2d 162]

In the second instance the discovery occurred in a darkened area and is parallel to stories about a rat sold as a piece of Kentucky Fried Chicken.[10]

The plaintiff, Ella Reid Creech, lives about a quarter of a mile from this store [where the Coca-Cola was purchased] and about 6 p.m. on the date last named [January 9, 1931] sent her sister Tillie to this store to get her two bottles of Coca-Cola. She got them and handed one to the plaintiff. The room was dark. Plaintiff opened and bottle and drank it. She became very sick and began to vomit. A light was turned on and she discovered a partially decomposed mouse in the bottle. Dr. Darnell was called and pumped and washed out her stomach. [Coca-Cola Bottling Co. of Shelbyville (Kentucky) vs. Creech, 53 S.W. 2d 745]

Multiple Origins and Urban Belief Tales

As noted above, few cases are appealed from the trial court decision. In Minnesota courts, for each case appealed in 1976, 412 cases were heard at the county or district level. Let me play with hypothetical statistics for a moment, recognizing the dangers involved. If only one mouse case was appealed for every 400 cases brought, there were 18,000 mice found in soft-drink bottles! One account suggests that for every ten claims brought to Coke's attention only one ends up in court.[11] This provides the astounding figure of 180,000 bottled mice, recognizing of course that some of these cases are illegitimate rip-off schemes by con artists.[12] Finally, if each of these individuals told twenty acquaintances about this remarkable, startling, and horrifying event, there may be as many as 3.6 million people who either heard a personal experience story from a victim or were victims themselves—approximately seventeen people in every thousand[13]—a figure which seems high, but probably is not outrageously so.

Whatever the actual number of bottled mice, many Americans have received these surprises or know someone who did. Because of the dramatic, horrifying qualities of the event, along with its functional value for expressing real fears about the industrialization of America, each of these versions is likely to be widely diffused. Thus, multiple creation and diffusion are likely to support each other in this instance. As the stories are spread by people who did not experience the events personally, they may be systematically altered to produce a better story. Similarly, when two of these conduits intersect, the future teller may combine elements from both versions, possibly assuming that they are accounts of the same event. As new cases are diffused, stories currently circulating will be altered to fit the new facts, as the continued diffusion is given impetus by personal experiences—spread orally or through the print media.[14]

I am not claiming that all urban belief tales are the product of actual events, or of duplications of these actual events. However, the data from the "mouse in the soft-drink bottle" story suggest that such an origin must not be discounted, as one diligent undergraduate student has done:

> There is a story that sometimes people find mice, cigarette butts, flys, and other foreign matters in their soft drinks and particularly in coca-cola. I have heard these mentioned myself but I was unaware that they were folklore and had very little if any basis in fact. [G. M. Jordan, Jr., April 1951, Michigan State University Files, Indiana University Folklore Archives]

Several conclusions are relevant: (1) polygenesis may explain the origin of some urban belief tales in that they may be based upon repeated events, (2) diffusion and polygenesis may jointly affect folklore and should be recognized by scholars interested in the creation and diffusion of modern folklore forms.

Notes

I wish to thank Anne Kaplan, Willard B. Moore, J. Sanford Rikoon, Arlette Soderberg, Donald Ward, and the Coca-Cola Bottling Company for help in the preparation of this paper.

1. Richard M. Dorson, "Introduction," in his *Folklore and Folklife: An Introduction* (Chicago: University of Chicago Press, 1972), 8; Alexander H. Krappe, *The Science of Folklore* (New York: Norton, 1964 [orig. 1930]), 70.
2. See Helen Gilbert, "The Crack in the Abbey Floor: A Laboratory Analysis of a Legend," *Indiana Folklore* 7 (1975):61.
3. Richard M. Dorson, *American Folklore* (Chicago: University of Chicago Press, 1959), 252.
4. See Lauri Honko, "Memorates and the Study of Folk Beliefs," *Journal of the Folklore Institute,* 1 (1964):12.
5. L. Michael Bell, "Cokelore," *Western Folklore* 35 (1976):62; repr. in *Readings in American Folklore,* ed. Jan Harold Brunvand (New York: Norton, 1979), 99–105.
6. Jan Harold Brunvand, *The Study of American Folklore,* Second Edition (New York: Norton, 1978), 111. Brunvand reports a mouse tail, not a whole mouse was found.
7. This is the standard legal notation for the citation of cases. In the case of (64 So. 791), the first number indicates the volume, the abbreviation refers to the regional reporter series in which the case is indexed, and the final number is the page number on which the printed decision begins. States are placed into nine regions in this system: Northeast (N.E.), New York (N.Y.S.), Northwest (N.W.), Atlantic (A.), Southeast (S.E.), Southern (So.), Southwest (S.W.), Pacific (P.), and California (Cal.). In addition, there is a federal reporter (F.) for cases in the federal courts system. The notation "2d" indicates that the case is located in the second series of these volumes (i.e., a relatively recent case).
8. By decade we find: 1914–20 (4 cases), 1921–30 (3), 1931–40 (9), 1941–50 (8), 1951–60 (15), 1961–70 (4), 1971–76 (2).
9. Alphabetically by states: Ala.-2, Ariz.-1, Ark.-3, Cal.-2, D.C.-1, Fla.-1, Ga.-1, Ill.-3, Iowa-1, Ky.-4, La.-1, Md.-1, Miss.-2, Mo.-4, Neb.-1, Nev.-1, N.Y.-2, N.C.-2, Okla.-1, Penna.-3, S.C.-1, Tenn.-3, Tex.-3, Va.-1.

10. See George G. Carey, *Maryland Folk Legends and Folk Songs* (Cambridge, Maryland: Tidewater Publishers, 1971), 71–72.

11. E. J. Kahn, Jr., *The Big Drink* (New York: Random House), 92.

12. Thus, some of these fraudulent claims may have been suggested by the existence of this traditional story, and by the perception that such occurrences are likely and can be faked.

13. Among other weaknesses, this does not consider the fact that these events occurred over a sixty-two-year period, and thus all who heard directly of these events were not contemporaries.

14. A printed account from the *Washington Post* (February 3, 1917) is cited by Carey, Maryland Folk Legends, 72–73.

5

Folklore Diffusion
Through Interactive Social Networks:
Conduits in a Preadolescent Community

How best to conceptualize patterns of folkloric transmission has proven to be a major difficulty for those attempting to examine social constraints on information diffusion. Linda Dégh and Andrew Vázsonyi[1] have taken an important step towards solving this problem by suggesting that folklore is transmitted through social conduits. Conduits, for Dégh and Vázsonyi, entail transmission of folklore between *interested* parties who have the opportunity to interact. Some individuals, they suggest, qualify neither as legend receivers nor as transmitters. This model of the transmission process is proposed as an alternative to that which suggests that folklore is like a raging stream that floods everything in its path—or at least is diffused with no discernible pattern. The conduit approach emphasizes that, even within a close-knit community, folklore transmission only occurs within sub-populations interested in the topic being discussed. Further, in any community, numerous folklore conduits operate simultaneously. To understand communication flow we must recognize both idiographic factors, such as interest and social proprieties, and social structural issues, such as opportunity for interaction. This essay examines empirically the conduit hypothesis proposed by Dégh and Vázsonyi, and it describes ways in which idiographic and social structural features determine the effects of conduits on folklore content.

C. W. Von Sydow realized that in order to comprehend the processes of folklore diffusion, the possibilities for interaction in a community must be understood.[2] Within any community a folk tradition may affect only a small percentage of the residents, and "[t]he various traditions differ both as to number and to kind of their bearers."[3] Von Sydow proceeded to describe the circumstances which affect the spread of information both within a community and between communities. This argument clearly presages the conduit theory proposed by Dégh and Vázsonyi.

Dégh and Vázsonyi's conceptualization of conduits as a social network was, despite the perceptive analysis of Von Sydow, the first significant attempt to conceptualize transmission in terms of patterns of social interaction; however, in their 1975 article no substantial empirical evidence was presented.

While the theory was appealing, one might have rendered a Scotch verdict: not proven.

Research in other social science disciplines provides evidence for the validity of Dégh and Vázsonyi's conception of folklore transmission. Most notably, a growing body of scholarship attempts network analyses of communities and social structures: this approach has recently had a major impact on both anthropology and sociology. Pioneered by J. A. Barnes, the network argument asserts that community structure can be specified by examining the linkages or relationships between individuals within a community.[4] These linkages serve as a means of describing social structure,[5] and also as a means of understanding communication flow within a society.[6] Both social structure and cultural content, while analytically separate issues, can be specified by means of this construct. The implications of a social network go beyond simple structural considerations, such as residence or occupation, to explain the effects of patterns of relationships. One area in which network analysis has been applied with considerable success is in the analysis of communication patterns. Studies of innovation,[7] rumor,[8] hysterical contagion,[9] and gossip[10] have demonstrated the potential of this approach in analyzing communication linkages as a function of interactional ties.

For the purpose of clarity, a distinction needs to be drawn between the concepts of network and conduit. By *network,* I refer in this essay to the entire set of relationships among individuals in the community population under discussion. *Conduit,* as used by Dégh and Vázsonyi, refers to a particular set of linkages that become activated in the diffusion of a folkloric element, and not to the entire set of relationships. The conduit is equivalent to the concept used in network analysis of a "network strand."

The circumstance that folklorists have not closely examined network analysis may be attributed to a tendency in network analysis which ignores or downplays the *content* of the interaction between individuals. Despite increasing attention given to the performance situation as a determinant of folklore, most folklorists would agree with D. K. Wilgus's claim that textual analysis is central to folkloric scholarship,[11] although it must be used in conjunction with an examination of performance. In order to be relevant to folklorists, network analysis must consider the content variation of information transmitted within its component conduits.[12]

The proposed type of analysis might be compared to macro-folkloric approaches that employ texts from societies and subsocieties as units of analysis and attempt to reconstruct changes in folkloric forms on the basis of discoverable alliances and routes of communication, trade, and migration. Network analysis, to be maximally useful to folklorists, should allow for a similar objective using the individual as the unit of analysis.

Research Site

The basic design of the study was to examine the behavior of preadolescent boys playing Little League baseball in one Minnesota community. It was argued that each team would develop its own group culture, and that this group culture would be affected by, and would in turn affect, the social structure of the group.[13] As the research progressed it seemed undesirable to limit the investigation to the interaction which occurred within those teams being examined. All teams in the league were part of a larger social system—that of the preadolescent society in the community studied. Communication patterns crossed team membership boundaries, and included individuals (girls, as well as boys) who did not play Little League baseball. An attempt to examine the total preadolescent society resulted, and the fieldwork expanded in magnitude. Over the course of a five-month period, approximately eighty days were spent in this community.

Sanford Heights,[14] a middle-class suburb of Minneapolis, has a population of slightly over thirty thousand with a 1970 median income for families of approximately $11,800.[15] Much of the suburb's growth has occurred since 1960, and consists largely of developers' tract homes.[16] The Sanford Heights Northern Little League consists of seven Major League teams, comprising ninety boys aged ten through twelve. Five AAA Minor League teams were organized for boys and girls deemed not sufficiently proficient athletically to play in the Major Leagues, as well as eight AA Minor League teams for eight and nine year olds.

From about four o'clock in the afternoon until nine at night during the spring and summer, preadolescents could be found at the Little League park, practicing or playing, watching others, participating in pick-up games, talking, or just hanging around. Frequently as many as fifty non-participating preadolescents were at the field during games, and if one included the players present, the number of children exceeded one hundred during any evening.

The primary methodological tool employed was participant observation;[17] I attended most of the games played during the season and told the players I desired to observe what they regularly said and did. While I focused my observations on two of the seven Major League teams, I spent time with all seven. In addition, I became acquainted with many preadolescents who were regularly present at the field, and my personal social network expanded as informants introduced me to their non-playing friends. Participant observation was supplemented during the season with brief sociometric questionnaires filled out by the players in the Major League. These techniques and data permit a fairly adequate composite portrait of the social world in which these boys participated.

In examining the conduit hypothesis, I shall first indicate the ways that friendship patterns can be predicted by knowledge of social structural features of a community and by the organizational affiliations of preadolescents. These structural ties and friendship ties will then be shown to affect the directions of folklore diffusion in the case of a simple culture item—the story of a window being broken at a local elementary school. Finally, a case of legend transmission is analyzed in terms of the way in which content variation occurs through folklore conduits. Each section of the study, therefore, builds theoretically on the section before—from the determination of friendship ties to the structure of communication conduits to processes of content variation in theses conduits.

Sociometric Patterns

Before examining folklore diffusion, it is important to recognize that friendship ties do not occur at random throughout a community, but that they are developed through interaction. We expect that friendships are more likely to occur within salient organizations than outside of them, and are more likely to be found among those who spend time with each other than among those who do not. In this research school, grade and team are expected to affect the patterns of friendship. These organizational factors only provide a guide to choosing friends—by limiting the potential friendship partners available; the particular boys chosen as friends will be selected on personal factors, including personality and ability.

Four times during the season Major League players were requested to complete a questionnaire listing their three best friends, their three best friends in the Major League and their three best friends on their own team. The following analysis will be restricted to the ratings provided in the midseason questionnaire, completed by all but two players.

By the middle of the season friendship patterns are dramatically influenced by team membership. Twenty-three percent of the players' best friends were chosen from among the twelve boys[18] on the chooser's own team. Because it is impossible to determine the effective population from which a child can choose his friends, no expected frequency for within-team friendships choices can be computed. When one asks a player who in the Major Leagues are his best friends, team membership has a similar effect. If best friends were named without reference to team membership, one would expect the number of within-team choices to be 13 percent—the number of possible within-team friendship choices divided by the total number of friendship possibilities (the number of players in the league excluding the chooser). The actual percentage of within-team choices is 51 percent, substantially higher than the 13 percent predicted if friendship was based upon a random choice of peers. Apparently the intensive personal interaction involved in team membership affects friendship choices.

Additional analyses indicate that the player's school and his grade level affect his friendship choices. Players are more likely to choose as best friends boys who are in the same grade,[19] and who attend their school (see Table 5.1).

The sociometric evidence indicates the importance of the structural characteristics of a preadolescent's social world in determining patterns of friendships. These intense friendships (and other acquaintanceship patterns which are less intense) provide potential channels for the transmission of cultural items. While behavior settings, such as school and team practice, allow for communication, perception of affiliation motivates conversation (and in turn rewarding conversation produces friendship). Friendships provide the milieu in which folklore is transmitted. While there are specialized folklore transmitters who communicate beyond their friendship net, affective patterns are excellent predictors of transmission.[20]

The Hiawatha Broken Window

To indicate the effects of social networks on diffusion, we have chosen to discuss a simple piece of information which spread through the preadolescent community in Sanford Heights during mid-June 1977. On the final day of school, shortly after the students at Hiawatha School (the school which 42 per-

Table 5.1 Expected and Observed Patterns of Friendship

	N	Expected Percentage[d]	Observed Percentage
Friends in League who are team-mates	90[a]	13	51
Friends in League in grade: 6th graders	48[b]	53	90
Friends in League in grade: 5th graders	27	29	59
Friends in League in grade: 4th graders	11	11	52
Friends in League in same school			
Hiawatha School	37[c]	40	88
Grove School	8	8	17
Cooley School	17	18	59
Buckminster School	13	13	72
St. Thomas School	8	8	42

[a]88 players completed the questionnaire
[b]47 players in the 6th grade completed the questionnaire
[c]36 players from the Hiawatha School completed questionnaires
[d]based on random choice of friends—possible friends in category divided by number of children in the sample

cent of the players attended) had been dismissed for the summer, a window was broken. Several boys, including four in the Major League and one in the Minor League, were questioned by the police. For several days the broken window was a salient topic of conversation which involved news, rumors (who had actually broken the window), personal experience stories (about the police interviews), and local anecdotes (about previous relevant events and about the experiences of other relevant individuals who had been questioned). In addition, the performance setting in which the story was transmitted was a folk gathering. The most notable traditional aspects of the tellings were the personal experience stories[21] told by those boys who were interviewed by the police about how they outsmarted the police, managed to escape blame, and proved their innocence. The importance of the personal experience story in the telling is attested to by the fact that these boys were asked by others exactly what the police said and did, and how they dealt with the situation—as others were convinced that they would be questioned next.

Perhaps because of the importance of the personal experience story associated with the event, those individuals who had been questioned by the police were most frequently reported as informants by their peers. This could be because the experience impelled these individuals to describe their adventures to others; because others who heard their adventures second-hand asked for a personal recounting; or because respondents, unable to recall from whom they heard it first, reported hearing it from these peer leaders. While it was impossible to observe where the information was first heard for each player, "suspects" did recount their experiences with the police, and on occasion were asked by others specifically what occurred. Reports of managing the police and convincing the "pigs" of their innocence were widely heralded, and over half (51 percent) of the players in the league who heard the news claimed to hear about it from one of the five police "suspects."

To determine the effect of social networks upon communication, all players in the league were asked verbally two to three weeks after the event whether or not they had heard about a window being broken at the Hiawatha School, and if so, from whom. For this analysis we are only concerned with the pattern of transmission, and not the content. Forty-one of the ninety players (46 percent) reported having heard about it. The issue in regard to a network analysis is whether certain segments of the preadolescent community were more likely to have heard of the event than others, and what characterized these segments.

School Effects. The event was widely known by boys who attended the Hiawatha School. Of the thirty-seven boys in the league from Hiawatha, twenty-five (68 percent) had heard of the broken window. However, of the fifty-three boys who did not attend that school, only sixteen (30 percent) had heard the story. A Chi-Square analysis[22] indicates that this difference in knowledge differs significantly from chance ($\chi^2 = 11.6$, df $= 1$, p $<.001$). The information spread differentially through the various subsegments of the Little League social system—although schools were closed. Apparently the story was spread to those most likely to be interested and affected.

Team Effects. Sixteen boys who had not attended Hiawatha heard about the broken window. The question arises as to how they received their information. Fourteen (87 percent) heard from other boys on their own team—indicating the importance of inter-team communication for the spread of knowledge. The two counter-examples, both on the same team, learned from a single source—a boy on a rival team before a game at which the two teams were to play.

Interestingly, this within-team communication is less likely to characterize the way Hiawatha students heard about the window. Of the eighteen boys who heard it from peers, only seven (39 percent) reported hearing it from team-mates. This pattern is significantly different from that revealed by the non-Hiawatha students ($\chi^2 = 8.4$, df $= 1$, p $< .01$), and suggests that a primary means of informal contact for the non-Hiawatha students with Hiawatha students is through Little League. On the other hand, the Hiawatha student has many occasions and numerous channels through which he can communicate with his fellow students, including geographical proximity of residence.

Grade Effects. Grade also affects the likelihood of having heard about the broken window and the stories associated with it. Of the thirty-seven boys at Hiawatha, twenty (54 percent) were in the sixth grade and seventeen (46 percent) in the fourth or fifth grades. Of the twenty-five Hiawatha boys who heard the story, nineteen (76 percent) were in the sixth grade and six (24 percent) in the lower grades. Thus, 95 percent of the sixth graders heard about the broken window, whereas only 35 percent of the younger players had. This difference is highly statistically significant ($\chi^2 = 15.0$; df $= 1$; p $< .001$).

This finding is reasonable when considering two factors. First, it was five sixth graders who were questioned by the police, and thus they were the ones most likely to transmit their personal experience story to friends and acquaintances. Second, because of the Sanford Heights police's interest in the "crime" and their suspicion that it was perpetrated by a sixth grader, it became particularly important for sixth graders to be aware of the on-going events.

Older players were slightly more likely to have heard the story even if they did not attend the Hiawatha School. Seventy-five percent of the twelve non-Hiawatha students who heard the report of the broken window were in the sixth or seventh grade, while sixth and seventh graders comprised only 60 percent of the total non-Hiawatha population.

Structural considerations play an important role in shaping diffusion. Access to first-hand information about the event motivates informational spread. The channels that this information takes are determined by factors which affect the acquaintance patterns of the players—school, grade, and team direct the flow of information through the larger preadolescent acquaintanceship net-

work. Much as geographical boundaries may provide barriers for folkloric diffusion, so may organizational affiliation, such as school or team.

Effects of Friendship. In addition to structural considerations, affective
relations have a significant impact on information transfer. Friends are more
likely to be reported as informants than other individuals.[23] Thirty boys reported hearing about the broken window from other boys in the Major League.
Of these thirty players, twenty-eight reported who their three best friends in the
league were. We would expect by chance that if diffusion was *unrelated* to
friendship, only 3 percent of the players would have heard the news from a best
friend in the league (i.e., 3 percent is the likelihood of any one boy being named
a best friend). Actually thirteen (46 percent) of the twenty-eight boys heard
from one of their best friends in the league. Seven boys (25 percent) claimed to
hear about the window from one of their three best friends (including those outside of the league structure). Within the Hiawatha sixth grade, seven of the nine
players who heard about the broken window through others in the league heard
it from one of their three best friends in the league (78 percent); six of the nine
(67 percent) heard about it from one of their three best friends in the world. One
must take into account the effect of common team membership and common
school and grade in determining the pure effect of friendship ties abstracted
from other structural consideration. Still, it appears that friendship, in conjunction with these structural factors which influence choice of friends, plays an
important role in the diffusion of information.

Pop Rocks Legends

In the analysis of diffusion about the broken window, no attention was paid to
content variation in transmission conduits, but these variations, additions, and
distortions are central to an understanding of folklore diffusion. In this example
two closely related stories will be examined particularly in terms of their content. These stories spread throughout Sanford Heights in late May and early
June 1977 and dealt with a novel candy, Pop Rocks. Pop Rocks, manufactured
by General Foods, are small sugar pellets treated with carbon dioxide so that
they tingle or, in the preadolescent vernacular, "explode" when put on one's
tongue. These sweets provide a unique sensation and became a valuable item in
the preadolescent economy of Sanford Heights. As one player put it: "These are
wicked, man."

The Natural History of the Legends. The first I learned of these candies
was on May 11, 1977, at a practice of the Dodgers, one of the Major League
teams being examined in detail. Stewart, the most popular boy on the team, had
purchased a package at the nearby PDQ (a convenience grocery store). He

doled out small portions to the other boys present—many of whom had not tasted the candy before. This pre-practice interlude revealed considerable excitement on the part of the players and was characterized by laughter, rapid speech, and comments of amazement ("This stuff is weird"; "This must have been made with some kind of acid"). During this period, one of the twelve year olds, Ronald, a relatively low status boy on the team, was the first to report that someone had died from eating them:

> Some kid took, you know, he took two packs of those things; he swallowed them, and he suffocated . . . somewhere in Montana. [Transcribed recording, May 11, 1977]

This narrative was told spontaneously in the presence of other members of the team. Two twelve year olds on the team responded by terming the story "a lie," but Ronald insisted on its accuracy. At the time, this appeared to be the first anyone on the team had heard of the story.[24]

According to the players, Pop Rocks were first sold in Sanford Heights only a few days previously, although some had received packages from out of town. Ronald claims:

> I was the first to get 'em around here, 'cause um they had them out in Washington State . . . They started out in Montana, then they came to Washington; now they came here. [Transcribed recording, May 11, 1977]

This narrative about a death from Pop Rocks is part of a tradition of food contamination stories which have spread about several products.[25] Jan Brunvand speaks of a type of legend termed urban belief tales, which include decomposed mice found in Pepsi bottles, a Kentucky Fried Rat, or a snake sewn into a garment in a local department store.[26] A few months previous to this research the national media reported that preadolescents believed that Bubble Yum, the best-selling gum on the market, contained spider eggs or caused skin cancer. In discussing the Pop Rocks death, one boy mentioned a structurally equivalent legend: "You can die from Alka-Seltzer. A person already died of Alka-Seltzer." The story, which the boy had heard from his father, is that someone had swallowed an Alka-Seltzer tablet whole, and its subsequent fizzing killed the victim. Like many legends found in contemporary society, it deals with the public ambivalence towards the effects of modern technology and products.

Eight days after the original story, Stewart claimed that he had heard the story two weeks previously—prior to the time Ronald's version was told and prior to the time Pop Rocks were supposedly first available in Sanford Heights. His source, a friend from school, claimed that the death had occurred in Avondale, a neighboring suburb. The localizing process cited as a characteristic of legend forms[27] is operating as the locale of the story shifts from a distant state to a neighboring suburb, Avondale, and subsequently to Sanford Heights itself (although the changes do not occur in the telling of a single individual).

By this time it became impossible to purchase Pop Rocks in Sanford Heights ostensibly because of a distribution problem, although the situation must have appeared ambiguous to the preadolescents. In this circumstance, details are likely to be added to the story, and one might expect the story to spread further. Within two days variants of the story were referred to on other teams. The detail that Pop Rocks had been declared illegal in Minnesota had been added—an example of what Gordon Allport and Leo Postman term "an effort after meaning."[28] On May 25th one player reported that he heard from a saleslady at a 7-11 (a local convenience grocery store) that Pop Rocks had been taken off the market:

> The lady at 7-11 says that a kid three blocks away from her about five years old . . . uh . . . He got a big . . . big Pop Rocks package and swallowed them and they popped in his stomach, and they made 'em illegal, and now they're off the market. Some stores still might have 'em, but they're illegal. [Transcribed recording, May 25, 1977]

An interesting though minor variant of the legend occurred when the author brought to Sanford Heights a package of Pop Rocks purchased in Colorado. Because the package had been exposed to excessive heat and moisture, the pellets did not pop, although they were still edible. Although this explanation was given at the time, the story soon spread that General Foods was going to start making Pop Rocks so that they no longer popped—again an "effort after meaning"—and this explanation was heard from other preadolescents not present at the time the candy was distributed. Thus, this inadvertent experimental manipulation by the researcher indicated an effect of additional evidence on the story content.

By two weeks after the "original" Sanford Heights version, the story was widely known. Among the locations where children were reported to have died were Sanford Heights, Avondale, Brooklyn Park, Brooklyn Center, Minneapolis, Minnetonka, Bemidji, Blaine, North Dakota, South Dakota, Montana, Washington, Michigan, and Massachusetts. Variants of the other details in this legend vary as much, with from six pellets to thirty-three packages causing death.

One day after the story was widely know, a player informed me that he had read an article in a medical journal which his mother had brought home from the hospital where she worked about Pop Rocks causing death. He assured me that the report was about a boy who had died from eating too many Pop Rocks, and promised that the following day he would bring a copy. Thinking for once that a folklorist might have discovered the legendary "kernel of truth," I waited with anticipation. The following day he brought an article which his mother had picked up at the hospital. However, this story in the June 13, 1977, issue of *Newsweek* made no mention of any death or injury from Pop Rocks, but did mention that some parents were needlessly concerned about possible danger.

The player admitted to me that he had not remembered the story correctly the previous day but knew the article had something to do with Pop Rocks. Attempts to track down an article in the Minneapolis paper about these "deaths," not surprisingly, proved fruitless.

A Systematic Survey of Legend Content and Diffusion. Most folklore investigations gather data through observation or in-depth interviews with a small percentage of the population being examined. Thus, one is not able to examine communication chains or content variations because there generally is a large number of linkages for which data is unavailable. In order to avoid this difficulty in determining the diffusion conduits and content variation of these legends, responses to a short questionnaire were collected from 203 preadolescents and early adolescents in Sanford Heights over a thirteen-day period from June 4, 1977 (three and a half weeks after the collection of the first story) until June 16, 1977. Eighty-nine of the ninety Little League baseball players completed the questionnaire at the same time as the midseason friendship survey. Most of the players in the AAA Minor League responded, as did three girls' softball teams. Other preadolescent respondents were asked to fill out the questionnaire as they became available. The sample represents a sizable segment of the preadolescent population of the north end of Sanford Heights. The Hiawatha School is the largest elementary school servicing the area, and questionnaires were collected from 12 percent of the fourth graders at Hiawatha, 29 percent of the fifth graders, and 33 percent of the sixth graders (46 percent of the sixth grade boys). As with the window breaking story, ethnographic evidence suggests a reasonable correspondence between field observation and survey responses. (For the specific questions asked, see the Appendix.)

Questionnaires allowed for a more complete and systematic collection of data than would otherwise have been possible. However, in doing this we have ignored the textual subtleties found in other studies (and in the observational part of this study), although the questions asked were developed from observing natural tellings of the legend. We have not collected natural texts through the questionnaire, even though the questionnaire responses do seem parallel to natural content. Asking an informant to recall a folklore item in any situation in which that item would not naturally occur has problems associated with it; however, the results do allow us to point to some important aspects of content stability and variation, which we can generalize to natural transmission. Asking identical questions to the sample of over two hundred respondents allows for quantification, impossible in observation and in-depth interviewing. It should be noted that while this research is systematic and the data collection technique "artificial," I deliberately attempted not to spread the story myself, just to listen and observe natural interaction, to ask non-directive questions when necessary, and not to provide any details that respondents had not heard. With the exception of the non-popping Pop Rocks (described above), I was successful in not directly influencing the stories. Thus, this was not "experimental" research in the social scientific meaning of the term, in that the subjects were not systematically manipulated by the researcher, although the data collection procedure was systematic.

Knowledge. The questionnaire results confirm that the Pop Rocks legends are widely known. Eighty-one percent of the players in the Major League have tasted Pop Rocks, as have 75 percent of the non–Major Leaguers. Sixty-two percent of the Sanford Heights Major Leaguers had heard about someone dying from an overdose of Pop Rocks; as compared to 50 percent of the rest of the sample. Among the Major League players, 49 percent had heard that Pop Rocks had been declared illegal in Minnesota as compared to 45 percent of the rest of the sample. Thus, the samples are generally comparable.

A further analysis suggests that the two stories did not always appear together, and thus are different items. Of the Major Leaguers, twenty-four had heard neither, twenty had heard about the death but not about Pop Rocks being illegal, eleven had heard that Pop Rocks were illegal but had not heard that anyone had died, and thirty-four knew of both stories. Of those who had heard both, only eighteen (53 percent) reported hearing them from the same source. Thus, it seems legitimate to suggest that while related, two separate folklore items are present and should be analyzed as such.

Judging from discussions with parents, the story does not seem to have spread widely among adults—the large majority of adults questioned had not heard the story—indicating the selective nature of cohorts in folklore diffusion.

Belief. Belief has traditionally been a definitional criterion for the legend,[29] although scholars such as Dégh and Vázsonyi and Robert Georges have come to doubt the necessity of this criterion.[30] These Pop Rocks stories are believed as true by a majority of those who have heard them. Sixty-two percent of the Major Leaguers (55 percent of the others) believe that Pop Rocks are illegal in Minnesota, and 61 percent are convinced that someone has died from eating too many of the candies (79 percent of the non-Major Leaguers). Boys were observed to tell others to be careful consuming Pop Rocks and to eat them only sparingly. One boy commented to friends that he knew from personal experience that one starts to choke if too many are swallowed at once. A Hiawatha student claimed that a student at the Buckminster School started choking on Pop Rocks and the school nurses made the students get rid of them, although Buckminster students denied any truth to this legend variant. Another boy commented that one should have the candy pop in one's mouth and not swallow them whole or they will explode in one's stomach. One boy did place a large handful of the candies in his mouth, at which point he was told by another with the mixture of aggression and concern characteristic of preadolescents: "You're crazy to put them all in your mouth. I hope you die."

Structural and Friendship Effects. As with the information of the Hiawatha broken window, team membership, grade, school, and friendship patterns affect transmission. Because this legend was spread while school was in session, it is not surprising that the results indicate that boys are particularly likely to hear it from schoolmates. Of the twenty-nine players who reported hearing the story of the Pop Rocks Death from someone inside the Major League, 66 percent claimed to have heard it first from a schoolmate. Seventy-one percent of the twenty-one players who heard that Pop Rocks were illegal in Minnesota heard this from a schoolmate. The figures for grade are similar: 72 percent of the Death stories and 67 percent of the Illegal stories were told by grade-mates. The figures for communication within both grade and school are 55 percent and 57 percent respectively. The structural network which characterized the window-breaking accounts is observed again; however, in the Pop Rocks stories the intra-school communication is not limited to Hiawatha School, but applies to communication within the Cooley and Buckminster schools.

Team membership also seems to play a significant role—as noted, if communication were based upon a random network we would expect approximately 13 percent of all versions from within the league to be from teammates, since 13 percent of the boys in the league are teammates of any one boy. Results suggest that team plays a much more significant role. Forty-eight percent of the Death stories from sources within the league were transmitted from teammates, as were 57 percent of the Illegal stories—substantially higher than the expected figures for within-league communication. No expected parameters can be computed for all communication, inside and outside the league, but the observed frequencies for within-team communication as a percentage of total communication are 26 percent (Death) and 24 percent (Illegal), well above the figures expected if all of a child's acquaintances were taken into account in determining a random communications net. Ethnographic evidence confirms that the team setting was the location at which many boys first found out about Pop Rocks.

In addition to team membership, friendship patterns also channel these legends. Considering only communication that occurred through intraleague channels, one would expect that with each boy choosing 3 percent of all others in the league as best friends (as they were limited to through survey design), if friendship did not affect folkloric communication, only 3 percent of the within-league communication should be from within-league friends. Actually 45 percent of the Death stories were transmitted by league friends, as were 48 percent of the Illegal stories. For the Death story, thirty-seven players named sources (excluding adults) for the story; ten (27 percent) of these informants were named as one of the boy's three best friends. The figures for the Illegal story are similar; nine (35 percent) of the twenty-six peer sources were named as a best friend.[31]

Inter-team transmission of the story seems to occur particularly through these friendship linkages. For the Illegal story, 70 percent of the inter-team transmission (seven of ten cases) was through friends, while only 27 percent of the intra-team transmission (three of eleven cases) was through friends.[32] The comparable figures for the Pop Rocks Death legend are 53 percent (eight of fifteen cases), vs. 36 percent (five of fourteen cases).[33] In cases of structured interaction, affective relationships seem less salient in the transmission of information than in conditions of free interaction.

Extent of Conduit Chains. In order to determine differences between hearers and non-hearers, and between active tellers and passive listeners, one must describe the extent of the communication chain. In the case of traditional legends one cannot speak of originators or first-order sources—no one actually witnessed the death or observed the ban making Pop Rocks illegal and no one in the sample created the story. However, for our analysis of this childlore, we shall assume that anyone who heard the story from an adult is a "first-order source," since preadolescents believe that adults expect their statements to be taken as "fact." Players who heard from these individuals are "second-order sources" and so on. Those preadolescents who cite a peer outside of the sample will be termed "*possible* second-order sources"—assuming, possibly incorrectly, that they would have recalled an adult informant. Any player who heard from these boys will be considered a "*possible* third-order source."

For the story that Pop Rocks are illegal, six players (13 percent) were "first-order sources" (four heard from employees at a 7-11 Grocery Store, one from a parent, and one reported hearing it from the author). Nine players (20 percent) claimed to have heard the story from one of the first-order sources; four "third-order sources" (9 percent) claimed to have heard the story from a "second-order source," and there was one "fourth-order" and one "fifth-order source" (2 percent each). Nineteen players were classified as "*possible* second-order sources" (42 percent); four (9 percent) claimed they heard the Pop Rocks were illegal from a "*possible* second-order source" and thus were "*possible* third-order sources." One boy (2 percent) was a "*possible* fourth-order source."

Similar figures describe diffusion of the Pop Rocks Death legend. Nine boys (17 percent) were categorized as "first-order sources" (four claimed to have heard it from 7-11, three from the author, and two from parents). Three of these boys were also "first-order sources" of the Illegal story. Ten players (19 percent) were "second-order sources," and six (11 percent) were "third-order sources." For *possible* sources, sixteen (30 percent), ten (19 percent), two (4 percent) and one (2 percent) were second-, third-, fourth-, and fifth-order sources respectively. Thus the transmission pattern for these stories appears relatively constricted.

Evidence suggests that boys who heard about either Pop Rocks story as first- or second-order (confirmed) sources had significantly more friends than those who had never heard the story. For the Death legend the mean number of friendship choices a first- or second-order source received when players were asked to name their three best friends in the world was 2.5; when boys were asked to name their three best friends in the league, these early knowers received 3.8 friendship choices. These figures correspond to 1.2 and 2.5 friendship citations for boys who had not heard the legend. A statistical analysis reveals that these are significant group differences (t = 2.65, df = 49, p. = .01 [best friends in the world] and t = 1.76, df = 49, p. = .08 [best friends in the league]).[34] An analysis of the report about Pop Rocks being illegal reveals similar results. First- and second-order sources receive 2.3 (world) and 4.1 (league) friendship choices, as compared to the non-hearers 1.2 (world) and 2.5 (league) choices. These group differences are also statistically significant (t = 2.70, df = 57, p = .01 [world]; t = 2.37, df = 57, p = .02 [league]).[35] These data support the research findings on innovation diffusion which suggest that early knowers (the first- and second-order sources) have higher social status and more social participation than do late knowers (the non-hearers).[36]

Of those individuals whom other Major Leaguers reported to have transmitted the stories, "active tellers" are more popular than others who had heard the story but who were not reported to have repeated it.[37] Twenty boys can be classified as active tellers of the Death story, while thirty-seven boys claimed to have heard the story but did not spread it. Active tellers received 3.0 (best friend in the world) and 4.8 (best friend in the league) friendship citations, compared to 1.1 (world) and 2.3 (league) for the passive knowers. These differences are statistically significant (t = 4.11, df = 55, p < .001 [world]; t = 3.39, df = 55, p < .001 [league]). A similar, though weaker, finding applies to the story of Pop Rocks being illegal. Here, the seventeen active tellers receive 2.5 (world) and 4.1 (league) friendship choices; as compared to friendship choices to the twenty passive knowers of 1.4 (world) and 2.9 (league) (t = 1.90, df = 45, p = .06 [world]; t = 1.43, df = 45, p = .16 [league]).

This statistical analysis supports Dégh's observation that folklore narrators are either highly respected or shunned by the community.[38] She suggests that the respected narrators remain active, while those who are shunned (perhaps through a lack of narration opportunities) become passive tellers. While structural factors, such as neighborhood layout or team personnel, may have influenced our results, ethnographic evidence clearly supports the importance of the respected teller as an effective transmitter of folkloric material.

Content Variation in Sub-Networks. Central to this investigation is an understanding of the variation in cultural elements in a social conduit and of the way in which particular content comes to characterize a legend conduit. In order to examine these issues, two sub-networks (characterized by the presence of Pop Rocks legend conduits) will be explored in detail. This in-depth analysis will allow for a coupling of the naturalistic observational data with the survey results. Because the Death legend is both more detailed and more traditional than the Illegal legend, the analysis will focus on the variations in its content in two particular sub-networks within the Sanford Heights preadolescent network. In each case I shall describe the ethnographic evidence and the structure of the legend conduits, and then analyze details of legend content.

1) THE ROSESBUDS: SIMPLE DIFFUSION

In addition to an active Little League baseball program, which is privately operated, the town of Sanford Heights organizes baseball and softball programs for preadolescents. Though these activities are not as structured and extensive as the Little League program, many local children participate in them.

As part of this research, contact was made with one of the preadolescent girls' softball teams in the area—the Rosebuds. Girls' softball teams are based on school attendance, and the ten Rosebuds questioned attended fourth grade (four girls) and sixth grade (six girls) at the Grove School. Nine of the girls had tasted Pop Rocks; two had heard they were illegal (both heard this outside the group), and six had heard that someone had died from eating them (four learned this within the group).

At least twelve days before the questionnaire was distributed, the stories about Pop Rocks had spread among this group—although we have no proof that those individuals who claimed not to have heard the story were present at that time. One girl, Janice, who seemed to know most of the story, commented:

> Janice: I heard from my brother there's this little boy way up north. He
> uh . . . GAF: North Minnesota? Janice: Yeah, way up . . . Up north Minnesota.
> He um . . . I don't know if it's a rumor or what, but uh . . . he had to have sur-
> gery 'cause um his stomach burst open because he ate . . . ate too many Pop
> Rocks, and then he swallowed them and they started popping in his stomach.
> [Transcribed recording, June 2, 1977]

None of the half-dozen girls present disputed this version, and no other facts were added, though prior to this recitation one of Janice's teammates mentioned that she thought they exploded in someone's vocal cords. The subsequent short discussion among team members dealt with how to eat this candy safely. One girl commented:

> You're supposed to chew 'em before you swallow 'em. You're supposed to suck
> on them . . . After they dissolve, you're supposed to swallow them. [Transcribed
> recording, June 2, 1977]

The functional value of this legend is observable in this warning—a frequent companion to a recitation of the story.

By the time questionnaires were completed, the details of the legend had stabilized to the point where it was clear that four of the six versions derived from the expansion of this story.

Figure 5.1
Rosebud Network

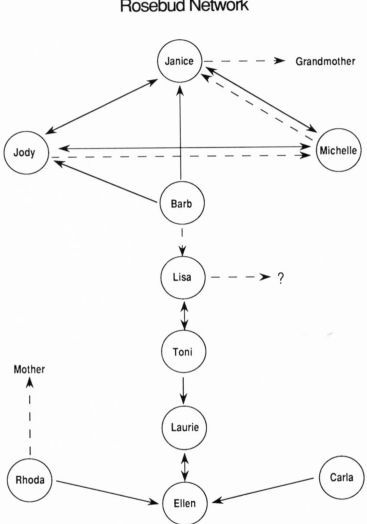

Solid arrows indicate friendship choices with arrowhead directed at chosen.

Although, because of time considerations, not every player on the Rose-buds could be questioned, the network presented (see Figure 2) shows a clear pattern. There are two cliques on the team, consisting of: 1) Janice, Jody, Michele, and Barb—which shall be termed Janice's cluster—and 2) Ellen, Laurie, Lisa, Toni, Rhonda and Carla—which shall be termed Ellen's cluster. All four members of Janice's cluster had heard of the Pop Rocks Death, while only two of the six members of Ellen's cluster had—both hearers were pe-ripheral members in that they were only chosen as friends by one other within the cluster. No member of one cluster chooses a member of the other cluster as one of her three best friends. This does not imply that there is hatred or rivalry on the team; rather, the division corresponds to age and grade. All of Janice's cluster are ten years old and in fourth grade; all of Ellen's cluster are twelve and in sixth grade. While the distinction between cliques does not indicate rivalry, it does correspond to different communication networks.

To exemplify how network analysis can apply to folkloristic research, the questionnaire responses of each of these girls shall be examined (see Table 5.2). Four of the questionnaire responses are close variants of the story told on June 2, 1977, by Janice. Much as in the methodology of the Finnish school, we can compare versions and suggest that Barb's story, despite her claim that she heard it from Lisa, was likely heard from Jody or Michelle, whose stories are most similar to hers.

The transmission conduit clearly includes Janice, Michelle, and Jody and although Barb claims that she heard the story from Lisa, her version surely was spread from within the clique. This again indicates the importance of friendship in folklore transmission. The stories of Rhoda and Lisa apparently were dif-fused from other directions, although there is no evidence to suggest that Rhoda's story did *not* originally derive from Janice's cluster. The individual de-tails in Janice's cluster's versions serve to indicate the potency of a network analysis for folklore, and it is to these details we shall next turn.

Analysis of Legend Components. Locale: In all four versions the victim is from Bemidji, which corresponds to the June 2nd account in which the boy was from northern Minnesota.[39] These four stories are the only ones collected in which Bemidji (or anywhere in northern Minnesota) is the locale, suggesting that this is a specialized version, and not simply a variant based on another Sanford Heights telling.

Age and sex: Janice and Michelle, the first two in the chain, state that the victim was eight years old; Jody and Barb suggest the victim was approximately eight years of age, indicating a detail which could be changed in future retell-ings. All agree that the victim was male, and this detail is common in versions from both males and females. In only four versions collected from the total sample was the victim female, and none of these narrators were part of a con-

Table 5.2 Questionnaire Responses of Sanford Heights Rosebuds

	Respondents Who Had Heard of Pop Rocks Death:					
	Janice	Michelle	Jody	Lisa	Barb	Rhoda
First source?	Grandmother from Bemidji	Janice	Michelle	?	Lisa	My mom
First heard?	A week ago	About 2 weeks ago	About 3 months ago	?	A few weeks ago	A week ago
Belief?	Yes	No	Yes	?	Yes	Yes
From whom first source heard?	Friend of hers	Her grand-mother	I don't know.	?	I don't know.	?
Who else told you?	Nobody	(blank)	No one	?	Nobody	?
Age of victim?	8	8	About 8	?	Around 8	?
Number of packs swallowed?	1	1	Don't know	1	I don't know.	?
Locale of death?	Bemidji	Bemidji	Bemidji	North Dakota	Bemidji	?
Sex of victim?	Male	Male	Male	2 girls	Male	?
Cause of death?	Stomach burst	Ate Pop Rocks and then drank pop. Stomach burst.	Ate Pop Rocks, then drank pop. Stomach broke open.	They ate away their vocal cords.	Because he ate Pop Rocks and then drank pop after.	He swallowed them. Stomach burst.

duit. Dying from candy is apparently a male prerogative—perhaps because males are seen as more willing to take a dare—or perhaps just less intelligent.

Sources: By the time the legend reaches the third-order sources (Jody and Barb) the original first-order source (Janice) is no longer named. This finding corresponds to Dégh and Vázsonyi's[40] suggestion that reports of memorate transmission chains frequently become simplified in the course of retelling.

Cause of death: An alteration occurs in the story in that, although Janice suggests in her questionnaire response that the boy's stomach burst (also reported on June 2nd), other versions suggest that the victim not only consumed the Pop Rocks but then drank pop. It cannot be ascertained from observation if: a) Janice ever mentioned this detail, b) it was an embroidered explanation added in the course of Michelle's retelling, or c) it was incorporated from other versions. The circumstance that these are the only three versions in which this detail appears vitiates the third explanation. The detail is consonant with other folkloric motifs, such as death produced by the mixture of aspirin and Coke. The conjunction of the popping of the drink and the popping of the candy indicates that even at this level an aesthetic of narrative content may exist.

Belief: Dégh and Vázsonyi[41] note that belief in a legend may vary from absolute acceptance to total skepticism. Further, levels of belief may oscillate within a transmission chain. In this instance, the chain is not sufficiently lengthy to determine what would happen if the story continued to spread; however, even in this short conduit, belief (in the form of responses to the binary question: Did you believe the story?) does vary. Michelle claims disbelief, while the other three accept the story. This parallels other conduits, in that some members may accept the account as meeting their standards of evidence while others remain skeptical or unconvinced, perhaps due to additional information or lack of trust in the narrator's judgment.

Date of the telling: Twelve days before the questionnaire the story was not being reported in its present form, and Janice, in her questionnaire response, claimed that she heard the story only a week before (perhaps her grandmother expanded on a story she had previously been told by her brother). Michelle claims that she heard this story from Janice two weeks before. Barb said she heard it a "few weeks ago," and Jody claims that she was told the story by Michelle three *months* before. These recollections should not be considered factual accounts, but rather seem to be part of the folklore. As the story moves from the original teller, the time frame of its existence lengthens, perhaps psychologically making it seem more stable and accurate by having been in existence longer.

The Rosebud network, and in particular Janice's conduit, provides an interesting case study of the subtle ways in which a folklore legend may become altered in transmission. While the Rosebud network is basically stable, some significant changes can be seen in the recounting of the story. In addition, this network indicates that we can determine patterns of diffusion through the examination of content in conjunction with the determination of friendship patterns; thus, we can say with assurance that Barb's version did derive from Janice's cluster, despite the contrary claim of the teller herself.

2) DODGERS NETWORK: THE EFFECTS
OF MULTIPLE VERSIONS

The entire Dodgers team can be viewed as comprising a preadolescent subnetwork. It was while observing the Dodgers that I first became aware of the story, and twelve of the thirteen team members heard the story (the only one who had not was the player who was late to that original practice). By definition the Dodgers can be termed a potential communications network, through the time spent together in games and practices. Players generally arrived at practice and at games fifteen to twenty minutes before the coach, which provided time to discuss the latest happenings. For reasons which the coach claimed were due to chance, the Dodgers had more players (seven or 54 percent) attending Cooley School than any other team in the league (the second highest team had only four Cooley players). This school attendance is associated with close friendship ties. The Dodgers chose relatively many team members as best friends,[42] and were known as a close-knit group. No one from outside the team reported hearing the legend from a Dodger team member.

Although the legend seems to have been first told on the team by Ronald, no member of the team cites him as even a secondary source, and the questionnaire responses do not clearly reveal his impact. The questionnaires indicate two major sources for the effective transmission of this story within the team—a primary and a secondary source. Because the narratives from these two sources were different in some respects, there occurred a relatively wide variation in detail from those who had heard the story and reported it on June 6th, twenty-six days after its original recitation (see Table 5.3).

The development of the legend in this social network is considerably more complex than in the Rosebud network. Having presented the data as collected by questionnaire on June 6th, let us reexamine the field observations. On May 11th, immediately before practice, Ronald told his story about Pop Rocks causing a death in Montana. Although eleven of the twelve other members were at practice, no one mentioned that he had previously heard a similar story. Frank and Harmon insisted it was "a lie."

The next significant discussion of Pop Rocks by the Dodgers occurred before practice on May 19th (two and one-half weeks before the questionnaire). I had brought a package of Pop Rocks to the field. Roy placed a handful in his mouth and started choking (not seriously); Stew told him that he should spit

Figure 5.2
Dodger Network

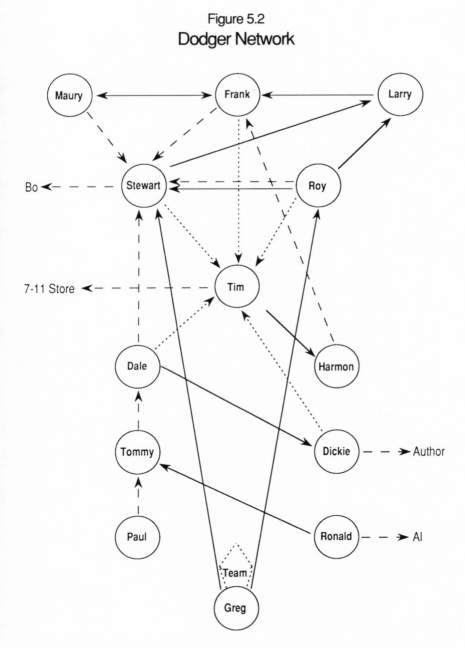

Solid arrows indicate friendship choices arrowhead directed at chosen;
maximum of three choices. Slashed arrows indicate main legend transmission
channel; dotted arrow indicates secondary transmission channel.

Table 5.3 Questionnaire Responses of Sanford Heights Dodgers

	Respondents Who Had Heard of Pop Rocks Death:					
	Ronald	Stewart	Tim	Roy	Maury	Frank
First source?	A friend, Albert	Bo	Bonnie, at 7-11	Stew	Stew	Stew
First heard?	—	3 weeks ago	2 weeks ago	1 month ago	1 week ago	3½ weeks ago
Belief?	Yes	No	Yes	No	No	No
From whom first source heard?	Beats me	—	—	—	Tim	His sister
Who else told you?	No one	Tim	Bonnie, at 7-11	Tim	Stew's sister	Tim
Age of victim?	I don't know.	12	11	12	Maybe 12	Maybe 12
Number of packs swallowed?	4	4	3	2	2 or 3	2
Locale of death?	Taylors Falls, MT	Avondale	Brooklyn Center	Avondale	I don't know.	Avondale
Sex of victim?	Male	Male	Male	Male	Male	Male
Cause of death?	Ate too many	—	Eating Pop Rocks	Ate too many	He ate too many.	Ate too many
School and grade	Buckminster, 6th grade	Cooley, 6th grade	Cooley, 5th grade	Cooley, 6th grade	Cooley, 6th grade	Cooley, 6th grade

Table 5.3 (*Continued*)

Respondents Who Had Heard of Pop Rocks Death:

	Dale	Tommy	Paul	Dickie	Greg	Harmon
First source?	Stew	Dale	Tommy	Gary (author)	Team	Frank
First heard?	1 month ago	1 week ago	About 2 weeks ago	A couple of weeks ago	1 week ago	3 weeks ago
Belief?	Yes	Yes	No	Yes	Yes	Yes
From whom first source heard?	I don't know.	I don't know.	No idea	I don't know.	I don't know.	I don't know.
Who else told you?	Tim	Nobody	No one	Tim	No one	No one
Age of victim?	I don't know.	Who knows?	I don't know.	I don't know.	I don't know.	I don't know.
Number of packs swallowed?	4	4	4	33	2	9
Locale of death?	I don't know.	I don't know.	I don't know.	Sanford Heights	?	—
Sex of victim?	Male	Male	Male	I don't know.	Male—I think	Male
Cause of death?	I don't know.	Eating Pop Rocks	From choking on them	They exploded.	?	Carbon dioxide
School and grade	Hiawatha, 4th grade	Buckminster, 4th grade	Junior High, 7th grade	Buckminster, 5th grade	Cooley, 5th grade	Hiawatha, 6th grade

them out because too many can kill you. I asked whether anyone had actually died from eating them, and Stew replied affirmatively and provided a version of the Death legend. Roy, Frank, and Maury—all Cooley friends of Stew—were present. All three claimed to have heard the story from Stew on the day he first brought Pop Rocks (May 11th)—the same day that Ronald told his story. However, unless this storytelling occurred after practice, the accuracy of the account is questionable. Stew claims, and repeats the assertion on the questionnaire, that he had heard about the death from his friend Bo before Ronald mentioned it. At this time Stew contends that the boy died from the carbon dioxide, and after some discussion in the group,[43] it is agreed that the victim ate four packs, though Roy suggests two packs. Stew comments that it happened in Avondale, and comments in terms of the story's credibility: "I heard a rumor . . . but I *know* it happened."

On May 23rd, Tim, the other major source, introduces his story, which he said he had learned from a cashier at 7-11. He claims that the Pop Rocks got caught in a boy's throat and killed him. Frank, who is present at the time of Tim's account, says that he heard a similar story from a boy at school and he makes no reference to Stew's version. Both Stew and Ronald then repeat the basic elements of their versions.

By May 23rd all the basic elements of the legend have been introduced to the Dodgers. While discussion of Pop Rocks continues intermittently between the 23rd and June 6th, no significant developments occur—at least as recorded in the field observations. It is not until June 10th that Maury reports that *two* kids had died from eating Pop Rocks; the Avondale death is reiterated, but Maury adds that a boy swallowed two packs of Pop Rocks and "croaked." When I asked him where the death occurred, he turns to Stew and asks him. Stew says that the second death was in South Dakota, or possibly in North Dakota.

On first glance at Figure 5.2, friendship might not seem to have had a significant effect on transmission among the Dodgers, and the time spent together in the Dodgers' practices and games deemphasizes the role of cliques and dyadic friendships. Only in one instance does a boy claim to have heard the story from another boy whom he considers to be one of his three best friends (Roy hearing it from Stew). However, all players were also asked to name their three best friends on the team (see Figure 5.3). Taking into account only the seven primary reports, six of these boys heard the legend from a team friend—three of these six cases (and the one counter-example) involve a relationship with Stew. Tim, the secondary source, is only chosen as a friend by one member of the team, and Ronald is chosen by fewer boys than would be expected through chance. These are within-team friendship ties, which, if not as strong as a best friend relationship, may serve to channel communication—through pre-game and pre-practice discussions.

Examination of the details of the Dodgers' versions indicates that Stew's

Figure 5.3
Dodger Network: Within Team Friendships

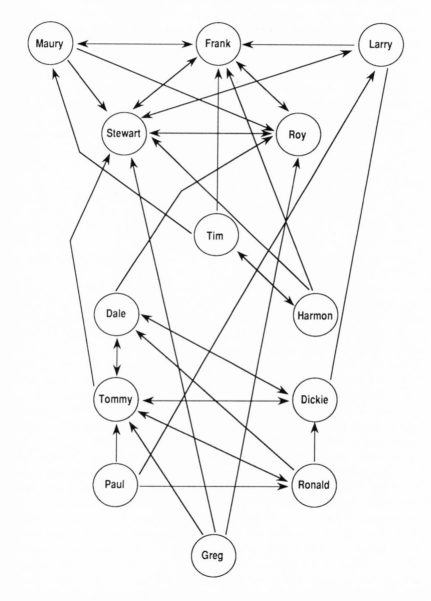

Solid arrows indicate friendship choices within team with arrowhead directed at chosen; maximum of three choices telling seems to have had the greatest impact on the team (with four players claiming to hear it first from him); some evidence, though not conclusive, suggests that the versions of Ronald and Tim may have had an effect as well. Unlike the Rosebuds, the Dodgers do not provide clear evidence of a multi-link transmission conduit; and analysis of the stories coupled with the field observations suggest that the three major single sources provided their versions to their teammates—and those were accepted or ignored. Only in the chain from Stew to Dale to Tommy to Paul do we have evidence of multiple stage transmission. However, Dale and the others report only skeletal versions—dropping victim's age and location, and, except for Paul's possible reconstruction, the reason for death.

Analysis of Legend Components. Source: Five Dodgers were in the sixth grade at the Cooley School during the 1977 season: Stew, Roy, Frank, Maury, and Larry. With the exception of Larry, who was not present throughout much of this period, the Cooley sixth graders report strikingly similar stories—the only details which differ concern the number of packs consumed. This consistency of the story content is undoubtedly shaped by Stew's multiple tellings. The version on May 19th was by all accounts not the original one, and this retelling provided reinforcement for the boys. On May 19th the Cooley sixth graders agreed with Maury's observation that the story was heard "through the grapevine." Stewart first called the account a "rumor," and only later recalled that he heard the story from Bo. Unlike the Rosebud chain, the prior link in Stew's story does not lead back to an adult source, and few players mention a prior source for the story beyond their immediate informant.

Because Stew's story was prior to Tim's, it is not surprising that his story is cited as the primary version. The two stories are not combined[44] by the team, perhaps because Tim is not popular, and his low sociometric status serves to decrease the likelihood of his version being adopted as a supplement to Stew's. Tim, however, is a loud and gregarious boy (an active teller) whose version from 7-11 would be recalled, even if not accepted. A geographical factor is that the boys from Cooley School live on the other side of a major dividing street from the Sanford Heights 7-11, and thus regularly patronize the PDQ store— thus decreasing the likelihood that they would have heard Tim's version reiterated by a 7-11 employee. Players were not asked where secondary sources had heard the story, but possibly more of Tim's hearers would have known his source, since he emphasized it as a means of stressing the legend's facticity.

Perhaps because of Ronald's relatively low sociometric status on the team and his diffidence, or perhaps because of the non-local setting of his story, no one names him as even a secondary source. While it is dangerous to overemphasize structural considerations in an idiographic analysis, note that unlike Stew or Tim, Ronald has no classmates on the team from the Buckminster sixth grade. Although Ronald publicly repeated his story at least three times, no mention of it is made in the verbal statements or questionnaire reports from his teammates. This selective recall of texts is an issue not only in questionnaire studies of diffusion but in field studies as well, where one relies on the selective memory of one's informant.

Belief: Although seven players claimed to believe that the death actually occurred, these believers were not randomly distributed in the team's communication structure. The five non-believers comprised the Cooley sixth grade group and included Paul, the only seventh grader on the team.

On May 19th, Stew assured me that the event described actually occurred, despite its "rumor" status. Some event in the following two and a half weeks altered opinions significantly, and indicated that the death was discussed outside of the author's presence. One might speculate that it was Tim's certainty about his version's veracity that produced a questioning of the legend. Older children seem particularly likely to question the veracity of a story told by a younger child, and are less likely to question the accuracy of the identical information revealed by someone older. In the three cases in which younger children claimed to hear from those older (Dale from Stew; Tim from the 7-11 employee; Dickie from the author), belief is expressed in the legend. This is despite the fact that Stew himself claims not to believe it, and whatever Dickie heard was not accompanied by the author's confirmation. In the only case in which an older boy (Paul) heard from a younger one (Tommy), the teller's belief is converted to skepticism by the recipient. While in the total sample there is insufficient evidence of what happens when a younger boy informs an older boy, evidence suggests that older non-family members tend to be believed. Of the eleven Major Leaguers who heard from an older, non-relative, ten believed the legend (91 percent), compared to only fifteen (60 percent) who believed the twenty-five peer versions ($\chi^2 = 3.45$, df $= 1$, p $< .10$).

Date of Telling: According to respondents' reports, the original teller may be the last to know—the same finding as on the Rosebuds. Each of the four Dodgers who names Stew as his original source claimed to hear it from him before he himself claimed to hear it. If May 11th is accepted as the original diffusion date on the Dodgers, those who suggested they heard it a month before the questionnaire were nearly correct, and Frank's estimate of three and a half weeks was actually more accurate than Stew's own three weeks estimate.

Age and sex of victim: Stew's group agrees that the boy who died was twelve years old, though Frank and Maury are not certain of this detail. It is an esoteric detail not recalled by the others on the team, who uniformly are not aware of the age—perhaps provided in a single retelling of the story when Stew suggested that the victim was "about our age." The detail is a likely social construction of the Cooley sixth graders at some point in their discussions, although not while filling out the questionnaire, since the sheets were completed individually in the author's presence. Stew's group was the only one in the total sample who claimed that a twelve year old died. Tim's assertion that the boy was eleven (his own age) is not mentioned by any other team members. Generally, few preadolescents mention the victim's age—in the Major League sample 24 percent (thirteen players) recall an age, as compared to 35 percent (nineteen players) who name a locale, and 69 percent (thirty-seven players) who know the number of packs consumed. Thus, the age of victim is not a central element to the story, and not easily transmitted or recalled. All respondents agree that the victim was male, with the exception of Dickie, who cannot recall.

Locale of the victim: Stew's group also indicates its cohesion in that Stew, Roy, and Frank agree that the death occurred in the neighboring suburb of Avondale. While Maury does not recall this on the June 6th questionnaire, by June 10th he reports this detail. No other respondent in the entire sample mentioned this location. The other major teller, Tim, claims the death occurred in Brooklyn Center, which is part of the version diffused from 7-11 employees. Ronald has now specified the Montana town in which his version occurred.[45] Dickie locates the story in Sanford Heights—consistent with the process of localization; although the proximate reasons for the change are not apparent.

Reason for Death: Unlike the Rosebud network, the Dodgers do not provide a very satisfactory physiological explanation. "Too many Pop Rocks" is a gloss for why the Pop Rocks killed the victim, and the specific organ destroyed. However, Stew's Cooley friends, Frank, Maury, and Roy, agree that the cause of death was too many Pop Rocks, although Stew does not name a cause. This reason is echoed by Ronald, and this detail in itself does not provide a clear means of differentiating this sub-network from others in the sample. This explanation may be a *post hoc* rationalization based upon one of Stew's comments or the extrapolation of his story by one of his three friends in the presence of the others. Some versions, such as the Rosebuds', provide an explanation which is central to the story, but that is not the case here, although both explanations warn preadolescents to consume the candy carefully and with discretion.

The other explanations: explosion (Dickie), choking (Paul), or carbon dioxide (Harmon) may have diffused from team tellings, from outside sources, or as personal extrapolation. On May 19th Stew mentions that the carbon dioxide killed the victim, and on the twenty-third, Tim mentions that Pop Rocks got caught in the victim's throat—thus possibly explaining the origin of Paul's and Harmon's explanations. All three explanations are mentioned by others in the sample, although no one with a friendship tie to these three respondents.

Number of Packs: The Dodgers generally are in agreement that several packs were eaten. Field observations indicate that Ronald mentioned on May 11th that the victim consumed two packs. Later, on May 19th, there was discussion of whether Stew's victim died from two or four packs, and four packs was finally agreed on. There is no record of Tim on May 23rd suggesting that the victim ate three packs, but this may have occurred, and Tim does mention this on his questionnaire.

On the questionnaire Ronald, perhaps as a result of the discussions within the team, claims that four packs were consumed by the victim. Stew continued to mention four packs, as does the conduit composed of Dale, Tommy, and Paul. Although details are eliminated (or "leveled" in Allport and Postman's terminology), the detail that remains is reported accurately from Stew's telling. Stew's own friendship clique has forgotten or discarded his version; Roy and Frank suggest that two packs were eaten, while Maury, possibly incorporating part of Tim's story, suggest two or three packs. Greg, who has heard the story from "the team," also reports two packs. These two-package versions may have developed from Ronald's early version or from Roy's disagreement with Stew.

While two pack versions are relatively common in the total sample, and seem to represent several conduits, four-pack versions are rarer. Of the eight four-pack versions collected, five (62 percent) are from the Dodgers, a sixth is from a version told by another Cooley sixth grader (although not directly traceable to this network), and the other two stories, presumably a separate conduit, are reported from two eighth grade friends at Sanford Heights Junior High (one reports hearing the version from the other). Thus, the prevalence of the four-pack version on the Dodgers, coupled with the Avondale locale and age of the victim, suggests that this story was shaped within the Dodgers' sub-network.

The two other versions, citing nine packs (Harmon) and thirty-three packs (Dickie), are idiosyncratic, and no other source mentions these numbers. The figure of thirty-three may be an expansion ("sharpening") of Tim's three-pack version, and nine may be a confusion of number of packs with age from some other version. Unfortunately, the source of these details and the versions as a whole remains obscure.

In summary, despite some inconsistencies, the effects of team membership on the Dodgers versions are clear. Stew is evidently the principal source—a situation produced by the friendship structure of the Dodgers and the localization of his story. Despite the circumstance that these boys reside in the same community as the Rosebuds, their stories are so dramatically different that it would be impossible to mistake a variant of one for a variant of the other. This gross difference between the sets of legends argues against their having any single progenitor within a few linkages of each other. The possibility of polygenesis, while unlikely, remains a task for those with resources to conduct a national search. At the point that they entered Sanford Heights they are effectively different stories which circulate in different conduits.

The data from the Dodgers also indicate the effect of contact of markedly different versions—one story often will achieve dominance over others (particularly when backed by the sociometric structure of the relevant population). Some alteration may occur, as with the addition of a second death or in variation in the number of packs, but on the basis of this evidence and that from other sub-networks a full meshing of the versions does not occur, and the original source will not be determinable—at least over a short-term period.

Conclusion

Even though the preadolescents examined in the Sanford Heights Northern Little League and in the northern half of Sanford Heights are a close-knit, interacting population, folklore does not spread through the community at random; there is sufficient segmentation in the community that several variants of the same basic folklore item may flourish simultaneously—even though there will be occasions in which conduits intersect and the parallel versions will be merged or selectively recalled.

Further, as shown in the window-breaking example, folklore-related items may spread only among sub-populations with particular interests or experience patterns, or according to group structures or friendship networks.

The data on both the window-breaking story and the two Pop Rocks legends provide support for Dégh and Vázsonyi's contention that folklore is spread through conduits, and not spread unsystematically within a community. This specification of folklore transmission patterns can significantly advance knowledge of diffusion processes, as it allows for a better conceptualization of the folklore role of social structures (schools, teams), affective ties (friends), and interaction potential (grade level, teams). While this study is intended to be exploratory, it is hoped that folklorists will utilize social science network models and methods of research. Few of these studies examine content *per se*, as attempted here; however, by looking at friendship ties, helping relationships, and corporate interlocks, these studies provide an approach which together with a qualitative orientation toward the folklore content can produce a greater understanding of the transmission of folklore forms within a community. A realization of the importance of social structures—both formal and voluntary—can help to explain the patterns affecting folklore diffusion and textual variation.

Notes

A preliminary version of this essay was presented to the Annual Meeting of the American Folklore Society, Detroit, Michigan, November 5, 1977. The author would like to thank Linda Dégh, Donald Bird, Raymond Bradley, Sylvia Grider, Janet Langois, James Leary, Philip Nussbaum, and Greta Swenson for their advice and criticism.

1.   Linda Dégh and Andrew Vázsonyi, "The Hypothesis of Multi-Conduit Transmission in Folklore," in *Folklore: Performance and Communication* (The Hague: Mouton, 1975), 207–51.

2.   C. W. von Sydow, "On the Spread of Tradition," in *Selected Papers on Folklore,* ed. Laurits Bodker (Copenhagen: Rosenkilde and Bagger, 1948).

3.   Ibid., 12.

4. J. A. Barnes, "Class and Committees in a Norwegian Parish," *Human Relations* 7 (1954):39–58. This community can be either geographically based or based upon common interests. See Beth Blumenreich and Bari Lynn Polonsky, "Re-evaluating the Concept of Group: ICEN as Alternative," in *Conceptual Problems in Contemporary Folklore Studies*, ed. Gerald Cashion, *Folklore Forum, Bibliographic and Special Series* no. 12, pp. 12–17, for a preliminary examination of the way networks influence individual folklore repertoire.

5. Harrison White, Scott Boorman, and Ronald Brieger, "Social Structure from Multiple Networks. I. Blockmodels of Roles and Positions," *American Journal of Sociology* 81 (1976):730–80.

6. Mark Granovetter, "The Strength of Weak Ties," *American Journal of Sociology* 78 (1973):1360–80.

7. James Coleman, Elihu Katz, and Herbert Menzel, *Medical Innovation: A Diffusion Study* (Indianapolis: Bobbs-Merrill, 1966).

8. Leon Festinger, Stanley Schachter, and Kurt Back, *Social Pressures in Informal Groups* (New York: Harper, 1950).

9. Alan C. Kerckhoff and Kurt W. Back, *The June Bug: A Study of Hysterical Contagion* (New York: Appleton-Century-Crofts, 1950).

10. A. L. Epstein, "Gossip, Norms and Social Network," in *Social Networks in Urban Situations*, ed. J. Clyde Mitchell (Manchester: Manchester University Press, 1969), 117–27.

11. D. K. Wilgus, "The Text is the Thing," *Journal of American Folklore* 86 (1973):241–52.

12. See, for example, Gyula Ortutay, "Principles of Oral Transmission in Folk Culture," *Acta Ethnographica* 8 (1959):175–221.

13. Gary Alan Fine, "Small Groups and the Creation of Culture: Determinants of the Development of Idioculture," unpublished manuscript.

14. All names used in this report referring to Sanford Heights and its inhabitants are fictitious.

15. This compares to the median income for families for the state of Minnesota of $9,931 (based on statistics from the 1970 census).

16. The geographic area covered in this study was the northern half of the suburb, which corresponds to the area covered by the Little League baseball program under examination. Four public elementary schools service most of the boys (and one girl) in the league, while two players attend the suburb's junior high school. Eight boys out of the 90 players in the Major League attended the Catholic parochial school in Sanford Heights.

17. Gary Alan Fine and Barry Glassner, "The Problems and Promise of Participant Observation with Children," *Urban Life*, 8 (1979):153–74.

18. This, and all future reference to boys, includes the responses of the one female player in the league.

19. C. Wayne Gordon, *The Social System of the High School* (Glencoe: Free Press, 1957); James S. Coleman, *The Adolescent Society* (New York: Free Press, 1961).

20. Von Sydow, "On the Spread of Tradition," 16–17.

21. Sandra Stahl, "The Personal Narrative as Folklore," *Journal of the Folklore Institute* 14 (1977):9–30.

22. The Chi Square statistic is a measure of association frequently computed by social scientists when examining nominal or ordinal data (e.g., categorical data or binary data). By using a Chi Square distribution table along with the degrees of freedom (df; a controlling parameter) one is able to determine the likelihood that a particular association occurred by chance alone. A low "p" value indicates that the result was not due to chance and thus

indicates that the result found was not a mere statistical artifact. A two decimal place "p" value indicates the number of times in a hundred cases that such a result could have occurred by chance; a three decimal place "p" value indicates the number of times in a thousand such a result could have occurred by chance. A "p" value of .05 or less is generally considered statistically significant. A "p" value of .10 to .05 is considered statistically marginal.

23. Linda Dégh (personal communication) has suggested that preadolescents may be more likely to communicate folklore to friends than are adults whose acquaintanceship patterns may be more specialized on the basis of perceived personality or interest. I have no comparative evidence to support or refute this assertion; however, it is clear that friendship linkages play an important role in adult interaction, even if its relative extent cannot be ascertained.

24. The story has been reported by a General Foods spokesman to have been spread elsewhere around the country as well. *The Nashville Tennessean* reported on Sunday, March 13, 1977 (p. 5), well before stories had spread in Minnesota, that the story of a child choking on Pop Rocks was widely known and believed in the Spokane, Washington, area. The Food and Drug Administration eventually tested the product and found them harmless. No injury has ever been traced to these candies.

25. Gary Alan Fine, "On Incredible Edibles: Legends of Fast Food Contamination," unpublished manuscript.

26. Xenia E. Cord, "Department Store Snakes," *Indiana Folklore* 2 (1969):110–14; George Carey, "Some Thoughts on the Modern Legend," *Journal of the Folklore Society of Greater Washington* 2 (1970–71):3–9; Jan H. Brunvand, *The Study of American Folklore* (New York: Norton, 1968), 91.

27. Brunvand, *Study of American Folklore*, 91–92.

28. Gordon W. Allport and Leo Postman, *The Psychology of Rumor* (New York: Holt, Rinehart and Winston, 1947), 5.

29. Maria Leach, ed., *Funk & Wagnalls Standard Dictionary of Folklore, Mythology and Legend*, 2nd vol. (New York, 1950), 612.

30. Linda Dégh and Andrew Vázsonyi, "Legend and Belief," in *Folklore Genres*, ed. Dan Ben-Amos (Austin: University of Texas Press, 1976), 119; Robert A. Georges, "The General Concept of Legend," in *American Folk Legend*, ed. Wayland D. Hand (Berkeley: University of California Press, 1971), 17.

31. Because the population parameters are indeterminate, no expected frequencies can be provided. Expected frequencies would be considerably lower than the 3% based upon within-league friendships.

32. The Fisher Exact Probability test, a measure of association used when a small number of cases are available, indicates that this is significant at the $p < .10$ level (i.e., marginally significant).

33. A Chi Square Goodness of Fit test reveals this trend to be insignificant, although it points in the expected direction.

34. A t-test is a measure of effect. In other words: do the two conditions have different effects on the respondents? This analysis need not imply causality. "p" values are interpreted as in a Chi Square analysis.

35. This analysis would have been inappropriate for the window-breaking story because of the segmental distribution of knowledge by school, and because the first-order sources were informed by an outside source on a criterion structurally irrelevant to popularity (i.e., rowdiness).

36. Everett M. Rogers with F. Floyd Shoemaker, *Communication of Innovations* (New York: Free Press, 1970), 108.

37. In this analysis we include all boys named by others as tellers—although in a few cases (3-Death; 2-Illegal) these boys denied knowing the story. It is unclear whether these boys had forgotten the stories or whether the other boys forgot who told them.

38. Linda Dégh, *Folktales and Society* (Bloomington: Indiana University Press, 1969), 51.

39. Bemidji is 214 miles north-northwest of Minneapolis, and approximately 100 miles south of the Canadian border.

40. Linda Dégh and Andrew Vázsonyi, "The Memorate and the Proto-Memorate," *Journal of American Folklore* 87 (1974):231.

41. Dégh and Vázsonyi, "Legend and Belief," 109–18.

42. Only one of the six other teams in the league had more within-team choices than the Dodgers when players were asked to name their three best friends in the world.

43. As discussed in Dégh and Vázsonyi, "Legend and Belief," 104–107.

44. Recall that on June 10th another variant was added by Maury and Stew.

45. Despite Ronald's assertion, no town named Taylors Falls exists in Montana; Ronald may have confused Taylors Falls with Thompson Falls. Taylors Falls, Minnesota, is a popular vacation area, not far from Minneapolis-St. Paul.

Appendix: Pop Rocks Questionnaire

1. Have you ever eaten Pop Rocks?
1a. Who gave you some Pop Rocks first?
1b. How long ago did you first taste Pop Rocks?
2. Have you heard that Pop Rocks are illegal in Minnesota?
2a. Who first told you this?
2b. How long ago did you hear this?
2c. Did you believe it?
2d. From who did that person hear it?
2e. Who else told you this?
3. Have you heard that someone died from eating Pop Rocks?
3a. Who first told you this
3b. How long ago did you hear this?
3c. Did you believe it?
3d. From whom did that person hear it?
3e. Who else told you this?
3f. How old was the person who died?
3g. How many packs of Pop Rocks did they eat?
3h. What city, town or state did this happen in?
3i. Was the person who died male or female?
3j. Why did the person die?

6

The Kentucky Fried Rat:
Legends and Modern Society

Although the existence of folklore was once considered a characteristic of rural, isolated groups, threatened by urbanization, no folklorist today would deny that tradition thrives in post-industrial society. Research on urban traditions has taken several forms during the past decade. Some studies focus on the folklore survivals of rural migrants to the city;[1] others have examined the transformation of folk traditions as a function of the urban environment;[2] still others collect traditions of subsocieties which have resulted from urbanization, such as factory workers,[3] hippies,[4] dieters,[5] or white collar workers;[6] a fourth approach assumes that modern society as a whole comprises the folk group under study.[7]

This article examines this fourth orientation—considering modern society as a "folk community" and examining the effects that massive relocations in the American social structure have had on individuals. New folklore content and the transformation of old themes are the expected consequence of large environmental changes. Contemporary folklore themes are the attempts of people to negotiate their current reality and to deal with changes in their personal environment.

Mullen has recognized difficulties with the use of the term "urban legend" to denote legends about contemporary events by correctly noting that these traditional stories are not localized to urban areas.[8] Many legends depict suburban lifestyles, and, as a result of the expansion of corporate franchising, the mass media, and advertising, urban legends may be collected in small towns and rural areas. If the geographical referent of "urban legends" is emphasized, the use of "urban" is unsatisfactory. Mullen suggests that "modern legend" is a more adequate description. However, the problem with this phrase, as with other temporally relative labels, is that they become outdated. Thus, the "young Turks" in folklore of the early 1970s[9] have become the "old boys"; their "new perspectives"[10] have become accepted dogma. Similarly, the *modern* legends of 1980 may be forgotten by 2020.

While there is a temptation to impose a neologism (mass legend, metropolitan legend, megapolitan legend), the term "urban legend" is serviceable so long as it is recalled that "urban" refers not to geography but to the socio-psychological conditions of urbanism.

The Great Change in American Community Life

Sociologists who have examined American community life have recognized that since World War II there have been massive structural changes in our society. These changes have been characterized in numerous ways, and, while there are disagreements about the content and extent of these changes, there is consensus on their outlines. For this analysis I shall adopt one widely utilized set of categories, formulated by Roland Warren, adding a folkloristic perspective. Warren has argued that in the post-war period, "changes on the community level are taking place at such a rapid rate and in such dramatic fashion that the entire structure and function of community living is being transformed."[11] He describes seven components of what he terms "the Great Change" in American community life.

1. Division of Labor. Modern society is increasingly characterized by the interdependence of individuals who supply each other with products and services outside their own occupational specialization.[12] While all societies have some distinct occupational roles, the wide diversity of work specialties is particularly characteristic of industrial (and post-industrial) society where technical specialization is emphasized at the expense of general competence. Related to this differentiation of skills is a lack of knowledge of other occupational specialties. This ignorance provides a fertile breeding ground for folk beliefs. For example, the belief that a kitten, puppy, or infant exploded when placed in a microwave oven results from this collective ignorance. The operation of a microwave oven is a contemporary equivalent of magic. In fact, although the kitten, puppy, or infant would cook, it would *not* explode.

2. Differentiation of Interests and Associations. Several decades ago the basis of community was spatial proximity—the neighborhood. This has changed with community now increasingly based on shared interests. It is not that "community" has declined, but only that community is no longer synonymous with neighborhood.[13] This change is partially a result of increased availability of transportation, additional leisure time, economic prosperity, and knowledge of numerous possible recreations, and is reflected in the transmission of urban legends about these specialized interest groups. The grotesque story about the hippie babysitter who cooks a baby rather than a roast is characteristic of the antagonism felt toward people of widely diverging lifestyles, and proceeds from the anxiety that outsiders feel about hippies.[14] Differentiation of interests also permits the development of subcultural folklore traditions—such as the folklore of dieters[15]—as folklore traditions develop within every group which strives to obtain a sense of community.

3. Increasing Systemic Relationships to the Larger Society. The contemporary image of a nineteenth-century American community is that of a nearly self-sufficient population center. Whatever the validity of this description, communities are now far less self-sufficient. Communities are increasingly connected to a nation-wide organizational network as a result of governmental intervention, industrialization, and national mass media. Community institutions have been displaced by national institutions. Whereas once the local school was a largely autonomous institution, during the past few decades it has been shaped by federal policy directives. Similarly, the local grocery store is likely to have been bought out or supplanted by the supermarket chain.

While there may be advantages to the transference of authority to the national level such as uniformity of service, equality of access, and increased choice of goods and services, psychologically this process seems to increase alienation from these institutions. Individuals feel they have little influence on decisions, and this psychological distance promotes "horror" stories which focus on the irresponsibility of these extra-community agencies. The accounts of McDonald's hamburger meat being composed of worms or that snakes were found in imported sweaters sold in discount store chains[16] are responses to this loss of community control.

4. Bureaucratization and Impersonalization. One component of the transition from local organizations to national ones is a shift from a personal relationship between client (or customer) and organizational employee to an impersonal one. While clients may be known personally in a large bureaucratic organization, organizational rules often provide that they must be treated identically to everyone else. Although this prevents prejudicial treatment against stigmatized groups, it may also prevent individuals from being treated according to their individual needs. As a result the organizational structure may be technically efficient but appear inefficient to those who have a special problem or require a unique solution.

Routine processing is not recalled as competence; however, isolated difficulties are long remembered and may be the basis for personal experience stories about inefficient or hostile bureaucracies. Folklore emerges which symbolically addresses the frustrations of encountering these monolithic, uncompromising structures. For example, stories or rumors are common about egregious government mismanagement and waste.[17] One rumor describes a lengthy and complex government regulation controlling a trivial item, such as heads of cabbage.[18] While bureaucracy in its ideal form is a rational and, thus, efficient organization,[19] it is not *experienced* as such. As a consequence of the fixed character of its operating procedures, it is perceived as inefficient and irrational, and this folk belief provides the legitimation for urban legends.

5. Transfer of Functions to Profit Enterprises and Government. A recent societal change is that government and profit-making organizations have assumed social functions which formerly the family, neighbors, or local charitable organizations had handled. Since the Depression, government has repeatedly established programs to aid "needy" individuals. Whatever the total effect on American society, one consequence has been to decrease the significance of local groups. Thus, there is less need for communal charity when indigents receive food stamps, aid to dependent children, or social security. To be sure, community-based systems did not work perfectly, and some individuals did not receive community support, consequently starving, or living in dire poverty. Yet, whatever the political virtue involved, this change in community structure produced a change in American folk culture.

Concurrent with the growth of government as a provider, there has been an increase in the role of profit enterprises. Once food was almost exclusively prepared and consumed in private residences. Now, more than one meal in three is served outside the home. The house call of the local general practitioner has been replaced by a visit to the health maintenance organization. Whereas once we spoke of a warm bedside manner, today we speak of efficient health care delivery systems. Insurance has replaced the community welfare fund and neighborly cooperation. Such trends affect folklore creation and variation. Stories about welfare cheats who drive Cadillacs and vacation in the Bahamas reflect concern over the unintended consequences of government interference, while the folk beliefs that fast food corporations willingly contaminate their food with worms (McDonald's), buckshot (Arby's), or dog food (Pizza Hut) criticize industry.

One set of beliefs about corporations *apparently* represents the opposite perspective. It is said that a particular corporation will donate expensive medical technology to help a sick person (often a child) if community residents collect an enormous number of product packages. These may be teabag labels, cereal boxtops, or bottle caps. A grimly apposite story concerns a tobacco company which was to supply a lung machine to a victim of cancer for several thousand cigarette package wrappers. Such beliefs are typically untrue, and embarrass the corporation which must deny them to the expectant community. However, they do reveal public expectations. At their best, corporations are perceived as paternalistic, having the resources to provide technology in exchange for product loyalty. These stories also indicate how neighborhood action can be integrated into the corporate state.

6. *Urbanization and Suburbanization.* Probably no change in American society has been as dramatic as the change in American residential patterns from small towns and rural areas to urban and suburban living. In 1790 only 5 percent of the population resided in towns or cities with more than 2,500 residents; by 1970 two-thirds of the American population lived in these "urban" areas.

If only the *geographical* location of people had changed, this process would be less culturally significant. However, residence affects social life. Sociologist Louis Wirth listed five components to urbanism: (1) anonymity, (2) division of labor, (3) heterogeneity, (4) impersonal and formally prescribed re-

lationships, and (5) symbols of status independent of personal acquaintanceship. As a result of these features, urban life may alienate individuals.

While some sociologists have challenged the validity of parts of Wirth's
argument,[20] these traits do apply in some urban settings. These anonymous,
impersonal settings provide the backdrop for numerous urban legends. What
could better serve as a metaphor for the city as a jungle than the belief that the
New York sewer system is filled with albino alligators, which swim through
toilet pipes and bite victims in public washrooms? While part of this story may
have a factual basis,[21] it is significant that the urban restroom is a prototype of
the anonymous urban setting.

Another widely known story describes a kidnapping from a shopping center restroom. Typically, the victim is a young girl whose mother waits for her
outside the restroom. After a long time, the girl emerges clearly drugged, accompanied by two women. The mother asks what is happening, to which one of
the women responds that this is her daughter who has been taken ill; the real
mother vehemently states that the girl is her own daughter, and the two women
escape. The mother subsequently learns that the women were planning to sell
the daughter into white slavery. This story is known throughout the nation and
causes shopping center operators and police departments considerable worry.[22]

7. *Changing Values.* Finally, there has been a massive change in values, although it is difficult to determine the precise content of this change. Despite
problems of interpretation, some value shifts are obvious. Over the past few
decades, Americans have emphasized play as opposed to work; there has been a
reshaping of gender role attitudes, increasingly open sexuality, and an emphasis
on consumption. These value shifts have unexpected effects, as members of a
society cannot alter their basic mores without some ambivalence. This ambivalence, often not talked about openly, is expressed indirectly through folklore,
which disguises the threat through the projection of the fear of a "real" occurrence. Values tend to lag behind social change, and some conflict is likely.[23]

The supposed factuality of legends is justification for their telling (whether
or not they are believed), although their criticism of contemporary values may
provide the unconscious rationale. Stories about corporations which manufac-
ture bathing suits that become transparent in water indicate a fear of the effects
of overt sexuality. Similarly, a legend about a cheerleader who has oral sex with
the members of her team and must then be rushed to a hospital to have her stomach pumped[24] depicts the dangers of changing sex roles and morality. Rumors
about Ray Kroc, the owner of McDonald's, being a member of the Church of
Satan, the rock group KISS standing for Knights In Satan's Service, or Procter
& Gamble being owned by Rev. Moon's Unification Church reflect threats to
traditional religion.

These seven components constitute the "Great Change" in American community life. By affecting the structure of community life they also affect cul-

ture. The acceptance and diffusion of beliefs, legends, and rumors are grounded in the folk's worldview[25]—or what actions are deemed "credible." Not every possible action makes sense, and only those stories that could happen will be accepted. Thus, legends which contradict our own "empirical" worldview, like "The Flying Dutchman," will no longer be accepted. Generally, urban legends are grounded in human baseness rather than in a belief in supernatural power.

Food Contamination Stories

Many urban legends deal in some way with food consumption.[26] Rumors and legends concerning poisoned foodstuffs, of course, are not only a contemporary phenomenon but reflect the innate human orientation toward orality.[27] During the Black Death in fourteenth-century Europe, Jews were rumored to have poisoned local wells, and mass poisoning is also associated with wartime sabotage. For example, the Chinese claimed Japanese saboteurs put ground glass in food tins during the Sino-Japanese hostilities in the 1930s. Likewise, American GIs warned each other not to drink Coca-Cola in Saigon because Viet Cong sympathizers placed ground glass in the soft drink. Soldiers sometimes believe that their military supervisors place chemicals in their food to dampen their sex drive.[28] The questioning of the ingredients of the "mess" (i.e., foodstuffs which cannot be easily identified by sight or taste) is a common topic for those whose food is institutionally prepared—e.g., servicemen, schoolchildren, or summer campers.

A key feature of many contemporary food legends is that they deal with corporate food products, and some may even affect sales. The *Wall Street Journal* reports:

> [R]umors are almost as much a part of the business life as profits and losses. A growing number of businesses are struggling to spike rumors in hopes of minimizing the harm they can do to sales, employee morale, and relations with stockholders and regulatory officials.[29]

Widely known food contamination beliefs assert that McDonald's hamburgers are made from worms; that decomposed mice are found in Coke bottles;[30] that Bubble Yum bubble gum is made from spider eggs, and that children have died from Pop Rocks.[31] Each story blames a large corporation—significantly, the leading seller of that class of food products. The account about wormy hamburger meat apparently was originally attached to Wendy's, a rapidly growing chain which advertises how *juicy* their hamburgers are. However, the target of the stories soon changed to McDonald's, the largest fast food franchiser in America. The frequency of attachment of an urban legend to the largest company or corporation is so common as to be considered a law of urban folklore. This seems to be a result of the expansion of a kernel story;[32] for example, if one recalls that a story is about a soft drink, it is likely that one will assume that Coke, the most popular soft drink, is involved.

Following Alan Dundes,[33] I contend that understanding the social-psychological meaning of legendary material is central to explaining its presence, popularity and persistence. Specifically, an examination of the urban legend about the Kentucky Fried Rat will expose how the characteristics of modern American life cited above affect folklore. Five of these factors are particularly fruitful for analysis: Increasing Systemic Relationships to the Larger Society, Impersonalization, Transfer of Functions to Profit Enterprises, Urbanization and Suburbanization, and Changing Values. As jokes permit individuals to express real fears in disguised form,[34] urban legends permit the teller to achieve some measure of "role-distance"[35] from the narrative by postulating that the events retold are true or at least credible.

The Kentucky Fried Rat

Few urban legends are as widely known as the one about a rat served as a piece of fried chicken. On the basis of questioning introductory sociology students, I estimate that approximately half the undergraduates (at the University of Minnesota) have heard a version of the story. During the past five years I have collected 115 versions of this urban legend from informants at Harvard University, Boston College, Auburn University, University of Rhode Island, Indiana University, Indiana University-Southeast, Central Michigan University, University of Minnesota, and at two California high schools. The popularity of the legend can affect its content. As Dégh notes:

> The greater the popularity of a legend within a group, the more functional it becomes, and the more and more conspicuous its incompleteness becomes. As it spreads almost like a rumor from person to person, it cannot reach a consistent form but often remains incoherent.[36]

While several of the accounts are lengthy narratives, others are mere statements of belief, unsupported by evidence. To the extent that rumor and legend can be differentiated on the basis of length and detail,[37] this corpus contains both rumors and legends, generated from the same set of folk beliefs.

Examples of the full version of the Kentucky Fried Rat story include:

> Before going to the movies, a young man and his date stopped at a fast-food chain fried chicken stand, purchasing a bucket of fried chicken to eat at the show. The girl complained that one of her pieces of chicken was rather tough and

"rubbery." Toward the end of the film she became violently ill. The boyfriend was so concerned at her sudden and intense condition that he drove her to the nearest emergency hospital. The examining physician said that she appeared to have been poisoned, and he asked the young man if he knew of any possible causes. The boy raced out to the car and began burrowing through the half-consumed bucket of chicken and discovered the odd-shaped piece, half eaten. He broke off the batter and realized it was the remains of a rat, poisoned and fried along with the chicken. The girl, receiving a fatal amount of strychnine from the rat's body, died. [38]

A lady was sitting in her living room watching TV and eating Kentucky Fried Chicken. She bit into it and after a couple of bites, she noticed that it tasted funny, and she turned on the lights and saw that it was a rat she was eating with extra-crispy coating on it. Later I heard a boy that worked at Kentucky Fried Chicken fried it for a prank. I can believe that it would be true. There are crazy people in this world. [39]

However, other versions are simple statements of fact:

Instead of a piece of chicken, someone got a Kentucky Fried Mouse. [40]

[Kentucky Fried Chicken] fries rats instead of chicken and sold them to customers. [41]

Most of the variants are brief, only providing the "kernel story." While this brevity in part derives from unnatural collecting settings (written documents and direct interviewing), many informants know only the outline of the story.

Kentucky Fried Content

Locale. As is typical in legends and rumors, localization occurred regularly. In fact, the accounts were situated in thirty-eight locales in fifteen states, the District of Columbia, and one Canadian province. [42] Although the specific sites are a result of the nature of the sample, they indicate the extent of localization of legendary material. [43] Focusing the story on a particular Kentucky Fried Chicken outlet emphasizes the presence of the corporation in the local community and recognizes systemic ties between local services and national organizations. [44] The legend describes the damage caused by this institution to a community resident, suggesting anxiety about the encroachment of big business on the community. Only 2 of the 115 accounts claim that the incident occurred at a local establishment.

The locale of the Kentucky Fried Rat story is particularly appropriate in light of the American economic system. Although food contamination stories have been collected in Western Europe, these stories typically implicate local ethnic restaurants. Stories collected in West Germany,[45] Great Britain,[46] and Sweden[47] have the same structure as the Kentucky Fried Rat legend, but typically deal with rats served in Yugoslavian, Italian, or Chinese restaurants. Because fast food is not as omnipresent in Europe, fast food stories are not common, although there is evidence that these stories are known to some Europeans.[48] In the United States these stories were once associated with Chinese or Italian restaurants[49] but are now primarily associated with fast food outlets. To the extent that folklore represents a means of dealing with anxieties in disguised forms, claiming that a fear is *real* and did *actually* happen provides us with a grim satisfaction that our fears are not groundless.[50] The target for our fears has shifted to corporations which, like foreigners, are outsiders to the local community (the accepted basis for standards and morality) and have not adopted moral injunctions.[51]

Contaminant. In all but two cases, informants report that a rat or mouse was battered and fried.[52] Three possible explanations for the centrality of the rat seem possible. First, rats *have* been found in milk cartons, pies, soft drink bottles, and other foods. Second, the structure of the story requires a substitute for a piece of chicken that could reasonably be taken as a piece of chicken and which might be found in a fast food establishment. Finally, a rat is symbolically appropriate in the legend. The rat is a common symbol of urban decay.[53] The rat, an animal attracted by filth, represents the decline of community and morality in the neighborhood or small town. Thus, this detail is appropriate in light of the legend's message that people who work at fast food chains do not care about their employer and do not keep the establishment clean.

Reasons for Contamination. Only sixteen (14 percent) of the informants explain how the rat got fried and sold. These explanations, while diverse on the surface, fall into two broad categories: (1) deliberate sabotage by employees, and (2) unintentional carelessness due to unsanitary conditions. The small percentage of explanations suggests that this normally is not an integral part of the story, but an expansion of the kernel story. As such, they represent "reasonable" explanations for a bizarre happening.

Deliberate sabotage. In one version presented above, the informant suggests that a prankster was responsible. This view is also expressed in the version about the fried cat:

> It seemed that a cat has wandered into the store, and when the employees ran across it, they took it upon themselves to offer the public a new finger-licking delight, that of fried cat. Naturally, when the public heard of this all the employees involved were fired along with the manager.[54]

One employee commented that he and his co-workers "wanted to try it as a joke" but apparently did not do so. Because of the impersonality of large institutions, workers do not feel morally attached to their supervisors or to those served. As a consequence, such events are believable.

Unsanitary Conditions. Some informants suggest that a rat got into the vat of chicken not out of human malice, but due to the unsanitary conditions in the restaurant.[55] This presence of filth occasionally is explicitly connected to the time pressures under which the employees work:

> One or some of the Kentucky Fried Chicken places were frying rats instead of chicken thighs and breasts. The factory places were so dirty that the rats accidentally got mixed in with the chicken and the people working there didn't bother to sort it out.[56]

> It is said that one of the cooks was in such a hurry that instead of grabbing a piece of chicken, he grabbed a rat.[57]

These versions suggest that Kentucky Fried Chicken outlets are perceived as unclean.[58] In this they are contrasted with the home kitchen, which may have more actual "filth," but is viewed as having less, perhaps in part because at home one can control and organize one's dirt. Anxiety and guilt arise from the change from eating personally prepared food to eating what profit-making enterprises serve; these emotions have been projected onto the commercial establishment, and transformed into fear.

Victim. In sixty-three cases the sex of the victim is indicated. Fifty-one of the victims (81 percent) are female, eight (13 percent) are male, and in four cases both males and females receive the rat. If we assume that these accounts do not derive from an actual occurrence (or occurrences) and that females do not eat more Kentucky Fried Chicken than males, two explanations seem plausible. First, women are perceived as more vulnerable to attack than men (e.g., "The Roommate's Death," "The Department Store Snake"). Second, if these legends do represent the longing for a lost community life, the woman as victim is symbolically proper. The woman by neglecting her traditional role as food preparer helps to destroy the family by permitting the transfer of control from the home to amoral profit-making corporations. Thus, the receipt of a rat is appropriate symbolic punishment.

Event. In a felicitous turn of phrase, Jeffrey Schrank describes Americans' attitudes to processed and fast foods as "eater's alienation."[59] We have become separated from the production of our food, unsure of its preparation, and consequently are willing to believe almost anything about it. Many of the collected versions are based on the belief that the chicken is not what it appears to be:

> An old lady ordered out for Kentucky Fried Chicken. She was eating along when she noticed teeth; she pulled back the crust and discovered she was eating a rat. She had a heart attack and died, and her relatives sued Kentucky Fried Chicken for a lot of money.[60]

> In Grafton, North Dakota, there is a Colonel Sanders' Kentucky Fried Chicken. One day a lady was eating her meal of the Colonel's home recipe. At one point in the meal she took a bite of a thick coated, fatter piece of chicken—she supposed it

was chicken. This prompted her into a more in-depth investigation into what she was eating. She found that what she had bitten into was a mouse and that the crispiness was not the coated batter, rather the bones of the mouse. Of course, the bone-biting was accompanied by hairs choking upon and guts spouting.[61]

These stories are sometimes accompanied by the warning that the only way this deception was detected was through an outside investigation:

Someone was eating a piece of chicken that was found to have hair. The health department analyzed this and rat hairs were found to be in the chicken.[62]

The Colonel had been convicted of mixing rat meat into barrels of chicken. The twelve secret spices camouflaged the rat. These rats were butchered so that only careful scientific analysis could reveal its true nature.[63]

This detail is parallel to other versions in which victims eat their chicken "in the dark." While the detail of darkness is structurally legitimate to explain why the rat was not recognized before being half eaten, it also is symbolically significant. It acknowledges the change of eating habits produced by contemporary time schedules. The family dinner, once a focal component of American cultural tradition, has been replaced by eating as a hurried secondary activity:

There was this lady and she went to Kentucky Fried Chicken and she went in there and she came out in the dark and it was raining, and she sat in her car eating a bucket of chicken and one of the pieces tasted funny. And she turned on the light in the car and saw a rat. She took it back in there and sued them.[64]

A lady was watching TV one night with her husband. They were eating Kentucky Fried Chicken. The room was dark. The lady noticed that her chicken tasted funny, so she turned on the light and discovered she'd been eating a rat.[65]

One account is explicit in blaming the wife for not performing her homemaking role properly:

There was a wife who didn't have anything ready for supper for her husband. So she quick got a basket of chicken and tried to make her dinner look fancy with the pre-prepared chicken. Thus, she fixed a candle-light dinner, etc. When her and her husband started eating the chicken, they thought it tasted funny. Soon to find out it was a fried rat.[66]

While the primary culprit is the national chain, implicit blame accrues to the decline of family eating traditions.[67]

Aftermath. The harmful effects of these changes in American life are dramatized in the episodes' conclusions. Fifteen (13 percent) of the accounts mention that the victim became ill, went into shock, never ate food again, or died. This detail characterizes the longer, more complete versions:

My sister told me that her friend told her that a lady went to Kentucky Fried Chicken. She was out in the car eating it and noticed that one of the pieces tasted funny. She looked and it had a tail. Then she looked again and saw it had eyes and was a rat. She threw up and went crazy and is in the State [Mental] Hospital in Kalamazoo. She won't eat any food.[68]

I first heard this in about 1970 from some friends at the University of Iowa, Iowa City. A friend of theirs had worked at a Kentucky Fried Chicken, and while there a woman had been served a fried rat and she had a heart attack and died.[69]

These accounts postulate a danger from corporatism, and one major way in which this can be combatted is through another modern institution—the courts.[70] Where such episodes once might have been handled locally and personally— perhaps only with a sincere apology—today we rely on the courts for judgment and settlement. Twenty versions (17 percent) mention legal action, either in progress or won by the victim, often with a large recompense for suffering:

A lady (older, in mid-60s) was eating Kentucky Fried Chicken at one of their stores. She took a bite of what she thought was chicken, but was really a rat. She brought it to the attention of the store's manager and she later sued Kentucky Fried Chicken for $500,000.[71]

An old lady in Florida went to a Kentucky Fried Chicken stand and she bought some chicken and there she bit into a leg and it was a rat. It was a rat with batter over it. Fried batter. And she sued them and won two hundred thousand.[72]

The cycle is complete in that extra-community degradation can only be corrected by extra-community defense, given the power structure of modern America.

Belief and Rationale. Some might see the possibility of a major restaurant chain serving a rat to a customer as ludicrous and beyond credibility. However, the legend is widely accepted. Of fifty-one respondents who indicated whether they believed their account, thirty-nine (76 percent) believed that the event definitely or probably happened. Several informants claimed to have read about the event in the newspaper, although attempts to track down the legend in the press proved, not surprisingly, unsuccessful. Some informants took their belief so seriously that they actually changed their eating habits:

A mouse jumped in the batter and the person working at Kentucky Fried Chicken put it in the deep-fat fryer. A customer was served the mouse and ended up taking a bite from it. . . . I believed it then: I believe it now . . . and I haven't eaten Kentucky Fried Chicken since that day.[73]

One time someone was eating at Kentucky Fried Chicken and they happened to look at what they were eating and saw it looked like a rat, and it was. I don't know if it's true, but it was told as true, and to this day I won't eat fried chicken.[74]

Frequently, the legend is narrated while eating or when thinking about food. Thirty versions (26 percent) were told while eating (often at fast food restaurants) or while deciding where to eat, and function (when told seriously) as a warning to avoid these establishments:

> All I remember is that the customer was horrified and I got the impression that it was somewhat the fault of Kentucky Fried Chicken, and it was a warning to watch out for that place.[75]

> I was cruising along the street one night and I said to my friend. "Let's stop and get some Kentucky Fried Chicken." And he said, "No way, ' cause I heard there was a rat found in one of their buckets of food. A customer bit into it and found it tasted funny." They closed the restaurant temporarily, but it reopened again. It really did happen in Wyandotte.[76]

The context of the performance of these stories is important for my interpretation in that they are told when the anxiety about food technology is expected to be particularly high.

The Kentucky Fried Rat and the Great Change

This set of Kentucky Fried Rat legends indicates that contemporary folklore content is responsive to environmental change and the psychological effects that are concomitant with this change. The public's malaise may be analogous to Alvin Toffler's notion of "Future Shock,"[77] a concept which indicates the difficulty some individuals have adapting to technological change. As I noted above, several versions are explicitly didactic, warning of the consequences of fast food. Others, while implicit, express a similar theme that the fast food establishments are settings of employee sabotage and corporate greed. The legend in addressing modern fears can be connected to several of the components of the Great Change described above.

The impersonalization of the fast food establishment is central to many accounts. Because of the structure of the restaurant, customers feel they are not treated as individuals, but as part of a mass. Workers are given little room to act at their own discretion, and in several fast food establishments, workers even are given set responses to customers' questions. Personal relationships are not permitted to develop between employees and customers. This impersonalization can be understood as representing a lack of concern, and other symbolic indications of a lack of concern—such as serving rats instead of chicken—become believable.

Related to impersonalization is the fact that Kentucky Fried Chicken is an extra-community organization, currently owned by a major American corporation, Heublin, Inc., the 227th largest corporation in America. The presence of national restaurant chains is one example of the increasing systemic relationship of the neighborhood to the larger society, with the residents of the local neighborhood losing control over decisions that affect their lives. This is contrary to the human desire for mastery,[78] and through psychological projection this legend depicts the harm which comes from a lack of personal control.

The growth of fast food chains represents a change of function in the direction of profit-making enterprises and away from home cooking and the community or church supper. By implication this change symbolizes the decline of the family, the church, and community organizations in their most basic function—that of nourishment. Nourishment is now provided by those who strive for economic gain, rather than personal satisfaction.

Although fast food outlets are a result of urbanization and suburbanization and, thus, are an effect and not a cause of metropolitan problems, they are seen as a particularly graphic embodiment of the changing environment. The anonymity of population centers facilitates the impersonality of the relation between servers and customers, and the decay stemming from size and a lack of concern is symbolized by the rat.

Finally, this legend reflects changing values. Fast food chains did not develop without public acceptance. The increased emphasis in American life on leisure and the changing roles of women make the fast food restaurant possible, and possibly necessary. Yet, these changes in value orientation did not occur without psychological effects, as individuals in transition have not completely reconciled themselves to the structural changes these new values imply.[79] The new values coexist with and, in some cases, contradict traditional values. As a result, these urban legends are conservative in implication, even when narrated by those who overtly accept the value change. Folklore is grounded in human experience and individuals deal with these experiences in a symbolic, expressive manner. By indicating the relationship between one widely known urban belief legend and major structural changes in American life in the past few decades, I hope to have illustrated an interpretation of folklore in light of its environment. However, this effort must not end here; other folklore content must be examined to determine if this legend represents an exceptional case. Further, greater attention should be paid to the performance features and context of urban folklore. For example, one might conduct an ethnography of fast food chains, recording the conversations among customers and among employees.

I have argued that understanding the relationship between social structure and communication content is a critical topic for folklorists. This relationship is mediated by individual perceptions and collective needs, and these mediating factors may be a particularly fruitful locus for investigation. Massive social structural changes do not just happen in isolation but produce a myriad of cultural effects, and the examination of this process will lead folklorists to the core of the meaning of modernity.

Notes

The author wishes to thank Donald Allport Bird, Jan Brunvand, Richard Dorson, Patrick Mullen, Marci Persky, and Donald Ward for their assistance in the preparation of this paper.

1. See Ellen Stekert, "Focus for Conflict: Southern Mountain Medical Beliefs in Detroit," in *The Urban Experience and Folk Tradition,* ed, Américo Paredes and Ellen J. Stekert (Austin: Univ. of Texas Press, 1971), 95–127.
2. Morton Leeds, "The Process of Cultural Stripping and Reintegration: The Rural Migrant in the City," in *The Urban Experience and Folk Tradition,* 165–73; Richard M. Dorson, "Is There a Folk in the City?" in *The Urban Experience and Folk Tradition,* 21–52.
3. Bruce Nickerson, "Is There a Folk in the Factory?," *Journal of American Folklore* 87 (1974):133–39.
4. Richard M. Dorson, *America in Legend* (New York: Pantheon, 1973), 257–303.
5. Elizabeth Tucker, "The Seven Day Wonder Diet: Magic and Ritual in Diet Folklore," *Indiana Folklore* 11 (1978):141–50.
6. Alan Dundes and Carl R. Pagter, *Urban Folklore From the Paperwork Empire* (Austin: American Folklore Society, 1975).
7. See Bengt af Klintberg, "Folksagner i dag," *Fataburen* (1976):294–96.
8. Patrick B. Mullen, "Modern Legend and Rumor Theory," *Journal of the Folklore Institute* 9 (1972):95.
9. Richard M. Dorson, "Introduction," in *Folklore and Folklife,* ed. Richard M. Dorson (Chicago: Univ. of Chicago Press, 1972), 45.
10. Américo Paredes and Richard Bauman, eds., *Toward New Perspectives in Folklore* (Austin: Univ. of Texas Press, 1972).
11. Roland Warren, *The Community in America,* 2d ed. (Chicago: Rand McNally, 1972), 53.
12. See Emile Durkheim, *The Division of Labor in Society* (New York: Macmillan Co., 1933).
13. Barry Wellman, "The Community Question: The Intimate Networks of East Yorkers," *American Journal of Sociology* 81 (1979):1201–31.
14. Sociologists term this process by which nonconformists are labeled as behaving in extreme and deviant ways "deviance amplification." See L. T. Wilkins, *Social Deviance: Social Policy, Action, and Research* (Englewood Cliffs, N.J.: Prentice Hall, 1965).
15. Tucker, "The Seven Day Wonder Diet," 141–50.
16. Xenia Cord, "Department Store Snakes," *Indiana Folklore* 2 (1969):110–15.
17. Dundes and Pagter, *Urban Folklore,* 126, 170; Donald Allport Bird, "Rumor as Folklore: Interpretation and Inventory," Ph.D. dissertation, Indiana University, 1979, 149–59.
18. Max Hall, "The Great Cabbage Hoax: A Case Study," *Journal of Personality and Social Psychology* 2 (1965):563–69; Ralph L. Rosnow and Allen J. Kimmel, "Lives of a Rumor," *Psychology Today* 13 (1979):88–92.
19. H. H. Gerth and C. Wright Mills, *From Max Weber: Essays in Sociology* (New York: Oxford Univ. Press, 1976), 196–98.
20. David Karp, Gregory Stone, and William Yoels, *Being Urban* (Lexington, Mass.: D. C. Heath, 1977), 48.
21. Loren Coleman, "Alligators-in-the-Sewers: A Journalistic Origin," *Journal of American Folklore* 92 (1979):335–38.

22. "Kidnap Rumor May Be Just That—Rumor," *Minneapolis Tribune*, 2 March 1977, 12C. For a French version with anti-Semitic overtones, see Edgar Morin, *Rumour in Orleans* (New York: Pantheon, 1971). This legend is similar to the castration motif in racial or religious legends; see Florence H. Ridley, "A Tale Told Too Often," *Western Folklore* 26 (1967):153–56.

23. For a valuable exposition of this point, see Clifford Geertz, *The Interpretation of Cultures* (New York: Basic Books, 1973), 142–69.

24. Gary Alan Fine and Bruce N. Johnson, "The Promiscuous Cheerleader," *Western Folklore* 39 (1980):120–29.

25. Alan Dundes, "Folk Ideas as Units of Worldview," in *Toward New Perspectives in Folklore*, 93–103.

26. For a discussion of food contamination as a legend type, see Susan Domowitz, "Foreign Matter in Food: A Legend Type," *Indiana Folklore* 12 (1979):86–95.

27. See Sigmund Freud, *Introductory Lectures on Psycho-Analysis (Part III)* (1917; reprint ed., London: Hogarth Press, 1963), 313.

28. George W. Rich and David F. Jacobs, "Saltpeter: A Folkloric Adjustment to Stress," *Western Folklore* 32 (1973):164–79; see Marie Bonaparte, *Myths of War* (London: Imago, 1947); Andrea Greenberg, "Drugged and Seduced: A Contemporary Legend," *New York Folklore Quarterly* 29 (1973):131–58. Greenberg suggests that teenage girls believe their boyfriends are willing to put Spanish Fly—an aphrodisiac—in their food or drink.

29. Jim Montgomery, "Rumor-Plagued Firms Use Various Strategies to Keep Damage Low," *Wall Street Journal*, 7 February 1979, 1.

30. This is a true story. See Gary Alan Fine, "Cokelore and Coke Lore: Urban Belief Tales and the Problem of Multiple Origins," *Journal of American Folklore* 92 (1979):478–79.

31. See Gary Alan Fine, "Folklore Diffusion Through Interactive Social Networks: Conduits in a Preadolescent Community," *New York Folklore*, 5 (1979):99–125.

32. Susan Kalčik, "'. . . like Ann's gynecologist or the time I was almost raped': Personal Narratives in Women's Rap Groups," in *Women and Folklore*, ed. Claire R. Farrer (Austin: Univ. of Texas Press, 1975), 3.

33. Alan Dundes, "On the Psychology of Legend," in *American Folk Legend*, ed. Wayland D. Hand (Los Angeles: Univ. of California Press, 1971), 21–22.

34. See Sigmund Freud, *Jokes and Their Relation to the Unconscious* 1905; reprint ed., New York: Norton, 1960); Roger D. Abrahams and Alan Dundes, "On Elephantasy and Elephanticide," *Psychoanalytic Review* 56 (1969):225–41.

35. Erving Goffman, *Encounters* (Indianapolis: Bobbs-Merrill, 1961), 105–10.

36. Linda Dégh, "The 'Belief Legend' in Modern Society: Form, Function, and Relationship to Other Genres," in *American Folk Legend*, 62.

37. Gordon Allport and Leo Postman, *The Psychology of Rumor* (New York: Holt, 1947), 154.

38. From the UCLA Folklore Archives, collected by Robert J. Williamson from a male, aged twenty-five, Santa Monica, California, January 1973.

39. Collected from a female, age eighteen, University of Minnesota, April 1977.

40. Collected from a female, Boston College, April 1975.

41. Collected from a female, University of Minnesota, February 1977.

42. Informants claim that the incident occurred in; Collegeville, Minn.; Iowa City; Owatonna, Minn.: Rockaway, N.J.; Minneapolis; Racine, Wisc.; Laramie; Dearborn Heights, Mich.; Pontiac, Mich.; Milwaukee; Pearl City, Hawaii; Washington, D.C.; Toronto; Davenport, Iowa; St. Paul; Blaine, Minn.; unnamed Alabama town; West St. Paul; Shakopee, Minn.; Roseville, Minn.; Bay City, Mich.; Wyandotte, Mich.; Atlanta; Richfield, Minn.; Detroit; Columbus, Neb.; Ypsilanti, Mich.; St. Petersburg; St.

Cloud, Minn.; Schenectady; Roslindale, Mass.; Springfield, Mass.; Salt Lake City; Lawrence, Mass.; Lakeland, Fla.; Eustis, Fla.; Grafton, N.D.; Kalamazoo.

43. Jan Harold Brunvand, *The Study of American Folklore*, 2d ed. (New York: Norton, 1978), 106.

44. Kentucky Fried Chicken is owned by Heublin, Incorporated.

45. Donald J. Ward, "American and European Narratives as Socio-Psychological Indicators," in *Folk Narrative Research: Some Papers Presented at the VI Congress of the International Society for Folk Narrative Research,* ed. Juha Pentikainen and Tuula Juurikka (Helsinki: Studia Fennica 20, 1976), 348–53; Graham Shorrocks, "Chinese Restaurant Stories: International Folklore," *Lore & Language* 2 (1975):30.

46. Paul Smith and Georgina Smith, "Notes," *Lore & Language* 1:7 (1974):25; Graham Shorrocks, "Notes," *Lore & Language* 1:8 (1974):28.

47. Klintberg, "Folksagner i dag," 295.

48. See Barbro Klein, "Food in Peasant and Post-Peasant Swedish Legends: The Folklore of Poverty and the Folklore of Contaminated Plenty." (Paper delivered at the annual meeting of the American Folklore Society, Los Angeles, October 1979.)

49. Domowitz, "Foreign Matter in Food," 94.

50. I am not discussing whether the story has a factual basis—that topic is beyond the scope of this article.

51. Skeptical attitudes about the role of corporate enterprises in food production have existed for many decades—as the popularity of Upton Sinclair's *The Jungle* attests. See William Bloodworth, "From *The Jungle* to *The Fasting Cure:* Upton Sinclair on American Food," *Journal of American Culture* 2 (1979):444–53. Yet at the turn of the century corporations were not as involved in serving food.

52. A cat and a frog were named by two informants.

53. See, for example, Israel Horowitz's drama, *Rats*.

54. Collected from a male, aged twenty-one, University of Minnesota, April 1977.

55. This is ironic in that fast food restaurants are continually being swept and mopped and are almost antiseptically clean.

56. Collected from a female, University of Minnesota, February 1977.

57. Collected from a male, University of Minnesota, February 1977.

58. See Mary Douglas, *Purity and Danger* (London: Penguin, 1966), 40–53, for a discussion of the symbolic meaning of dirt and defilement, which suggests that such beliefs about these restaurants have more than an empirical referent.

59. Jeffery Schrank, *Snap, Crackle, and Popular Taste* (New York: Delta, 1977), 43.

60. Collected from a female, Indiana University, November 1976.

61. Collected from a male, age twenty-one, University of Minnesota, October 1979.

62. Collected from a female, age twenty-seven, University of Minnesota, April 1977.

63. Collected from a male, age nineteen, Harvard University, April 1975.

64. Collected by Marci Persky from a male, age eighteen, Central Michigan University, April 1976. See also, George Carey, *Maryland Folk Legends and Folk Songs* (Cambridge, Maryland: Tidewater Publishers, 1971), pp. 71–72.

65. Collected from a female, Boston College, April 1975.

66. Collected from a female, age nineteen, University of Minnesota, April 1977.

67. A cartoon by Trosley in the February 1978 issue of *Hustler* magazine pictures a black child holding up a "fried rat" at a filthy Kentucky Fried Chicken restaurant, while his mother looks on in horror. This offensive cartoon plays off several stereotypes about blacks: their love for fried chicken, their dirtiness and, significantly, the breakdown of the black family.

68. Collected by Marci Persky from a female, age twenty-four, Central Michigan University graduate, April 1976.

69. Collected from a male, age thirty-one, University of Minnesota, October 1978.
70. The themes of hospitalization, death, and legal action have parallels in other urban anxiety legends, such as that dealing with department store snakes; see Patrick B. Mullen, "Department Store Snakes," *Indiana Folklore* 3 (1970):214–28.
71. Collected from a male, age nineteen, University of Minnesota, April 1977.
72. Collected from a male, University of Minnesota, January 1977.,
73. Collected from a female, age twenty-two, University of Minnesota, April 1977.
74. Collected from a male, age twenty-one, University of Minnesota, April 1977.
75. Collected from a female, University of Minnesota, October 1978.
76. Collected by Marci Persky from a male, age twenty, Central Michigan University, May 1979.
77. See Alvin Toffler, *Future Shock* (New York: Bantam, 1970).
78. See Alfred Adler, *The Practice and Theory of Individual Psychology* (New York: Harcourt, Brace, 1927).
79. See Geertz, *The Interpretation of Cultures*, 169.

III DANGEROUS CAPITALISM

7

The Goliath Effect:
Corporate Dominance and Mercantile Legends

From Upton Sinclair's grisly description in *The Jungle* (1906:102) of how workers who fell in vats of fat emerged as Durham's Pure Leaf Lard to the recent belief that McDonald's uses worms in its burgers, one of the most prevalent folk ideas in twentieth-century American life is suspicion of big business.[1] This heritage of political progressivism and muckraking journalism remains a cornerstone of American folklore.

Although these attitudes had their roots prior to 1900 (Simpson 1983), much twentieth-century folklore can be understood by reference to American ambivalence toward bigness. I suggest that in their folklore Americans focus on the biggest or best-known corporations, and that these corporations will often be portrayed in a negative light as amoral or as distinctly malevolent. Specifically I propose a set of propositions collectively termed the *Goliath Effect,* arguing that a larger percentage of American legends than predicted by chance refer to the most dominant corporation or product in a particular market (e.g., legends will deal with McDonald's or Coke rather than with Burger King or Pepsi more than would be expected from their respective market share); that legends naming the largest corporations will be more widely disseminated than those referring to smaller corporations; and that legends may change target from a smaller corporation to a larger one. Similar effects are predicted for the most prestigious corporations or products in a market. Here, I attempt to demonstrate the plausibility of the Goliath Effect by analyzing several collections of data.

Folklore and Modernity

Because of the economic and social changes that have affected the United States, a set of legends and folk beliefs has become widely known that indirectly addresses these changes. Although some of these narratives have earlier roots, they are particularly characteristic of the post–World War II period. These stories reflect the conditions of modernity and raise the concerns of the age. They represent attempts by the public to deal with the massive social dislocations affecting them (Fine 1980; Warren 1972). Folklore cannot be divorced from the ideological perspectives of its tellers and audiences. Legends that folklorists have characterized as "urban" frequently feature businesses and corporations as central images and actors. I have chosen to describe this sub-class of urban belief tales as "mercantile legends."[2]

Mercantile legends typically posit a connection between a corporation and some harmful situation or event. Among the best known of these are the Kentucky Fried Rat (Fine 1980), the Mouse in the Coke bottle (Fine 1979a; Domowitz 1979), and the Death Car (Dorson 1959:250; Brunvand 1981:20). Other mercantile legends include stories of worms in McDonald's hamburgers, spider eggs in Bubble Yum bubblegum, deadly exploding Pop Rocks candy, snakes in K-Mart clothing, or Jockey shorts that cause sterility. These mercantile legends can be seen as mini-docudramas in which something dreadful happens to a naive victim: a person buys an inexpensive product but discovers it is horribly defective. Even the Death Car, whose defect cannot be attributed to the greed or negligence of the manufacturer, follows this pattern. In this legend, the car is inexpensive because an anonymous, unnoticed death—perceived as characteristic of modern life—previously occurred in it. Although a few mercantile legends mention court settlements, in most the purchaser can do nothing to prevent similar occurrences.

I classify these legends into three types in terms of the source of the contamination: The Evil Corporation, the Deceptive Corporation, and the Careless Corporation.[3]

The Evil Corporation. These legends proclaim that the corporation is consciously evil, although the product itself is not condemned. The belief that the late Ray Kroc, the president of McDonald's, was a member of the Church of Satan is a widely known example. Similar stories claim that Uncle Ben's gives money to the Palestine Liberation Organization; Procter & Gamble is owned by the Unification Church ("Moonies"), a satanic cult, or a witches' coven; and Schick Razors aided the Nazis during World War II.

The Deceptive Corporation. The second set of stories claims that a company regularly adulterates its products. A recent example is the contention that McDonald's adds worms to their hamburgers (Domowitz 1980). Some contend that Chanel No. 5 gets its distinctive odor from *eau du chat* (Domowitz 1980). Related are accounts of the long-term effects of commonly used products. Consumers say that Bubble Yum bubblegum (Cooney 1977) and Kool-Aid (Domowitz 1980) are carcinogenic. Others speak of the debilitating effects of colas (Bell 1976) and microwave ovens (Brunvand 1981:62–65). Whether such stories are true in whole or in part is a question for epidemiologists. However, the ready acceptance of such grim conclusions is significant to folklorists. These stories reflect the public's implicit conclusion that the post-industrial state is dangerous, since greedy corporations do not care about the health of the general public. In the phrase of Robert Nisbet (1976), the public perceives "the Rust of Progress." Progress does not only bring better times; it has a dark underside that creates tragedy. Technology is a distinctly mixed blessing (Sherry 1984).

The Careless Corporation. A third set of stories depicts one-time product contamination. One popular example is the Department Store Snake (Cord 1969; Mullen 1970; Brunvand 1981:160–71). A woman goes shopping at a discount department store and is bitten by a venomous snake or insect while examining the merchandise. Accounts of the Mouse in the Coke Bottle and the Kentucky Fried Rat are also of this type. Typically the corporation is not blamed for being intentionally evil but is seen as lacking concern, being careless, and employing apathetic and indifferent workers. Although these disturbing events are reported as isolated, people see them as characteristic of American corporate life. The events are shocking but are not really surprising given the shoddiness of our age.

All three groups of legends, when taken together, reflect the American mistrust of business. In a recent Gallup survey of Americans' confidence in their institutions (Gallup 1979), only 32 percent of the public reported having confidence in big business (less support than any other institution, including organized religion, the military, Congress, organized labor, or television). Bigness seems to trouble many Americans. This attitude is paradoxical in light of the American worldview, which emphasizes progress, newness, and size (see Dundes 1971; Dorson 1959). How can this apparent contradiction be resolved? We must recognize that emotional themes need not be responded to consistently. That is, people are ambivalent; although Americans revere size, technology, and innovation, these very traits also provoke fears (see Marx 1964; Harris 1981; Taviss 1972).

The Goliath Effect

Americans' fear of bigness is reflected in folk narrative in a pattern I term the *Goliath Effect*. A large proportion of American mercantile legends do not deal just with large corporations but, when they name a firm or product, name the one with the largest market share in that product area. The general public focuses its attention on this corporation or product, which galvanizes its fears and mistrust. If size per se did not have an effect, then the percentage of tales about any corporation or product would generally reflect its market share. This, however, is not the case. Because of its symbolic significance as the market leader, the largest (or, in some cases, the most prestigious) corporation or product is the target for more of these stories than expected.[4] I do not accept the unproven claim that these tales are usually tools of corporate espionage or conscious manipulations of public opinion by disgruntled consumers or employees (Rowan 1979; Klintberg 1981:156). Rather, these stories make sense because corporate leaders serve as the targets.[5]

I formally present the Goliath Effect through the following propositions:

P1.   The largest corporation (or product) in terms of market share in a particular product area will be mentioned in more versions of a mercantile legend than would be expected by share of the market alone.

P2.   The largest corporation (or product) in terms of market share in a particular product area will be mentioned in more individual mercantile legends than would be expected by share of the market alone.

A corollary of these propositions reflects changes in these legends over time:

C1.   Mercantile legends will tend, over time, to switch the corporation (or product) named in them from a smaller corporation (or product) to a larger one.

I have stated these propositions as precisely and as formally as possible so that other researchers can gather evidence supporting or disputing them, knowing they are examining the same propositions. Each proposition is a probabilistic statement; not all mercantile legends follow these patterns.[6] I do claim that more legends than expected by chance will follow these patterns. Also, I only refer to those legends that cite a particular corporation or product; many refer to the industry as a whole. Finally, I recognize that the primary social-psychological force involved is not actual market share, but market share as *perceived* by the public. This means that a folklorist who wishes to test these propositions must specify which audience is being considered and the time frame for analysis. Targets for these legends may change as corporate dominance shifts. I do not claim to have proven these assertions. Rather, I hope to demonstrate their plausibility by subjecting my data to interpretations based on social psychology.[7]

From the perspective of quantitative social science, the ideal means of examining these claims is to sample randomly a large collection of legends systematically collected from a large population. Unfortunately, since folklorists rarely collect texts systematically, such a collection does not exist. In attempting to assess the validity of the Goliath Effect, I have relied upon two data sources. First, during 1981–82 I requested 102 students in four classes at the University of Minnesota to complete a short questionnaire asking if they had heard of a set of mercantile legends and, if they had, which company was named. While this is not a random sample, I have no reason to believe that this group would be more likely to name large corporations than would a random sample of the population. Second, I reviewed major published accounts for examples of mercantile legend texts and searched systematically through the Indiana University Folklore Archives looking for items that mention corporation[8] names. Although this sample is neither complete nor unbiased, I find no reason to believe this bias would lead to a selection of texts that would unduly support the Goliath Effect.

The questionnaire distributed to students requested information about twelve mercantile legends. Of these, only six legends were known by at least 10 percent of the sample, the figure I used as the criterion for inclusion in the analysis. These were: (1) the mouse in the soft drink bottle; (2) the rat fried as chicken; (3) spider eggs in gum; (4) worms in hamburgers; (5) cat and dog food used in a pizza parlor; and (6) the car sold cheaply because someone died in it.[9] The results of this questionnaire lend support to my claim that the largest corporation will be named as the target of these legends. Coca-Cola, Kentucky Fried Chicken, Bubble Yum, McDonald's, and Pizza Hut are named most often for the first five legends (87.7 percent of all corporations named). The sixth legend is more complicated in that three students named the Corvette, possibly because it is a prestigious sports car. However, the Chevrolet line is also the largest selling car line. If we add the three who named Corvette to the one who named Chevrolet Camaro, four of the ten Death Car citations involve Chevrolet. Another respondent cited the prestigious Cadillac. The evidence thus suggests that more widely known legends refer to the largest firms, supporting Proposition P1.

I requested information about twelve legends. Significantly, only the aforementioned six were known by even one-tenth of the sample. The dynamics of recall in response to a questionnaire should be generally similar to natural recall. That people think "Coke" when they think "soft drink" applies to narration as well as to answering questionnaires.

One feature makes these findings less clear-cut than desirable, despite the statistical support cited above. Many of the stories have received media attention, and so, one might argue, the mass media have appointed one company as the "official" target. This certainly applies in some measure to all but the pizza parlor stories and the Death Car. Yet, media selection of a particular corporation is not as damaging to Proposition P1 as might appear. After all, newspapers and magazines do not create these stories; they report the fact that many people believe and are spreading them with a particular corporation as the target. Although the media may have expanded the number of people who heard the story and may have homogenized popular memory, there is no evidence that any of these mercantile legends were reported before they were in wide oral circulation. These stories are libelous, and newspapers or television would not name the target unless a popular consensus had developed.[10] Folklorists who examine contemporary beliefs must remember that oral tradition and media diffusion play off one another (Attebery 1970).

My second data source is an assortment of texts culled from a search of the

Indiana University Folklore Archives, a review of the literature on "urban" legends, and mercantile legends I have collected during a decade of research. The majority of these stories name the largest corporation or product in the market area. The exact figure is uncertain, given the difficulty of obtaining statistics on corporate market share at any given time; ideally one must consider the market share both at the time the story was first heard and when it was collected. Often such information is proprietary or otherwise unavailable. Despite these limitations, I am confident that a comparable analysis of other collections of texts will confirm my conclusion. I have compiled a table listing the major urban legends, the corporations about which these legends have been told, and whether the most frequent target for the story is the largest company in its area. A company with 25 percent market share should have 25 percent of the stories if the telling of such stories was a purely random phenomenon. These data support Proposition P2 in that the largest corporations appear to be mentioned in more legends than expected by chance. Although this is not a scientific survey, it does suggest that an empirical regularity is operating. Combining legends dealing with the largest corporation with those involving the most prestigious corporation (to be discussed below), one finds that more than two-thirds of the sample falls in one of these two categories.

Corporate Dominance

Some companies so dominate their product areas that their names are almost generic (Bell 1976). We refer to Xerox machines rather than copiers, Jell-O rather than flavored gelatin, Kleenex rather than facial tissues, or Oreos rather than sugar cream sandwiched between two chocolate wafers. People use these names even when they refer to other brands because these corporate names symbolize the products. In legends and rumors dealing with these products ("Xerox machines cause cancer") we use the corporate name without necessarily claiming that the corporation named is the only corporation involved. When informants talk about "Jell-O" hardening into rubber and being indigestible, the target of the story may not be General Foods. However, the mention of such corporate names reflects their psychological dominance. If asked directly which corporation was involved, informants typically confirmed that it was the corporate leader even though the source for the account might have used the product reference generically.

 Although their names are not synonymous with their products, some corporations are perceived as so dominant that they are the logical targets of such stories. This is particularly evident in regard to Procter & Gamble, one of the largest American consumer products corporations. Procter & Gamble was the target of rumors that it is controlled by Satanists, a witches' coven, or by the Unification Church. A survey by *Advertising Age* (1982:1) demonstrated that 79 percent of the public could not name any specific product of Procter & Gamble. Yet, the psychological dominance of the corporation as a whole made such beliefs credible for more than half the sample. Such rumors need not be grounded in knowledge, but only in general emotions about the corporation.

The effect of dominance is particularly evident in fast foods. People recognize that "Kentucky Fried Chicken" or "Colonel Sanders" is a corporate trademark, but they use it to refer to those establishments that sell take-out fried chicken. Many Americans cannot name a second fried chicken firm. In my collection of 115 versions of the Kentucky Fried Rat story (Fine 1980), not one informant named any other fried chicken chain, while 65 specifically named Kentucky Fried Chicken as the establishment where the rat was sold.

Similarly, many Americans see McDonald's as the quintessential fast food establishment. When Americans think of fast food, McDonald's is the company that comes to mind. As befits a corporate giant, many stories are told about its activities. Among those I have collected are the beliefs that founder Ray Kroc is a member of the Church of Satan and that McDonald's hamburgers are made from worms, rat hairs, sawdust, horsemeat, or even cardboard. Other stories claim that employees spit on the hamburgers or drop them on the floor. A tooth, a compressed rat, and a cat's eye have reportedly been found in McDonald's hamburgers. Their fish filets are supposedly made from carp, and rats are reported in the french fry oil. This large collection of stories is striking in contrast to the paucity of tales about Burger King, the second largest hamburger chain. I have collected only one mercantile legend about Burger King— that there are cockroaches in its hamburgers. Although the precise number of texts is not important, most stories that name a fast food hamburger restaurant name McDonald's. The corporate dominance of McDonald's preempts legends about other establishments.

The effect of economic dominance can be observed in the "natural history" of the claim that McDonald's uses worms in their hamburgers. According to an investigative account in the *Wall Street Journal*, "McDonald's believes that the worm rumor originated in Chattanooga, Tennessee, sometime last summer in connection with Wendy's. By November it was hurting business at more than 20% of McDonald's outlets, mostly in the Southeast, forcing the company to mount a counterattack that it tried to confine to the affected territory" (Montgomery 1979). Both Domowitz and I have found the story reported about Wendy's although most accounts named McDonald's (Domowitz 1980). Why should the worms crawl from Wendy's to McDonald's? At the time, Wendy's was the fastest-growing hamburger chain in the United States and was particularly concentrated in the Southeast. Wendy's advertising emphasized that its hamburgers were "hot and juicy." Emphasizing the "juiciness" (and, hence,

Table 7.1 Mercantile Legends

	Heard of Legend[a]		Named specific company	Corporations named	% of cases	% who named leading corporation	Estimated % market share
	Number	(%)					
Mouse in soft drink bottle	52	(51)	48	Coca-Cola	46	96	24[b]
				RC	2		
Rat fried as chicken	60	(59)	58	Kentucky Fried Chicken	57	98	59[c]
				Banquet	1		
Spider eggs in gum	22	(22)	19	Bubble Yum	10	53	25[d]
				Bubblicious	3		
				Hubba Bubba	2		
				Others (4)	4		
Worms in hamburger	40	(39)	38	McDonald's	34	89	45[e]
				Wendy's	2		
				Burger Chef	1		
				White Castle	1		

Table 7.1 (Continued)

Pizza parlor uses pet food	19	(19)	16	Pizza Hut	10	62	47[f]
				Shakey's	4		
				Sambo's	1		
				Big B's	1		
Car sold cheaply because someone died in it	19	(19)	10	Corvette	3		
				Ford	3		
				Cadillac	1		
				Others (3)	3		
				Total Chrevolet	4	40	17[g]

[a] 102 students are in the sample.
[b] Cited in "The CU Cola Challenge" (1984:67), "recent industry estimates."
[c] Cited in "Continued Expansion Planned . . ." (1983:88), 1981 data.
[d] Cited in "Bubble Yum . . ." (1980:10), 1979 data.
[e] Cited in Edwards (1983:79), 1982 data.
[f] Cited in "Overall, New Pan Pizza . . ." (1983:93), 1981 data.
[g] Cited in World Motor Vehicle Data, 1982 Edition (1982:336), 1981 data.

Table 7.2 Mercantile Legends and Their Targets

Type	Corporation
Mouse in soft drink bottle[a]	Coca-Cola, Pepsi, 7-Up
Death from exploding candy[a]	Pop Rocks
Rat fried as chicken[a]	Kentucky Fried Chicken
Red Velvet Cake[b]	Waldorf Astoria
Alligator in restroom[b]	Waldorf Astoria
Cement car[b]	Cadillac
Death car[b]	Corvette, Buick, Cadillac, Thunderbird, Porsche, MG
Corrosive soft drink[a]	Coca-Cola
Undershorts cause sterility[a]	Jockey
Spider eggs in gum[a]	Bubble Yum
Company giving money to PLO[a]	Uncle Ben's
Finger in sausage	Wardinski
Worms in hamburger[a]	McDonald's, Wendy's
Satanic cult[a]	McDonald's, Procter & Gamble, KISS
Carp in fish filet[a]	McDonald's
Rat found in french fry oil[a]	McDonald's
Compressed rat in hamburger[a]	McDonald's
Tooth in hamburger[a]	McDonald's
Horsemeat in hamburgers[a]	McDonald's
Employees drop hamburgers on floor[a]	McDonald's
Sawdust in hamburgers[a]	McDonald's
Cardboard in hamburgers[a]	McDonald's
Cat's eye in hamburgers[a]	McDonald's
Moonies control company[a]	Procter & Gamble, Entenmann's Bakery
Witch coven controls company[a]	Procter & Gamble
Dog or cat food on pizza[a]	Pizza Hut, Shakey's, Charlie's
Department store snakes[a]	K-Mart, others
Beer bottle label trade for sex	Olympia
Leper in cigarette factory	Chesterfield
Rat feces in hot dog	Weiner King
Cat odor in perfume[a]	Chanel No. 5
Drink mix causes cancer[a]	Kool-Aid
Worms in oatmeal[a]	Quaker Oats
Shoplifting error[a]	Marshall Field
Poisoned dress[b]	Marshall Field
Supporter of gun control[a]	Anheuser-Busch, Coors
Tobacco company owning marijuana fields	R. J. Reynolds
Worms in fish	H. Salt
Rat in fish	H. Salt
Garbage on pizza	Siano's Pizza

Table 7.2 (*Continued*)

Type	Corporation
Company giving money to Nazis	Schick
Finger in Chinese food	China Inn (Lansing)
Worker found in pickle barrel	Aunt Jane's Pickles
Cockroaches in hamburgers	Burger King
Bug in peanut butter cup[a]	Reese's Peanut Butter Cup
Rat hair in hamburger	Kelly's
Mouse in canned food[a]	Libby's
Dog food in hamburgers	Sandy's
Gelatin becomes rubber[a]	Jell-O
Urinating on hamburger grill	Henry's, Perkins
Garbage in cookies	Keebler
Cat food in Mexican food[a]	Zapata's/Zantigo
Garbage in canned corn[a]	Green Giant
Aphrodisiac candy[a]	M & Ms
Predicting gender of unborn child[a]	Drano

[a]Refers to largest corporation or product—regional or national.
[b]Refers to most prestigious corporation or product—regional or national.
Note: Corporations are listed in approximate frequency of mention.

that squooshy wetness) provided an aesthetic context in which the belief that they used worms was more credible. However, in accordance with Corollary C1, this belief was unstable because Wendy's is only the third largest franchiser. It is thus not the company one typically thinks of for fast food hamburgers. In time, the target became McDonald's. The original account may have dealt with worms in Wendy's hamburgers, but the listener may not have registered the detail that the hamburgers were from Wendy's. When the story was recalled later, the details would be reconstructed. The dominant corporation (McDonald's) would be named both because it is the largest and, thus, the most likely to have been involved. More significantly, because it is the dominant corporation, it is a symbolic representation that could "reasonably" be placed in this story slot. The change from Wendy's to McDonald's conforms to the process of how people recode information.

Regional Dominance

Some corporations are dominant only within a region and not nationally. Legends about such companies are spread within their economic territory; outside that region, either the story is not spread, or it is spread with the name of the leading corporation of *that* region.

Regional breweries are a case in point. Although the market structure of beer sales has become increasingly national during the past decade, some local breweries have regional marketing strategies and inspire community loyalty. In one story, a male was said to be able to get "a piece of ass" if an Olympia beer bottle label had a special code on its back (Preston 1973). These stories were originally known in Washington state where Olympia beer was very popular. When Olympia was marketed in Colorado, the story followed.

Perhaps the best examples of the regionalization of mercantile folklore are the stories about department store snakes (Domowitz 1980; Cord 1969; Mullen 1970; Brunvand 1981:160–71):

> A girl went into Hill's at Columbus [Indiana] to try on coats. While she was trying one on she felt something prick her arm. She just thought it was a pin prick and didn't bother about it. Later than night she got very sick and when they called the doctor he said it acted like a poisonous bite from a snake or something. They got the store manager and went back into the store and found the coat and in the lining of that coat in the sleeve there was a whole nest of baby snakes. The coat had come from the Far East, I think Hong King, and the snakes had gotten into the coat while it sat on the dock waiting for shipment. The girl was awful sick but she recovered. They said since they were only baby snakes they weren't poisonous enough to kill her. If it had been a grown snake she would have died. [Reported by Margaret O. McDonald, fall 1974; from IU Archives]

While Hill's is a major store in Columbus, Indiana, legends from other areas of the country cite different local or regional stores. I collected similar accounts in Massachusetts which name Zayre, the largest discount department store chain in that region; in Minnesota many consumers name Target, which is similar to Zayre. Although K-Mart is the largest chain of discount department stores in national sales, in areas where regional or local stores are dominant, these stores may be targets. Of course, because of the size and dominance of K-Mart, it is also a frequent target.

More problematic in terms of the Goliath Effect are mercantile legends that refer to local establishments. Most mercantile legends name national or regional chains, but some narrators name local businesses. For example, while most of the stories about dog food used as a pizza topping cite such major franchisers as Pizza Hut and, to a lesser extent, Shakey's, some blame local pizzerias such as "Charlie's Pizza." Since the targets of mercantile legends are selected because of their perceived appropriateness, it is not surprising that local establishments are the targets for some of these stories. This is especially true when a local establishment is perceived as having the characteristics of the national chains. The same outrages that happen in national chains can happen in local stores, although for psychological reasons they are seen as less likely. Of course, if a narrator is describing the event to someone from elsewhere, he or she may change the target either deliberately or unconsciously so that the audience will appreciate its significance. In order for a story to make sense, both teller and audience must share a "universe of discourse" (Berger and Luckmann 1966) about its major features. The central images and symbols must be meaningful to the audience. Because of their national scope, dominant corporations are appropriate in these legends whereas local concerns are not, except when neighbors are conversing.

Novelty and Innovation

Over time the public comes to take innovation for granted. Changes in product design or in technology present a psychological challenge ("future shock") to consumers, who may respond with narratives emphasizing the dangers of a new design or a poorly understood technology. One group of mercantile legends that reflects this fear of novelty and technical innovation concerns the dangers of microwave ovens. I have collected accounts of wet infants, kittens, and puppies that exploded when placed in a microwave oven to dry off. Another microwave story describes a restaurant worker who, to save time, removes the oven door. The system works well for a few weeks, but then he experiences digestive difficulty. When his abdomen is x-rayed, the doctors discover that his stomach has been cooked. These legends reflect a public perception of danger concerned with the misuse of new technology. In them a manufacturer is not named, perhaps because the sale of microwave ovens is not perceived to be dominated by a single brand. Although there is mistrust of this new technology, the market is not such that any one brand is thought to represent the industry.

In other technological innovations, the brand is an important part of the story; Bubble Yum was the first "soft" bubble gum marketed, and this innovation proved immensely popular among children. Bubble Yum quickly became the best-selling brand of bubble gum (Cooney 1977:1). Shortly after Bubble Yum appeared, rumors spread among the gum's young consumers that it caused cancer or that it contained spider eggs or spider legs:

> Last weekend at the Harvard Market I asked the clerk (a friend of mine) if Bubble Yum was any good. He said I'd love it because it has spider legs in it. Apparently some little kids in either New York or Chicago started telling people that the reason Bubble Yum was so soft was because the gum has spider legs in it. It spread around all over the country apparently because as I was chewing a piece of Bubble Yum talking to the clerk, someone came in and asked for some Spider Leg Gum. [Collected by Gary Alan Fine, from female respondent, age twenty, University of Minnesota, April 1977]

People needed to explain why this new gum, so different from traditional gums, felt and tasted as it did. Even after similarly soft rival gums, such as Bubblicious or Hubba Bubba, appeared, the story "stuck" with Bubble Yum.

Another example of a technological innovation stimulating mercantile legends involves Pop Rocks candy (Fine 1979b). Pop Rocks, manufactured by General Foods, are small sugar pellets treated with carbon dioxide so that they tingle or, in the words of their preadolescent consumers, "explode" when put on one's tongue. The action of this unusual candy is inexplicable to its consumers, and in an "effort after meaning" (Allport and Postman 1947), stories spread about its power. One preadolescent told a friend, "This must have been made with some kind of acid." Related to these folk beliefs was a set of stories that identified Pop Rocks as the cause of a child's death. A young girl reported the following version of this legend:

> Janice: I heard from my brother there's this little boy way up north. He uh . . .
> GAF: North Minnesota?
> Janice: Yeah, way up . . . up north Minnesota. He um . . . I don't know if it's rumor or what, but uh . . . he had to have surgery 'cause um his stomach burst open because he ate . . . ate too many Pop Rocks, and then he swallowed them and they started popping in his stomach. [Collected by Gary Alan Fine, from female respondent, age ten, Minneapolis suburb, June 1977]

Some children claim that drinking soda pop while eating Pop Rocks makes the popping hazardous. Children do not understand the mechanics of Pop Rocks, and, as with many mysteries, they create explanations to account for the candy's effect and simultaneously to warn about the danger. The dynamics of such legends are parallel to those about modern technology in tribal societies.

The rumors and beliefs about what causes cancer or sterility (Bubble Yum, jockey shorts, radio waves) are dramatic examples of fearing material change or technological innovation. Likewise, consumers gain comfort from the "fact" that "natural" products such as orange juice (Vitamin C), carrots (Vitamin A), or apricot pits (laetrile) can prevent or cure cancer. What technology causes, nature can cure. Although not all Americans accept these beliefs, many sense that technology is a major cause of disease and that harmony with nature contributes to the cure. As is evident in several of these examples, the technical leader—the company that first produced this class of products—is blamed for the damage. In their rush for profit the pioneers have not checked their research carefully enough, and, because of this "folk motivation," the public infers devastating side effects. There seems to be an implicit worldview that there is nothing new *and* good under the sun—change is the devil's handiwork. This belief may be the functional equivalent to claims made in modern Mexican treasure tales that sudden wealth is a sign of some nefarious activity (Foster 1964:42–43).

Those stories that do deal with the positive effects of technology typically suggest that the new technology has been suppressed or overpriced because of corporate greed. Some point to the new cancer-fighting drugs, others to new fuels or automobile motors. This theme is also found in rumors prior to the introduction of products which suggest that they will be grander, more powerful, or less expensive than they are, implying that the best products have been kept from the public.

Prestige Legends

Size is not the only factor influencing mercantile legends. A second characteristic of corporations that seems to affect the content of such legends is prestige. Specifically I propose the following two propositions:

P3. The most prestigious corporation in a particular product area will be mentioned in more versions of a mercantile legend than less prestigious corporations.

P4. The most prestigious corporation in a particular product area will be mentioned in more mercantile legends than less prestigious corporations.

A corollary of these propositions notes that a change in target is possible:

C2. Mercantile legends will tend over time to switch the corporation named in them from a less prestigious corporation to a more prestigious corporation.

Aside from the problems with testing folkloric propositions generally, there is a special problem in operationalizing prestige. There is no objective measure of prestige, and there have been no systematic surveys indicating which companies or products the public sees as the most prestigious. For this reason my analysis will be impressionistic. In Table 7.2, six of the mercantile legends deal with companies and products that are not the largest but probably the most prestigious (Cadillac, Corvette, two about the Waldorf Astoria Hotel, and two stories about Marshall Field).[11] In those markets in which the largest corporation or best-selling product is not widely known, the most prestigious corporation may become the target. Furthermore, the content of some of these legends is such that the stories make sense only with the "best" product or corporation, as in the series of British stories about Rolls-Royce automobiles (Sanderson 1969:246–47).

Among the best-known American examples of legends that attach themselves to prestigious corporations are two legends about the Waldorf Astoria. Although today the Waldorf has slipped from its position as the preeminent New York hotel, the name "Waldorf Astoria" is still synonymous with luxury hotels, fine service, class, and wealth. The first legend is about the Red Velvet Cake recipe the Waldorf is supposed to have sold to customers for an outrageous price—several hundred dollars. According to some accounts (Brunvand 1978:111) the recipe is simply an ordinary cake with red food coloring added. The Waldorf swears that there is no truth to the story—they have never sold Red Velvet Cake nor do they charge for recipes from their kitchen—but the story has remained vigorous. The second story is a variant of the legend about albino alligators found in the New York City sewer system (Coleman 1979). One version has the alligator crawling through the plumbing and biting a woman's buttocks in the Waldorf's ladies' room. These stories, so far as I am aware, have not been attached to other hotels. The Waldorf, the symbol of luxury hotels, claims a permanent place in American folklore.

Another legend, published in the 1950s, involves the exclusive Chicago department store Marshall Field. The story, considerably abridged (for the full text see Carter 1953:5), concerns a woman who had received a beautiful inlaid compact from a friend. This compact was reported to be an original creation. One day while this woman was shopping in Marshall Field, she noticed an expensive compact that looked just like hers; when she compared the two, she found they were identical. As she was leaving the store, she was approached by a store detective who accused her of stealing the compact, which Field believed to be an original with them. When the store detectives called her friend, they were told that a rival store (Peacock's) carried the same compact, and this was confirmed. The store officials were terribly embarrassed and offered the woman anything she wanted in the store. The woman admitted that she really wished for a grand piano but knew that was out of the question. When the woman arrived home, she found men delivering a grand piano.

In this mercantile legend, the store does attempt to atone, perhaps because it is perceived as having enough class to admit it was wrong. However, this conclusion needs to be tempered by a second legend, The Poisoned Dress. A young woman purchased an evening gown from Marshall Field. One evening while out dancing, the woman felt faint, collapsed, and died. Upon investigation Field discovered that the dress had originally been purchased by a black woman as her wedding gown. When she died before the wedding, her family decided to bury her in the dress. Before burial they removed the dress because they felt that it was too expensive to clothe a corpse. The dress was returned to Field, which resold it. The company reportedly "paid . . . to keep the entire incident quite" (Hochsinger 1945:33).[12] In the first legend the store officials seem genuinely concerned about their reputation and about the woman they accused; in the second, no concern is shown. Whether prestigious corporations are treated "better" in mercantile legends than companies that are merely large is an empirical question, requiring systematic research.

In several tales about luxury products unavailable to the public, there is ambivalence between a desire for the product and a fear of obtaining it. This is evident in those stories about the Death Car, a legend whose target changes as perceptions of prestige change. A classy contemporary sports car is sold for a ridiculously low cost because someone died in it, and the stench of the dead body will not vanish. For example:

> Did you hear about the brand new Thunderbird which was selling for $200? Someone had died in it, and the body was not found for several weeks, and the smell was so bad and couldn't be removed that it was sold for only $200. [Collected by Gary Alan Fine, September 1979, from male radio broadcaster from Thunder Bay, Ontario, who first heard the story in high school during the early 1960s]

People experience psychological tension, envy for those who can own the car and an unconscious recognition that wealth does not prolong life. The smell is perhaps not only of death but of filthy lucre. The prestigious sports car symbolizes wealth; the legend suggests that the only way working-class people can obtain such a product is if it is defective—in other words, if it *stinks*.

A similar theme is evident in the legend of the Solid Cement Cadillac (in which an angry husband fills the new Cadillac parked outside his home with cement, assuming his wife is having an affair with its owner, only to discover it is his own birthday gift). Like the Corvette or Thunderbird, the Cadillac is not the best-selling automobile, but it has an aura of prestige. (Narrators and audiences find it appropriate that a Cadillac owner[13] is the amoral adulterer; the proper retribution is for the irate truckdriver husband to fill the car with cement (Sanderson 1980; Brunvand 1978; Toelken 1961). The inclusion of the Cadillac and the Truck reflects Olrik's Law of Contrast (1909), exemplified here as the contrast between "the seducer and the cuckold, the man at leisure and the man at work, the moneyed man and the weekly wage-earner, the private motorist with the expensive car and the transport driver employed trucking cement" (Sanderson 1980:381). Of course, the legend text warns against too great a reliance on these oppositions. After all, the husband destroys his own Cadillac; the man with his wife was but a worker—a car salesman. Although there is evidence that a DeSoto was actually filled with cement in Denver (Attebery 1970), the legend was collected prior to this event, and the DeSoto may have been filled with cement as a result of the legend. Still, the fact that a DeSoto was the actual target of the cement-dumper (although not for revenge) reminds us that the recalled target may shift from a relatively less prestigious product to a more prestigious one. The account would not make "sense" with a DeSoto.

Understanding the Goliath Effect

Having examined some of the forms the Goliath Effect takes, I ask what causes this folkloric regularity. First, memory is structured in ways that contribute to this effect. People do not recall events or stories verbatim; rather, stories or events are reconstructed.

> Suppose an individual to be confronted by a complex situation. . . . We saw that in this case an individual does not normally take such a situation detail by detail and meticulously build up the whole. In all ordinary instances he has an over-mastering tendency simply to get a general impression of the whole; and, on the basis of this, he constructs the probable detail. Very little of his construction is lit-erally observed and often . . . a lot of it is distorted or wrong so far as the actual facts are concerned. But it is the sort of construction which serves to justify his general impression. [Bartlett 1932:206]

Dégh and Vázsonyi (1975) concur with Bartlett's conclusion that the teller's attitude affects what is recalled. Further, as Dégh and Vázsonyi (1976:107–109) point out, legend-telling is not the smooth narration that characterizes other tales; legends are communicated in conversation. The details are often constructed in the course of talk.

Mercantile legends are altered to conform to community standards of ap-propriateness. Individuals forget the details of stories, particularly as there may be long periods of time during which they do not narrate them. When a recita-tion is given, the story must be reconstructed, often with the naming of a large or prestigious corporation. This helps explain why such legends can change to name these companies and why the stories are remarkably stable once the cor-porate name is introduced. Even if one forgets that it was Kentucky Fried Chicken that served a rat, that detail will be reconstructed.

For some individuals the name of the corporation or product may be a central part of the "story kernel" (Kalčik 1975). A story may be encoded, say, as a story about Kentucky Fried Chicken and rats. Alternatively, it may be en-coded as a story about rats served as fried chicken which, when retold, will name the fried chicken establishment that first comes to mind in conversation. This makes a good story in performance, and situates the narration—in this case, it is usually Kentucky Fried Chicken. The inclusion of the corporate leader makes sense in that these legends typically expose the transgressions of businesses. The leader in that market segment epitomizes the dangers of corpo-rate ownership and control.

The popularity of mercantile legends suggests that the public is sensitive to the nuances of corporate capitalism. The legends reveal attitudes within mod-ern capitalism that cannot be easily and directly expressed. These stories not only inform us about the dynamics of memory but also about the perception of the economic order. Most of these narratives are identical thematically: there is danger from corporations and danger in mass-produced and mass-distributed products. In some legends the corporation itself is guilty for producing a shoddy product; in others an employee is to blame for a specific episode; in still others the connection between motivation and product is indirect but harm results nonetheless. In few stories can the corporate entity be considered heroic (as in the legend of the corporation that provides a community with medical technology), and even here the stories revolve around the enormous size, power, control, and wealth of the corporation. In American mercantile legends there is a strong undercurrent of fear and suspicion of size and power (Sherry 1984).

The social-psychological rationale of these attitudes seems based on the separation of the public from the means of production and distribution (Fine 1980). Corporations are perceived as caring primarily about profits and only secondarily about the needs of customers. The trust individuals place in their neighbors (and in businesses owned by neighbors) is not extended to large corporations in which consumers have little confidence. Marx was correct in claiming that separating people from the means of production under capitalism will result in alienation; this alienation provides a psychological climate in which bogey legends can flourish.

Recognizing the psychological motivations behind these legends, we must also recognize their ultimate political impotence. They do not provide for the solidification of class consciousness but only express a fleeting disrespect, which many informants claim not "really" to believe. Although some of these stories may have caused corporate headaches for short periods—McDonald's announced their sales were off by 33 percent when people said their hamburgers were laced with worms—they have little lasting effect on corporate profits. Even though corporate executives claim to live in fear of such stories, I am not aware of any case in which a popular product was destroyed by a rumor or a legend (see *Advertising Age* 1982)—even Tylenol, a product with real problems, has regained most of its market share. These folk narratives are temporary outpourings of frustration but ultimately only strengthen the right of corporations to exist since, in time, the legends are seen by the public as unfair.

To accept this role of mercantile legends, one need not accept the validity of a Marxist critique of society, particularly not a Marxist view of the best means for ameliorating social ills. However, one must accept that the "folk" (in this case the post-industrial public) are capable of conceiving folklore content in economic terms that reflect the structure of mass capitalist society, feeling constrained, at least subconsciously, by their own lack of control. The resultant sense of constraint and frustration explains this pattern of mercantile legends that is so prevalent under American capitalism.

Notes

A version of this paper was presented at the American Folklore Society meetings, San Antonio, Texas, October 1981. The author wishes to thank Donald Allport Bird, Jan Brunvand, Linda Dégh, and Michael Preston for their helpful comments.

1. Simpson (1983) demonstrates that some examples of mercantile folklore were known in pre-Victorian Britain and were included by Dickens in *The Pickwick Papers*, Dickens (through Sam Weller) cites the man ground into sausage meat and the piemaker who used seasoned catmeat instead of veal. Simpson notes: "Whereas we would now regard the products of a local pieman, cooked on his premises, as superior to those from a factory, Sam distrusts them because he contrasts them with genuinely homemade pies individually prepared by some woman personally known to the eater of the pies" (1983:463–64). The theme of greedy businessman versus trustworthy housewife has roots older than the development of large food corporations.

2. For the purposes of this analysis, I shall sidestep the debate over the best generic term for these folk traditions—urban legends, modern legends, belief legends, etc. I use the term "mercantile legends," which captures the economic and corporate implications of this body of material. I use "mercantile" as an adjectival description, rather than to proclaim a new genre. In addition, I shall not distinguish among the precise genres into which each of the examples I use should properly fall—legend, rumor, or memorate.

3. I will not discuss a fourth class of legends which pictures corporations more positively; those legends claim that a particular corporation will supply expensive medical technology to a community if the community collects a large number of product labels, boxtops, tea bag tags, etc. Thus, technology is exchanged for product sales. There has not been, as yet, any systematic study of these legends, and, until we have a corpus of texts, it is difficult to ascertain their symbolic meaning or to know whether some companies are seen as "good" in the folk imagination. Such stories paint corporations in a paternalistic light, suggesting that they have immense power to do good or ill.

4. Some evidence cautions us against saying the effect is universal. Brunvand (1981:130–32) presents an account of the Solid Cement Cadillac collected in Norway in which the Cadillac is replaced by a Volkswagen. He suggests that the switch from the Cadillac to the VW reflects the differences in lifestyles between the nations. This story is not about the car per se, but the make is symbolic. Apparently there are some accounts in the United States that also mention a VW (Dégh, personal communication, 1983). Ward (1976) notes that equivalents to the Kentucky Fried Rat stories are told in Germany about small Yugoslav restaurants (see also Klintberg 1981). These American mercantile legends are transformations of some of the xenophobic legends of the past.

5. The aesthetic characteristics of a good story influence its popularity (Oring 1975). A story will only be told and retold if it makes sense and is seen as interesting and noteworthy. The fact that Ray Kroc, the late president of McDonald's, had a foreign name which, perhaps because of the /k/ phonemes or its homophonic character, sounds "evil," makes the connection with Satanism more believable. It would be more difficult to believe that Ray Appleseed was a member of the same devil cult. The nature of the corporation and the content of the story are relevant to the analysis. Still, stories can be shaped on any subject matter, and while this story might not have been spread, others could have taken its place.

6. Obviously not every corporation is now a victim of these legends. Yet, the range of possible mercantile legends is enormous; new legends are regularly being created and contemporary ones discovered. My argument is not that most dominant corporations will be targets, but that most targets will be dominant corporations. Individual legends deserve analysis by themselves as well. This analysis does not replace—but only supplements—research on particular legends. I ignore the nuances of detail of these tales in this treatment; such details may explain why some tales are matched with some products.

7. The concern with bigness does not exhaust the claims of social psychology; corporations may be feared for other reasons, a topic for further research.

8.   For ease of reference, I will use "corporation" to refer to "corporations and products."
9.   The six legends that did not meet the 10% criterion of recognition were: (1) the snake or insect found in department store; (2) beer company supports gun control; (3) cat odor in perfume; (4) company that gives money to the PLO; (5) hotel that sells the Red Velvet Cake recipe; and (6) finger in Chinese food. The sixth was specifically included because this mercantile legend is almost always told in reference to a local establishment. Only one student claimed to have heard that legend and didn't report what establishment it was told about. I attempted to include a representative sample of mercantile legends, not only those that attached themselves to the corporate leader. However, the others were less widely known, which gives indirect support to the Goliath Effect hypothesis.
10. The political use of mercantile legends and similar material that Klintberg (1981:159) notes in Europe does not seem to be common in the United States.
11. This is obviously a subjective figure, since prestige is a matter of judgment and statistics on relative corporate market share change over time and are hard to measure.
12. This legend appears to be a precursor of The Department Store Snake, in that a customer is killed by a piece of clothing. It also shares with The Death Car the motif of a transfer of "death" from a person to a commodity.
13. In Britain the car is usually the prestigious Jaguar (Sanderson 1980:381).

References Cited

Allport, Gordon, and Loe Postman. 1947. *The Psychology of Rumor.* New York: Holt.
Attebery, Louie W. 1970. "It Was a DeSoto." *Journal of American Folklore* 83:452–57.
Bartlett, Frederic. 1932. *"Remembering."* Cambridge: Cambridge University Press.
Bell L. Michael. 1976. "Cokelore." *Western Folklore* 35:59–64.
Berger, Peter, and Thomas Luckmann. 1966. *The Social Construction of Reality.* New York: Anchor.
Brunvand, Jan. 1978. *The Study of American Folklore,* 2nd ed. New York: W. W. Norton.
———. 1981. *The Vanishing Hitchhiker.* New York: W. W. Norton.
"Bubble Yum Not About to Gum Up Works." 1980. *Advertising Age* 51 (July 28):10.
"The CU Cola Challenge." 1984. *Consumers' Reports* 49 (Feb.):66–70.
Carter, Albert Howard. 1953. "Some Folk Tales of the Big City." *Arkansas Folklore* 4:4–6.
Coleman, Loren. 1979. "Alligators-in-the-Sewers: A Journalistic Origin." *Journal of American Folklore* 92:335–38.
"Continued Expansion Planned in Foreign, Domestic Markets." 1983. *Nation's Restaurant News* 17 (Aug. 1):88.
Cooney, John E. 1977. "Bubble Gum Maker Wants to Know How the Rumors Started." *Wall Street Journal* (March 24):1.
Cord, Xenia. 1969. "Department Store Snakes." *Indiana Folklore* 2:110–14.
Dégh, Linda, and Andrew Vázsonyi. 1975. "The Hypotheses of Multi-Conduit Transmission in Folklore." In *Folklore: Performance and Communication,* ed. Dan Ben-Amos and Kenneth S. Goldstein. The Hague: Mouton.
———. 1976. "Legend and Belief." In *Folklore Genres,* ed. Dan Ben-Amos. Austin: University of Texas Press.
Domowitz, Susan. 1979. "Foreign Matter in Food: A Legend Type." *Indiana Folklore* 12:86–95.

————. 1980. "To Eat or Not to Eat: Wormburgers and Related Legends." Unpublished manuscript, Indiana University.

Dorson, Richard. 1959. *American Folklore*. Chicago: University of Chicago Press.

Dundes, Alan. 1971. "Folk Ideas as Units of World View." In *Toward New Perspectives in Folklore*, ed. Americo Paredes and Richard Bauman. Austin: University of Texas Press.

Edwards, Joe. 1983. "McDonald's: Reluctance to Change Gradually Eroding Huge Customer Base." *Nation's Restaurant News* 17 (Aug. 1):78–79.

Fine, Gary Alan. 1979a. "Cokelore and Coke Law: Urban Belief Tales and the Problem of Multiple Organs." *Journal of American Folklore* 92:477–82.

————. 1979b. "Folklore Diffusion Through Interactive Social Networks: Conduits In a Pre-adolescent Community." *New York Folklore* 5:87–126.

————. 1980. "The Kentucky Fried Rat: Legends and Modern Society." *Journal of the Folklore Institute* 17:222–43.

Foster, George M. 1964. "Treasure Tales and the Image of the Static Economy in a Mexican Peasant Community." *Journal of American Folklore* 77:39–44.

Gallup Opinion Index. 1979. "Confidence in Institutions." Report #166 (May):1–11.

Harris, Linda. 1981. "Public Ambivalence Towards Science and Technology." Unpublished manuscript, University of Minnesota.

Hochsinger, Gloria. 1945. "More About the Poisoned Dress." *Hoosier Folklore Bulletin* 4:32–34.

Kalčik, Susan. 1975. ". . . like Ann's Gynecologist or the Time I Was Almost Raped: Personal Narratives in Women's Rap Groups." *Journal of American Folklore* 88:3–11.

Klintberg, Bengt af. 1981. "Modern Migratory Legends in Oral Tradition and Daily Papers." *Scandinavian Yearbook of Folklore* 37:153–60.

Marx, Leo. 1964. *The Machine in the Garden*. New York: Oxford.

Montgomery, Jim. 1979. "Rumor-Plagued Firms Use Various Strategies to Keep Damage Low." *Wall Street Journal* (Feb. 7):1, 19.

Mullen, Patrick. 1970. "Department Store Snakes." *Indiana Folklore* 3:214–28.

Nisbet, Robert. 1976. *Sociology as an Art Form*. New York: Oxford University Press.

Olrik, Axel. 1909. "Epic Laws of Folk Narrative." Translated by Jeanne P. Steager. In *The Study of Folklore*, ed. Alan Dundes. Englewood Cliffs, N.J.: Prentice-Hall. (1965).

Oring, Elliott. 1975. "Everything is a Shade of Elephant: An Alternative to a Psychoanalysis of Humor." *New York Folklore* 1:149–59.

"Overall, New Pan Pizza Proves Big Boost to Lunchtime Sales." 1983. *Nation's Restaurant News 117* (Aug. 1):93.

"P & G Rumor Blitz Looks Like a Bomb." 1982. *Advertising Age* 53 (Aug. 9):1, 68–69.

Preston, Michael. 1973. "Olympia Beer Comes to Colorado: The Spread of a Tradition." *Western Folklore* 32:281–283.

Rowan, Roy. 1979. "Where Did *That* Rumor Come From?" *Fortune* (Aug. 13):130–37.

Sanderson, Stewart. 1969. "The Folklore of the Motor-car." *Folklore* 80:241–52.

————. 1980. "Why Was it a DeSoto?" In *Folklore Studies in the Twentieth Century*, ed. Venetia J. Newall. Woodbridge, Suffolk: D. S. Brewer.

Sherry, John F. 1984. "Some Implications of Consumer Oral Traditions for Reactive Marketing." In *Advances in Consumer Research Vol. II*, ed. Thomas Kinnear. Ann Arbor: Association for Consumer Research.

Simpson, Jacqueline. 1983. "Urban Legends in *The Pickwick Papers*." *Journal of American Folklore* 96:462–70.

Sinclair, Upton. 1960. *The Jungle*. New York: New American Library. (1906).

Taviss, Irene. 1972. "A Survey of Popular Attitudes Toward Technology." *Technology and Culture* 13:606–21.

Toelken, Barre. 1961. "The Solid Cement Cadillac." *Oregon Folklore Bulletin* 1:5–6.

Ward, Donald. 1976. "American and European Narratives as Socio-Psychological Indicators." In *Folk Narrative Research: Some Papers Presented at the VI Congress of the International Society for Folk Narrative Research,* ed. Juha Pentikainen and Tuula Juuvikka, Helsinki: Studia Fennica.

Warren, Roland. 1972. *The Community in America,* 2nd ed. Chicago: Rand McNally.

"World Motor Vehicle Data, 1982 Data." 1982. Detroit: Motor Vehicle Manufacturers Association.

8

Mercantile Legends and the World Economy: Dangerous Imports from the Third World

During the past several centuries, the nations of the world have been tied together through an international trading economy in which products and resources are sold from land to land. Over the past few decades this trend has become increasingly prominent, and, during this time, themes of mercantile legends have changed accordingly. This trading system, often labeled "the world economy," refers to the interrelationships among national trading partners. Once periphery nations ("the Third World") primarily sent natural resources to core nations (or "the First World"), and received manufactured products in exchange. Since the end of the Second World War, and particularly in the last twenty years, this one simple picture has become increasingly complex. Manufacturing jobs are flowing from the United States and Europe to the "periphery continents"—to the Little Tigers of Asia (Hong Kong, South Korea, Singapore, and Taiwan) and other Asian, South American, and, even, African nations. The increasing American trade deficit of the 1980s is testimony to the role that manufacturing plays in the Third World, and the threats it poses to the "advanced" Western nations. Given the wage structures of our competitors, it becomes more difficult for advanced nations to compete.

Such a situation poses economic and social-psychological threats to Western populations, in addition to the challenges that it poses to the rapidly industrializing Third World. In this essay, I examine how this threat is expressed through mercantile folklore, particularly rumors and legends that deal with imports from overseas. First, I examine a set of legends that involve the importation of manufactured goods from overseas, then I focus on legends about the importation of raw materials, and finally I examine legends that describe threats to the United States from Mexico.

The Department Store Snake

One of the most widely reported mercantile legends is the claim that a shopper in a department store was bitten by an insect or serpent that was sewn into or otherwise hidden in an imported product. This legend type has been collected widely throughout the United States for approximately two decades and is known "generically" as "The Department Store Snake" or "The Snake in the Blanket" (Mullen 1970; Carey 1971; Cord 1969; Carpenter 1976; Stevens 1981; Brunvand 1981; Smith 1983:58–59; Koenig 1985:85–86).

I collected the following version from a Boston college student in 1975:

> The rumor I heard was a strange, true story about a woman being bit by a snake. The woman was taken to Norwood (Mass.) Hospital because of a bite on her arm. It was diagnosed as a snake bite and it wasn't understood how she got it. She was asked to report her doings during the day and she reported that she had tried on coats at Sears. The coats she tried on were then searched and in one coat was found a snake on the sleeve lining. This coat was made in Taiwan and somehow the snake got in the lining of the coat.

Brunvand claims that the legend was newly minted in late 1968 or early 1969. There is only negative proof for this assertion in that we have no texts from before that period and suddenly a large number collected at the time. However, even if the legend were not created in the late 1960s, its popularity should lead us to examine that time period carefully.

This period is the height of the war in Vietnam, and Asian dangers are very much on the minds of Americans. While these products did not originate in Vietnam, as Vietnam was not a manufacturing nation, the fact that these products are from nations in close vicinity to Vietnam suggests that the symbolic salience of the Asian origin, coupled with their menace, may have contributed to the development of these narratives.

Yet, despite the similarity of timing, we would be mistaken to conclude too rapidly that the existence of the war in Vietnam explained the whole of this mercantile legend. Certainly the war sensitized us to the relevance of Asia to the lives of Americans, but if the narrative were about the effects of the war, we might expect other legends that spoke more directly to these issues, rather than a legend about dangers from the import-export market. One might imagine legends of terrorism by Viet Cong saboteurs, but such accounts were rare except in Vietnam (e.g., ground glass in Coke bottles). To understand the meaning of a narrative, an explanation must deal with the details—both their internal consistency (can most of the details be explained?) and their external validity (does the explanation make sense in light of what else is happening at the time?) (Fine 1984).

In Brunvand's account of the development of this legend, he notes that constituent details vary widely: the type of poisonous animal, the object in which the animal is hidden, the country from which the object was imported, the name of the store, and the outcome. However, despite this variation some elements remain constant. Invariably the imported object is from Asia—particularly that arc from Japan and the Philippines to India, Pakistan, and Iran. The danger is from Southern to Eastern Asia. Significantly the danger is *not* as one might expect from nations that are "truly" backward or from nations that produce shoddy goods, but precisely from those nations that pose economic challenges to America.[1] Rather than suggesting that these stories reflect the "basic cultural mistrust of the mysterious East" (Mullen 1970:228), it is more plausible to suggest that the primary mistrust is economic.[2]

The snakes and spiders typically do not come from nations from which we get raw materials, but from those nations from which we receive manufactured goods. The goods in which these snakes and spiders are found are products that once were made in the United States but are increasingly manufactured abroad. Furthermore, these products (blankets, carpets, rugs, blouses, and coats) are "warm" and "soft"[3]—a symbolic contrast with the threat hidden within: the iron fist in the velvet glove. One 1969 informant made the moral explicit by advising, "don't buy Japanese goods," and, indeed, some people claimed to have altered their buying habits (Mullen 1970:228).

The vendors from whom these manufactured items are purchased are typically large American department stores, often discount department stores, such as K-Mart. An irony is evident: American corporations provide the distribution system for products that originate elsewhere, and the American manufacturing base is weakened as a consequence. In those legends in which consumers gain revenge through court action, the *American* store is sued, not the anonymous foreign business that manufactured the product.

The late 1960s and early 1970s demonstrated the increasing economic power of nations of eastern and southern Asia. By the late 1980s many manufactured products are primarily produced on the Pacific rim: motorcycles, clothing, steel, textiles, and television sets. The transfer of manufacturing was evident by the late 1960s.[4] Unlike mercantile legends about raw materials (that typically do not name Asian nations), these legends seem to derive from a fear of foreign competition or even a suspicion that American firms are capable of engaging in such practices as a marketing ploy. This legend effectively underlines the change in the American economy from one based on manufacturing to one concerned with service. Brunvand (1981:161) suggests that by the early 1980s the Department Store Snake legend no longer had the potency that it had a decade ago—whether this is because the story has been widely circulated and disproved, having saturated its audience, or because it is no longer as psychologically credible is hard to determine. The war against manufactured goods from Asia has been won—by them.

Raw Material and Raw Rumors

The Department Store Snake legend differs from other legends of the world economy in that it specifies that the snake is found in manufactured goods. Often the offending animal hides in raw products. The tarantula, spider, or snake in the banana is such as example, and is known in Europe (Campion-Vincent 1989:103) and the United States. Bengt af Klintberg (1985:275) collected the following text in Stockholm:

> My wife came home last week from work and told me about a woman, a friend of a friend's, who had been out driving with her family. The two children were sitting in the back seat. The kids became hungry, and she gave each of them a banana. All of a sudden one of the kids says: "Mum, the banana bit me!" The parents didn't pay any special attention to it. After a while, however, upon turning around, the mother found one of the kids lying there unconscious. They hurried to the hospital, but the doctors could not save the child, who died some hours later. One of the doctors told them that three or four similar accidents had happened before. There seemed to be some poisonous snake that laid eggs in bananas, which hatched into the peels.

Growing up in New York in the late 1950s, I heard (and spread) stories about people fatally bitten by tarantulas hiding in bunches of bananas imported from Central America. This has also been reported from Davenport, Iowa in 1933–34, where the victims were fruit handlers in New Orleans and the insect was a black widow spider (Hiner 1982).

Accounts of deadly spiders found in yucca trees (or cacti) also suggest the inherent dangers when citizens of industrialized nations purchase items from the Third World. Like the threat from bananas, narratives about yucca trees are international. Brunvand (1986:83–84) reports a text from England about yuccas from Africa, Campion-Vincent (1989:103) finds that the spiders in yuccas were widely known in France in 1986, and Klintberg (1985:281) presents texts from Sweden and Finland from the 1970s and 1980s about yuccas and cacti imported from Central America. The following American text from Kalamazoo, Michigan, is presented as a first-hand story, reported by a spouse of the co-worker of the "victim":

> We (she and her husband) purchased a cactus from Frank's Nursery and Crafts (in Kalamazoo).[5] When we took it home, I noticed that it seemed to move on its own. My husband said it was all in my imagination. The next day he decided that it was indeed moving. We called Frank's and they said that it couldn't move on its own. A while later, they called back and said to get out of the house at once. People from Frank's arrived and said that the motion was caused by a tarantula having babies inside the plant. [Miller 1989]

The purchaser is not injured by the spider, although it is generally similar to legends and rumors of foreign snakes and insects.

On the surface these legends might seem parallel to the Department Store Snake in structure, but they reflect different psycho-economic dynamics.[6] In the Department Store Snake the focus is on the store rather than the product. The kernel of this story is about a woman going into a store, touching or trying on an item, being bitten, and (sometimes) suing the store. The stable elements are the snake/spider, the Asian origin, and the department store.

Contrast this with the banana or yucca legend in which the raw material is the central focus of the story. The kernel of this banana narrative is the banana, the child (often the victim), and the spider. The location from which the bananas are purchased is not central and often not mentioned. The kernel of the yucca narrative is the plant, the snake/spider, the call to an expert (a local museum, mail order company, or florist), and the dramatic killing. In both legends the origin of the plant or fruit is vague. The bananas are from a tropical rain forest; the yuccas are from a desert. These locales do not provide economic competition with American industry. In neither case does the episode occur within a store, suggesting the danger is from the exotic locale rather than from economic competition. The central theme is the conflict between the dangerous wilderness and the tamed urban environment. The interstices of nature and culture are a critical node for danger.

THE MEXICAN CONNECTION

Mexico is the portal to the Third World for the United States. We are sandwiched between Mexico and Canada and have friendly, if prickly, relations with both, but our images of our neighbors diverge markedly. Could one imagine customs at the Mexican border run like those at the Canadian border? Could one imagine that twenty years ago young men would have attempted to avoid the draft by fleeing to Mexico? Multiple factors produce this differential treatment: race, language, culture, poverty, prejudice, and historical suspicion, but, whatever the case, the differences are both real and powerful. Americans see Mexico as both an underdeveloped nation—an exotic location filled with danger and poverty, and recently as an economic rival. These themes are evident in two "threats" from Mexico: the Mexican Pet and Urine in Corona Beer.

The Mexican Pet. This legend, nearly as widely known in the 1980s as the Department Store Snake was in the late 1960s, depicts tourists returning from Mexico with a small, cute pet. One extended newspaper account of the Mexican pet reads:

> A couple who lives somewhere in the vast plains of the state of North Dakota recently quit those endless horizons for a time to vacation in Mexico. It is believed that they stayed in the city of Oaxaca, far in the southern reaches of that country. In their hostel, they summoned a dinner from room services and, having dined, placed the dishes outside their door, to be fetched away. Some time later, on emerging from their room, they found those dishes still awaiting. But attending to the remnants of the repast was a tiny dog. A Chihuahua, they discerned imme-

diately . . . was nervously nibbling away at their table scraps. Though it made to escape at the sight of them, the little animal found itself swept up into the woman's arms and into the hearts of both the travellers. It was so small, so obviously fearful and disquieted, that they stroked and petted it and calmed it with their soothing words and manner. . . . As with all things good, the idyll drew to a close and the vacationers faced a dilemma. The law proscribed transporting their beloved friend across the border. Yet, they could not bear to part with it. . . . Praying that no yips or barks betray their mission, the woman secreted the quivering, precious bundle deep in a large purse. . . . Back home in North Dakota, the pair romped and frolicked with the new addition to their household. . . . Mindful that it had borne no tags when they discovered it, and eager to ensure the wellbeing of their friend, they took it to a veterinary clinic for immunizations. They said they would return on the morrow. Within hours, a vet called them on the telephone. "Are you certain," he said, "that you want to keep this animal?" Of, course, of course, they replied. What could prompt him to raise such a question? "Because," he said, "this is not a Chihuahua. This is not a dog. This is a Mexican water rat." [Kelly 1983:n.p.]

Brunvand (1986:21–22) reports that he began hearing this legend around 1983. Why 1983? This corresponds to the period at which the problem of undocumented aliens was receiving extended attention in the United States[7] (and elsewhere).[8] If nothing else, the Mexican pet is an undocumented alien. The rat is a scavenger—a homeless animal which survives on its wits. It has a deceptive, harmless appearance, but is frightening and dangerous (in several texts the rat attacks or eats the family pet). Occasionally the rat is rabid.

The role of the tourists is crucial to the story. While the North Dakota locale is not common, the detail seems strangely apt to symbolize the contrast between cultural safety and wild danger. These tourists are late twentieth-century "innocents abroad." They avoid government regulations out of naive humanitarianism. Their pity defeats their sense. The tourists are aware of the illegality of their acts, but conspire to deceive the authorities—in some versions by smuggling the animal under a woman's coat or sweater.

The rat provides a dramatic warning not to become too attached to innocent-appearing Mexicans. Like many contemporary legends about social change, the text has a conservative theme, revealing the dangers of unthinking internationalism. Those cute little Mexican dogs are really rats. While they are perfectly unexceptional in the streets of Mexico City, Oaxaca, Tijuana, or Acapulco, they—like Mexican workers[9]—have no place in the United States.

Urine in Corona Beer. The second "Mexican" text is a rumor: Corona Beer is contaminated with urine—Mexican workers urinate into bottles shipped to the United States, giving the beer its distinctive bright yellow and copious foam. The information was allegedly heard on "60 Minutes" "20/20," or "Nightline." I have no narrative versions and doubt that this rumor will evolve into a legend.

It appears to have emerged in 1986 or 1987 in California. The rumor was traced to a competing beer wholesaler in Reno, Nevada, who was sued for $3 million by Corona's importer. In an out-of-court settlement, Luce and Sons, which carried other imported beers, but not Corona, declared publicly that Corona was "free of any contamination" (Peterson 1987:1). It is unlikely this company began the rumor, although perhaps their salesmen spread it vigorously. However it began, the rumor caught on rapidly, and by 1987 was known in Boise, Phoenix, Seattle, Minneapolis, Milwaukee, and Chicago. At that time Corona's importer went public, denying the rumor in news accounts (Peterson 1987; Joseph 1987).

As I have argued in describing the "Goliath Effect" (Fine 1985), Corona Beer fits a particular market niche. At the time at which the rumor was at its peak, Corona was the fastest-growing imported beer, having increased its sales by 170 percent in 1986, passing Molson's to be the second-largest-selling imported beer in the United States (only the Dutch Heineken's sells more). Further, Corona was considered a high prestige brew, sometimes called the "Yuppie Cocktail," and for a time in 1987 the demand outpaced the supply of the beer (Rozsa 1987). Beer companies have been traditional targets of rumor, as tales about Coors, Stroh's, and Anheuser-Busch attest.

The Corona text depends on believing that contaminating beer with urine is plausible. The credibility of the story is enhanced by the bright yellow beer in a clear bottle (Anderson 1988), and possibly some prankster may have served urine as beer or claimed beer was urine. The belief that consuming beer produces copious urination is a well-known theme in barroom conversations. Further, Corona beer is the best-selling beer from the Third World in the United States. In 1987 Corona sold nearly three times as much as the second and third most popular Third World beers combined.[10]

Underlying these facts is the reality that United States citizens find it credible that Mexican workers might be capable of such an act of contamination and motivated to do it.[11] The Latin nations, particularly Mexico, may be beginning to replace the nations of the Far East in terms of our fears of competition. Mexico combines the general, dangerous characteristics of tropical nations with the specific immorality associated with Hispanics through our racial prejudice. With public concern over disease from "bodily fluids," this rumor reflects the fear of sexual diseases and lack of proper hygiene. What could be a more archetypal body fluid than urine?

A *Mexican connection* exists in North American folklore—a connection associated with our fear of Mexican aliens in the United States, by our fear of Mexican lack of hygiene, and by our fear of Mexico's economic competition. Mexico represents the Third World in our midst—neighbors who are strangers.

We live in a shrinking world. We know each other better than ever. Yet, this does not necessarily make us feel good about this closeness. Interconnections tug at the strings of nationalism, and undermine the control of dominant so-cieties. Hegemony can no longer be taken for granted in a world of free and open trade and in a world in which industrial technologies are exported and adopted abroad. If the middle third of the twentieth century witnessed the rise of American industrial and political power, the final third reflects the cracking of that industrial dominance. As the reality of this disintegration filters to the gen-eral population, warnings emerge through folk narrative. The world has be-come "decentered," but this loss of centrality is not an easy thing for those who used to be in control to come to terms with.

The first sign of this change was the influx of goods from foreign shores; along with goods came people, given the change of American immigration laws. Unlike nations of Europe, we have no nativist parties, protesting against immigration, but our feelings are displayed without our folklore. Hidden within the world economy is danger—spiders, germs, disease, and unwanted immi-grants. These outsiders are functionally similar. They represent a hidden "inva-sion" of one part of the world by another. Citizens of the First World worry that Third World problems may be becoming First World problems.

The second theme—reflected in the Corona Beer rumor and the Depart-ment Store Snakes legend—is that the material advantages of the First World are flowing to the Third World. The economic base of the entire world is begin-ning to look very similar, or so our fears suggest. Further, we contribute to our own demise by selling products from overseas in competition with our own manufactured goods. We are poisoning ourselves in the name of profits, and we suffer the consequences.

These two themes—fear of contamination and fear of competition—indicate how we are coming to terms with the world economy through folklore. These texts demonstrate collectively how great the change has been in the last few decades, and how far we have to go. As the economy shifts, so does our social psychology, and so do our narratives.

Notes

I wish to thank Jan Brunvand, Linda Dégh, Mark Glazer, Janet Langlois, W. F. H. Nicolaisen, Paul Smith, and Richard Sweterlitsch for their help in the preparation of this essay.

1. Up until the mid-1960s the phrase "Made in Japan" was a joke to indicate a poor quality item, but by the end of the 1960s that had changed dramatically.

2. Recent versions no longer mention Japanese goods, which are now frequently seen as a better quality than American goods. Persian carpets from Iran are no longer mentioned, because of the diplomatic breach between the two nations.

3. Brunvand (1987) cites an account of snake-infested merry-go-round horses that were imported from India that "bite" unsuspecting children at amusement parks. The theme

of the snake in the amusement park is a common theme (e.g., Mullen 1970:224–26), even when no explicitly foreign origin for these exotic animals is named.

4. Imports from East and South Asia increased by a total of 399% from 1965 to 1973, whereas exports increased by only 213%. This compares to a general increase in imports during this period of 324% and an increase of exports of 260%. The Taiwanese case is particularly dramatic. In 1965 the United States exported $234 million and imported only $93 million. By 1973 the figures were $1.168 million and $1.773 million. Imports from Taiwan far outstripped exports to Taiwan by the early 1970s (U.S. Bureau of the Census, 1974:792–95).

5. The story is widely known in Kalamazoo, according to the manager of Frank's Nursery and Crafts (collected, March 1989). In his version the workers are always "two men in white suits." He insists that while tarantulas can live in desert cacti, they purchase their cacti from greenhouses in Florida, emphasizing that they are American-grown. He added that some women have been afraid to enter the store because of fear of tarantulas. In line with the Goliath Effect, Frank's is part of the largest nursery chain in the United States, and this store is the largest nursery in Kalamazoo.

6. A related version is the "snake in the greens." Detweiler (1983) reports the legend from Atlanta: "My wife, who works as a therapist at the Emory University Hospital, learned of a woman shopping for collard (or mustard or whatever) greens at the Dekalb Farmers' Market, felt a sharp prick in her finger as she dug around in the greens, became ill, went out to her car, was found there dead by her husband, etc. Later a baby rattler was found in the greens. Everything was hushed up by the market, of course, for fear of losing business. . . . Within a few days the same thing was reported at other Atlanta markets, and soon after that a woman 'died' at a supermarket down in Savannah." Miller reports an essentially identical rumor from a low-income black area of Dayton, Ohio, where it was alleged that "a poor old woman had died after being bitten by a poisonous snake in the produce section of a supermarket commonly patronized by west Dayton residents" (Miller 1988:1). Unfortunately it is not reported where the "greens" originated or how the snake found its way into the market, but it has elements from both the banana legend and the department store snake.

7. The Gallup Poll reports that the response to the question of whether it should be against the law for employers to hire undocumented aliens reached its peak in 1983 with 79% in favor of penalties (The Gallup Poll 1985:250–51).

8. A related version of this tale is spread in France in the mid-1980s, at the time that Jean-Marie Le Pen and his nativist National Front emphasized the problems allegedly caused by African and Near Eastern immigration into France. According to Campion-Vincent (1988:10): France was also telling in 1986 the story of the very small, very nice (sweet?) pet dog, brought back from a holiday in West Africa . . . by a young couple touched by this lovely small pet who followed them affectionately during their holiday. They enter it clandestinely but, after a few days, they find the new pet has slit the cat's throat. Consulted the vet identifies the animal: not a dog, but a big ill rat.

9. A parallel legend concerns the existence of the "Buffo Frog" in South Florida in the early in early or mid 1960s. According to Farley Snell, who resided in South Florida at this time: "Someone's dog bit or attacked this frog and then died, so that the assumption was that it was poisonous." (Collected Taylor, Texas, March 1989). These large frogs apparently arrived with exiles from Cuba.

10. Both of these beers—Tecate and Dos Equis—are Mexican beers, but the rumors have only attached themselves to Corona, the most popular Mexican beer.

11. A. H. Tellier (1987) computed the amount of urine that it would take to contaminate a vat of beer. Using a detection level of 100 parts per million and a beer vat of 20 feet in

diameter and 20 feet high, he estimates that it would take 75 bladders filled with urine to make a noticeable difference. Of course, given that we confiscated all Chilean fruit because of "two lousy grapes," even one contaminated bottle might be more than enough.

References Cited

Anderson, June. 1988. Personal communication to Jan H. Brunvand.

Brunvand, Jan H. 1981. *The Vanishing Hitchhiker*. New York: Norton.

———. 1986. *The Mexican Pet*. New York: Norton.

———. 1987. "Amusement Park Stories Aren't Funny." *Desert News* (June 12):n.p.

Campion-Vincent, Véronique. 1988. "Conspiracies and Warning: Urban Legends in the City." Unpublished manuscript.

Campion-Vincent, Véronique. 1989. "Complots et Avertissements: Légendes Urbaines dans la Ville." *Revue Français de Sociologie* 30:91–105.

Carey, George G. 1971. *Maryland Folk Legends and Folk Songs*. Cambridge, Md.: Tidewater Publishers.

Carpenter, Ann. 1976. "Cobras at K-Mart: Legends of Hidden Danger." *Publications of the Texas Folklore Society* 40:36–45.

Cord, Xenia. 1969. "Department Store Snakes." *Indiana Folklore* 2:110–14.

Detweiler, Robert. 1983. Personal communication to Jan H. Brunvand.

Fine, Gary Alan. 1984. "Evaluating Psychoanalytic Folklore: Are Freudians Ever Right?" *New York Folklore* 10:5–20.

———. 1985. "The Goliath Effect: Corporate Dominance and Mercantile Folklore." *Journal of American Folklore* 98:63–84.

Gallup Poll. 1985. *The Gallup Poll: Public Opinion 1984*. Wilmington, Del.: Scholarly Resources.

Hiner, Jim. 1982. Personal communication to Jan H. Brunvand.

Joseph, Scott. 1987. "Urine No Danger." *New Times* (July 29–August 4):18.

Kelley, Mike. 1983. "Love Leads into Rattrap." *Austin American-Statesman* (Sept. 23):n.p.

Klintberg, Bengt af. 1985. "Legends and Rumors about Spiders and Snakes." *Fabula* 26:274–87.

Koenig, Frederick. 1985. *Rumor in the Marketplace*. Dover, Mass.: Auburn House.

Miller, Dan. 1988. " 'Snakes in the Greens' and Rumor in the Innercity." Unpublished manuscript.

Miller, Geoffrey M. 1989. Personal communication to Jan H. Brunvand.

Mullen, Patrick. 1970. "Department Store Snakes." *Indiana Folklore* 3:214–28.

Peterson, Jonathan. 1987. "Brewer Will Battle False Rumor about Its Product." *Los Angeles Times* (n.d.):1–2.

Rozsa, Lori. 1987. "Corona Leaves 'em Foaming at the Mouth." *Miami Herald* (August, n.d.):n.p.

Smith, Paul. 1983. *The Book of Nasty Legends*. London: Routledge & Kegan Paul.

Stevens, Charles W. 1981. "K-Mart Has Little Trouble Killing Those Phantom Snakes from Asia." *Wall Street Journal* (Oct. 2):31.

Tellier, A. H. 1987. Personal communication to Jan H. Brunvand.

U.S. Bureau of the Census. 1974. *Statistical Abstract of the United States: 1974*. Washington, D.C.: Government Printing Office.

9

Among Those Dark Satanic Mills:
Rumors of Kooks, Cults, and Corporations

> And did the Countenance Divine
> Shine forth upon our clouded hills?
> And was Jerusalem builded here
> Among those dark Satanic mills?
> —William Blake, "Milton"

Of all the crimes of which large corporations might be accused, being in league with Satan is among the most peculiar. Large businesses would seem, on the surface, to be institutions devoted to economic rationality *par excellence*. Why they might be in league with the devil is not usually stated, although even the devil requires capital. The profit motive swamps all else. It is slightly more credible to believe that large corporations might be owned by or contribute monies to extreme political organizations or controversial social movements. To accept that a large fast-food chain is owned by the Ku Klux Klan requires a leap of faith, but religious and political organizations do make investments in corporations, and most corporations contribute to charities.

It is impossible to know *for certain* whether these claims, implausible though they are, are true, and this is not my interest here. After all, if Procter & Gamble *were* to be owned by the Church of Satan, their denials would be as vigorous as if they were not. My intention is to understand what the range of rumors that connect corporations to religious and political movements announces about how people view the economic structures that surround them. While my sample is drawn from American sources, I do not believe that this is a purely American phenomenon. A comparative analysis of mercantile legends would demonstrate that such stories are found in all industrialized nations (Fine 1985). In Great Britain Marlboro cigarettes are alleged to have three *K*'s (symbolizing Ku Klux Klan) on the packaging and Special Service cigarettes are said to be connected to the Catholic Church.

For a person to accept these stories implies a certain set of beliefs about corporations, about religious and political movements, and about the relationship between the two. First, they assume a belief that these economic institutions can be deliberately evil; second, they claim that these movements have great power within the economic structure; finally, they presume that these con-

nections can be kept secret from the general public. I do not claim that the
rumors that I will discuss are believed *as facts*, but they are communicated in
such a way that they are seen as plausible arguments.[1]

Many widely known belief legends and rumors portray corporations as engaged in nefarious activity. Sometimes the action is a direct result of corporate
policy, as in the rumor that McDonald's uses red worms in their hamburgers.
On other occasions the stories focus on the doings of alienated employees, as in
the narrative that a Kentucky Fried Chicken outlet served a fried rat to a customer. I have argued that as modes of production and service have moved outside of the local community and are perceived to be controlled by impersonal
forces, it has become increasingly likely that folk beliefs that question the legitimacy and morality of the firms will grow (Fine 1980).

The rumors that I examine in this analysis connect to this belief structure.
These rumors claim that a company is directly in league with a social organization that much of the general public believes is outside of the mainstream of
legitimate political or religious discourse. This organization may be the Nazis,
the Ku Klux Klan, the Church of Satan, the Unification Church,[2] the Jews, the
Mormon Church, the Mafia, or the Communist Party.

These conspiracy stories, at least in their general outlines, have a long history in capitalist, industrial society. It was a common belief that many companies (most notably banks) were controlled by Jews (see, for example, *The
Protocols of the Elders of Zion*). The fact that until recently Jews were excluded
from the centers of American banking did not curtail the stories. Some Americans believed that significant portions of the economy were controlled by Ma-
sons or members of the Catholic Church. Members of the public contended that
each of these groups has considerable internal coherence and an ability to maintain collective secrecy from scrutiny by outsiders. Finally some Americans believed that members of these groups actively worked against the interest of
other members of society. They were credible targets.

I do not emphasize the historical development of urban belief legends
(Simpson 1983) but rather their contemporary characteristics. By associating
corporations with extreme religious and political groups, believers are saying,
in effect, that these corporations are outside of the moral boundaries of society.
By depicting the range and content of theses stories, I hope to suggest some
ways in which mercantile folklore is employed in a capitalist economy.

Much of the data for this paper derive from written and oral responses by
several hundred students at the University of Minnesota to requests for information about the existence and content of rumors connecting corporations with
extremist groups.[3] The data presented here are not representative, even though I
have no reason to believe that they are systematically biased. Students probably
do differ from a broader sample in being more critical of the likelihood of these
stories being true and there is likely a range of belief among the student sample,

but I have no specific evidence on this point. Although a few targets are widely known as victims of these stories (Procter & Gamble, McDonald's, Coors Beer), students named twenty-one corporations. As noted above, I have no evidence that could definitively prove that these stories are false. However, on their surface they seem implausible, no concrete evidence is presented to support them, and the range of targets suggests that these rumors are relatively easy to believe or at least to be communicated to others. Most of the targets are corporations that deal directly with consumers—often producers of foods or household products. Further, many of these targets are corporations that are leaders in their product areas (Fine 1985)—either in sales or prestige. The corporations that were named and the organizations that they are allegedly associated with are listed in the accompanying table.

Generally there seem to be two broad categories of rumors. One suggests that a corporation is involved with what the teller considers a religious fringe group. These groups include the Church of Satan, the Unification Church, and the Mormons. To be sure, what constitutes a religious fringe group is not always clear. Thus, the Mormon Church is named by several students as the owner of businesses (although I did not receive nominations of either the Catholic Church or the Jews). Some still consider the Mormons to be a "cult" religion, while many see them as mainstream religion. The members of the Unification Church (the so-called "Moonies") define themselves as a legitimate religion, though others see them as a cult.

In contrast, another set of stories name political groups: the Nazis, the Ku Klux Klan, the Moral Majority, and the John Birch Society. Companies such as Procter & Gamble that are plagued with religious rumors do not appear to have problems with political rumors; likewise, groups that are plagued with political rumors have not been the victims of religious rumors. The two are essentially different folk traditions.

The corporation that is named most frequently as the target of religious cult rumors is Procter & Gamble—at least during the period that this research was being conducted (in 1985–1987).[4] In a press release in May 1985 Procter & Gamble reported having received 100,000 calls and letters about allegations that they are involved in Satanism. (Interestingly these press releases do not discuss the related rumor that the company is owned by the Unification Church, perhaps because the Unification Church is perceived as a more legitimate institutions or perhaps because the rumors about it were not as intense.) The rumors reached their peak in 1982; then they subsided for a while and emerged again in 1985, especially in the New York area. The rumors reemerged for a while in the spring of 1987, but by the summer had entered a period of remission (Sussman 1987). They appear to be a classic case of the "diving" or "cyclical" rumor (Allport and Postman 1947)—a rumor that emerges briefly and then

Table 9.1 Mercantile Rumors Linking Corporations
and Extremist Groups

I. Religious Rumors	
Arm & Hammer	Satanists
Celestial Seasonings	Unification Church
Century 21	Unification Church
Coca-Cola	Mormons
Exxon	Satanists
Gorton Seafood	Unification Church
Johnson & Johnson	Satanists
McDonald's	Satanists
Marriott Hotels	Mormons
Ralph's Super Market	Mormons
Safeway	Mormons
Wendy's	Unification Church

II. Political Rumors	
Adolph Coors Company	American Nazi Party
	Contras
	Iran Arms Sales
	Ku Klux Klan
	Moral Majority
	Gun Control
Church's Fried Chicken	Ku Klux Klan
Kentucky Fried Chicken	American Nazi Party
	Ku Klux Klan
Pepsi-Cola	PLO
R. J. Reynolds Company	Contras
Stroh's Beer	Gun Control
Uncle Ben's Rice	Ku Klux Klan
	PLO
Welch's Food	John Birch Society

lies dormant until a spark brings it to life again, often in a new locale and with new details (see Goldstein 1972 on active and inactive traditions).

Procter & Gamble is the largest American corporation producing cleaning and food products, with sales of $12.9 billion in the 1984 fiscal year. Their corporate dominance makes them an easy target for rumors—the Goliath Effect (Fine 1985). In this regard it is significant that occasionally the focus on Satanism specifically names Crest toothpaste, which is one of Procter & Gamble's most dominant products in terms of market share and public perception.

The rumor can be subdivided into two parts; the first describes the Satanic symbolism of their product logo, and the second alleges that the man in charge of the company (that "president" or "owner" is never named, since this individual has had a low public profile) appeared on a leading television talk show (usually the "Donahue" show, but occasionally "60 Minutes," "20/20," or "Merv Griffin") and announced that the company was in league with the devil, or associated with the Church of Satan, adding that there weren't enough Christians in American to affect their sales. Taken together these rumors present the claim that Procter & Gamble is in some way associated with the Church of Satan (Brunvand 1984:169–186).

These rumors did not appear suddenly, fully formed. They responded to folk traditions and to popular knowledge. The rumors may appear highly implausible, or, less politely, "crazy," but they are not unique and the fact that they attached to Procter & Gamble should not be considered entirely coincidental.

The rumor complex apparently was first noticed in 1978 (Cohen 1985). At this point the rumor focused entirely on the symbolism of the company trademark—the now famous (or infamous) Moon and Stars. The rumor, then being spread primarily in the Southeast and the Midwest, alleged that the company had been purchased by the Unification Church. The interest in the symbolism of the rather odd-looking moon makes sense in this context, and the rumor has a certain plausibility to it, particularly as the Unification Church was known as a wealthy organization, committed to American-style capitalism. During this period other corporations were also alleged to be owned by the highly controversial Unification Church, including Entermann's Bakery, Celestial Seasonings, and Gorton's Seafood. The connection of "Moonie" involvement with capitalist enterprises had been made.

According to material distributed by Procter & Gamble, their symbol originated around 1851 as a simple cross used to designate boxes of Star brand candles. In 1882 the trademark with a moon and thirteen stars was officially registered with the U.S. Patent Office; the current version of the trademark as designed in 1930 and is among the most intricate and artistic corporate trademarks. (Because of the controversy, the company removed the trademark from some of their packages in 1985.) Yet, there is enough detail that one can see (if one uses his or her imagination) the unlucky number 13 in the 13 stars or the number 666, the symbol of the Antichrist from the Book of Revelations in the outline of the stars (or in the outline of the moon's beard).

At the same time that this rumor was being spread about Procter & Gamble, a related rumor was being spread about McDonald's. According to one account of the growth of the rumor, "it had reached the West Coast, where it collided with a rumor that McDonald's Corp. had achieved success not because it was frying billions of hamburgers a year but because of a strange alliance with the devil. What evolved was a rumor that a P&G executive (or president, as was often claimed) had appeared on the Phil Donahue show to 'come out of the closet' and proclaim himself a follower of Satan. 'The way we see it, somehow their Satan rumor got mixed up with our corporate symbol rumor, [Bill] Dobson [a P&G spokesman] said" (Madigan 1982). This rumor was attached in 1977 to Ray Kroc, the well-known president of McDonald's. Kroc's foreign name, coupled with the evil-sounding "k" phoneme and his appearance on the "Donahue" show, made him a plausible target (Brunvand 1984).[5] This helps to explain why the *name* of the president of Procter & Gamble is never mentioned. As far as the public is concerned the president (or "owner") of Procter & Gamble is a nonentity.

This rumor that alleges that the president admitted that he had sold his soul to the devil is, of course, a version of the Faustian legend—its pedigree is immaculate. Yet, it has the twist that the president is willing to admit this fact publicly on nationwide television because he claims that "there aren't enough Christians in the world to make a difference" (Solomon 1984:1). In a sense the rumor attacks American secular humanists as much as it attacks Procter & Gamble. It then becomes something of a game or test for the Christians to prove that this executive is wrong (Bird 1979). Given that Procter & Gamble sales have not declined, the game has surely not been won.

Still, one wonders how Procter & Gamble, a well-respected corporate citizen in the Cincinnati, Ohio, area with strong connections to the Episcopal Church, became linked to the Church of Satan. During the early 1980s a controversy occurred that may have provided a basis on which the rumor could have spread—the "fact" that linked Procter & Gamble to anti-Christian activity. In 1981 after the rumors were first reported, but before they became widely diffused, the company was boycotted by the Rev. Donald Wildmon's Coalition for Better Television and by other fundamentalist religious leaders for sponsoring allegedly violent and sexual television shows (Hornblower 1985). It is significant in light of later events that Procter & Gamble subsequently withdrew sponsorship of some fifty network television shows because of their gratuitous sex and violence (Draper 1982). However, the company had already been linked with anti-Christian activity in the minds of some fundamentalists.

By spring of 1982 the rumor was spreading widely, so widely that by June 1982 Procter & Gamble was receiving twelve thousand calls and letters a month. Although there was no evidence then (and is still no evidence today) that the rumor has affected sales, since sales of Procter & Gamble products steadily increased during this period, the company decided to fight back aggressively (Freund 1987).[6] Traditionally companies ignore rumors or respond only in the areas most affected; Procter & Gamble both in 1982 and 1985 responded by issuing national press releases along with letters from prominent clergymen

(Billy Graham, then-Archbishop Joseph Bernardin, Jerry Falwell and others), and they even instituted lawsuits against those who were spreading the story, including some distributors of rival Amway products.[7] They also invited writers from the *New York Times* (Salmans 1982) and the *Chicago Tribune* (Madigan 1982) to view their rumor-fighting operation. In 1985 when the rumor appeared again the company made a point of noting that they had hired detectives from the Pinkerton and Wackenhut agencies to track down the rumor-mongers (Hornblower 1985), apparently seeing the rumors as a form of corporate sabotage though consumers sometimes see the rumor as sponsored by the corporation (Soloman 1984:21).

It is very difficult to know whether these actions had any effect. Experimental control in such a circumstance is impossible. *Advertising Age* published the results of a survey they commissioned suggesting that few individuals believed the rumors (3 percent nationwide) and fewer still changed their buying habits (5 percent of the 3 percent of the believers) ("P&G Rumor Blitz" 1982). Further, the article claimed that it was the company who spread the rumor to many who had been unaware of it previously. Most of the respondents (79 percent) were unable to name a single product made by Procter & Gamble, which usually maintains a low corporate profile.

The rumor had had active periods and periods of quiescence. After the spring of 1985 the rumor subsided (although throughout most of 1986 the company was receiving over one thousand calls and letters each month—a total of more than sixteen thousand. In March 1987 the rumor flared again but by June had died down. Typically these rumor outbursts are regional or local. The rumors in 1984 spread to Roman Catholics in western Pennsylvania (whereas previously the rumor had been largely confined to Protestants). In 1985 New York City and New Jersey were affected. In the summer of 1987 calls were centered in Kentucky and West Virginia.

Bill Dobson, a P&G spokesperson noticed: "We watched it jump all over the place. Usually, you would see a jump after a weekend. That probably meant people were talking to relatives by phone" (Madigan 1982). In addition, copiers were important in the transmission of this "Xeroxlore." Rumors circulated in written form, and Procter & Gamble maintains a file of such flyers. Although the eight circulars Procter & Gamble sent me were individually typed, the wording on these circulars was very similar, indicating diffusion.[8] Circulars may have long lives, always capable of being distributed again. Currently (Spring 1989) the rumor is quiet compared to its heyday in 1982 and 1985, but the rumor could easily spread again.

In contrast to Procter & Gamble, rumors relating to the Adolph Coors Company tend to be more diffuse, less detailed, less "newsworthy," more based in fact, and the company chose to respond to them less visibly. Most of the rumors and beliefs about Coors beer allege a connection between the company and extreme right-wing politics. Yet the versions of the rumor that I have collected present few facts and informants have little detailed knowledge. Rumors claim that the Adolph Coors Company is involved with "right-wing groups," Iran arms sales, the Contras, the Moral Majority, white supremacists, the American Nazi Party, and the Ku Klux Klan—in other words with a panoply of groups on the conservative side of American politics, ranging from the respectable to the extreme fringe.

Unlike the Procter & Gamble rumor in which the entire story is highly implausible, the Coors family (who own most of the company stock) are known for being politically conservative. (Joseph Coors is a close friend of former President Ronald Reagan.) The company has taken a strong and principled anti-union position and acknowledges contributing to the National Right to Work Committee. As a result of a vote by their workers, the brewery workers' union was decertified at the Coors plant in Golden, Colorado. The then-chairman of the board, Bill Coors, noted: "If organized labor is in command, we no longer have a free society" (Michelson 1978:434).

In addition, Joe Coors, the former company president, has contributed to such organizations as the John Birch Society, STOP ERA, and the Heritage Foundation, a conservative think tank, and is known for his support for the Nicaraguan Contras (Michelson 1978). This does not mean, of course, that he or his company is closeted with the Ku Klux Klan or the American Nazi Party, but it does provide a plausible basis to associate the company with the extreme right. Likewise, it led some people to believe that Joseph Coors owned an airline that flew over the Mexican-American border shooting at illegal aliens entering the United States. Further, certain of Joseph Coors remarks about blacks were taken as reflecting racist sentiments. The company denies this point and now contributes to many black organizations. The name "Adolph" Coors and the politics of the company may have been associated in some minds with German anti-Semitism. The company also was a focus of controversy for insisting that employees take lie detector tests that included personal questions.

Although Coors is not the largest brewer in the United States (in 1987 it was the fifth largest), for many years and particularly at the time that the rumors were first circulating in the mid-1970s, it was the most prestigious domestic beer. Coors was sold only in the American West, and college students and presidents (Gerald Ford, notably) brought back cases of Coors from their trips across America. Drinking Coors was seen as a mark of taste. The prestigious quality of Coors makes it a prime target for mercantile rumors (Fine 1985).

The rumors have been circulating for well over a decade and were known even before the 1977 strike and 1978 union decertification election that caused much controversy (Shook 1987). Coors officials emphasize that the union boycott of Coors and union rhetoric in general did much to help spread the rumors. Bill Coors claimed: ". . . as far as the union is concerned, anything goes. No lie is too great to tell if it accomplishes their boycott objectives" ("Coors Beer" 1978:71).

The rumors have diminished in strength, but Coors officials say that they still hear these rumors every day. They are particularly strong in areas in which Coors is marketing their products for the first time. In 1987 Coors started selling their beer in New York and New Jersey, and the rumors spread in those areas. Like the Procter & Gamble rumors, these rumors are relatively localized and are diving rumors—disappearing in one area, then appearing fresh in another.

Another political rumor affects Coors and other beer companies (e.g., Anheuser-Busch and Stroh's). This rumor claims that the company supports gun control legislation. These rumors are particularly ironic for Coors which is not only politically conservative but gives money to the National Rifle Association. Peter Coors, Coors corporate vice president, has appeared in advertising for the NRA. Although this rumor is apparently not as troubling for the company, it still surfaces occasionally. Its existence emphasizes the blue collar, "pro-gun" sentiments of beer drinkers, who by spreading this rumor, proclaim that they oppose gun control.

In contrast to Procter & Gamble, Coors has taken a decidedly low profile in handling these rumors. Although they established a consumer hotline in 1987, they have not made any broad public pronouncements. Perhaps significantly Coors recently hired a woman from Procter & Gamble to oversee their public relations, possibly recognizing her experience in dealing with troubling mercantile rumors. Although the union boycott itself has taken an economic toll on the company (at the height of the controversy sales of Coors were down 15 percent in California ["Bitter Beercott" 1977]), the rumors have apparently had little effect apart from the boycott.

The rumors about Procter & Gamble and Coors, coupled with the rumors about the association of Church's Fried Chicken with the Ku Klux Klan, well documented by Patricia Turner (1987), remind us that the public has religious and political concerns and can be motivated to express these concerns through rumors—whether or not these rumors are believed as "fact." The existence of these rumors, their spread, and their longevity is a consequence of the heterogeneity of American society. We live in a society in which there *are* Nazis, Satan worshipers, Klansmen, and "Moonies." If they exist, isn't it plausible that they are in charge of corporations?

But, of course, the claims go deeper than that. The rumors spring from uneasiness about what is perceived to be the complete amorality of American corporate life. The fact that Satanists (an exaggerated form of secular humanists) can be believed to have such power suggests that not only is government separated from religion but business is as well. In fact, large corporations, hoping to gain the allegiance of all customers, play down the idiosyncratic beliefs of their managers. Can one now imagine Ford, IBM, or even Procter & Gamble referring to themselves as a "Christian" corporation—something that might have been said in previous generations. Secularism has become the religion of commerce. This secularism takes the form of what sociologists refer to as the "Civil Religion," a general belief in an anonymous "God-figure" and the claims of a normative system of moral beliefs (Bellah and Hammond 1980). Deep religious beliefs have long been banished from the marketplace, leaving a fertile ground in which rumors about religious "deviance" can take root.

American politics is likewise removed from the center stage of commerce. Most corporations do not advertise their stands on controversial political issues. More typically when they enter the political arena they contribute to nonpartisan "political" issues such as the rededication of the Statue of Liberty, the Olympics, measures for combatting illiteracy or supporting the responsibility to vote. Just as there is a "Civil Religion" in America, so is there a "Civil Politics." Yet the American public sees the potential political diversity in America, thanks to the media that tend to emphasize such divergences. They assume that it is plausible that some of these political extremist groups can control corporations and so look for hints, such as connecting Robert Welch with the Welch's corporation that makes fruit juice,[9] or connecting Church's Fried Chicken with the Ku Klux Klan because of the number of outlets in minority communities (Turner 1987).

All of these deviant groups have common elements. First, they are believed to be secret, with rites and rituals of which the public is largely unaware. They have kept their activities out of the public eye, and, so, the public can believe nearly anything of them. They are characterized by high levels of *secrecy*. Second, members of these groups are believed to share common goals and values and to hold these strongly. Members are highly committed to the group and are willing to do whatever the authorities in the group ask. The groups are characterized by high levels of *internal cohesion*. Third, these groups are believed to be working against the interests of most Americans. This provides a need for secrecy and internal cohesion. These groups are perceived as *hostile*. These three factors taken together explain why certain collections of individuals become focal points of such rumors and others do not.

The companies that are at the center of such rumors are, in contrast, companies that are well known and that deal almost exclusively in consumer products and services rather than in heavy manufacturing. Therefore, there is the paradox of well-known companies directed by little-known forces. Such is symbolically the case in much of American industry, in that the real managers of corporations are typically unknown. These rumors symbolically mirror the ambivalence between knowledge of the product and ignorance of the individuals who direct the creation and marketing of these products. In those cases in which owners are known (Lee Iaccoca, Joseph Coors, Ray Kroc, Armand Hammer), rumors do develop which question whether we know them as well as we think or whether our knowledge of them is just as surface as our knowledge of their products.

Just as we find an exaggeration of religious diversity, we also find an exaggeration of political diversity. Americans worry through these mercantile rumors that there exist more powerful extremists than the weight of the evidence will bear. The rumors, though perhaps not the reality, speak to fears of diversity in a society that has moved from its relatively homogeneous moorings. While the population is heterogeneous, our value systems appear to be even more so. Assumptions of value congruency are now no longer perceived to be tenable, and, hence, the rumors can develop freely. We imagine ourselves in a society in which anything goes, particularly with regard to those whom we perceive as controlling us, such as large corporations. Satan and the Ku Klux Klan are *both* social demons, bedeviling a society in which members have lost faith in each other.

Notes

My thanks to Linda Ulrey and Pam Sussman of Procter & Gamble and Don Shook of Coors Beer for their help in preparing this analysis. The comments of Frederick Koenig, Patrick Mullen, Brian McConnell, Paul Smith, and Hugo Freund helped to sharpen my arguments.

1. Patrick Mullen suggests (personal communication 1989) that there may be different levels of belief within the sample and among the rumors. Still, these are seen as the type of communication that can be reasonably reported, whether or not they are seen as likely to be true.
2. I use the label Unification Church to characterize that religious organization founded by Sun Myung Moon, the Korean evangelist. The term "Moonies," commonly used to describe the members of this group, is pejorative.
3. In this article I do not draw upon the performance context of these rumors and legends. One makes a trade-off in collecting a large body of material as opposed to collecting data from small groups contexts.
4. I am grateful to Linda Ulrey for making company documents available for this research project.
5. Another rumor spread during this period claimed that the name of the prominent rock group KISS stands for Knights in Satan's Service. Later it was claimed that the Smurf cartoon characters are demonic. These rumors are also linked to the belief widely held in the fundamentalist community that the Federal Communications Commission is considering banning religious programming on television (see Brunvand 1984:184).
6. There are individual instances in which stores have refused to stock Procter & Gamble products (Madigan 1982); in one instance a man returned a can of Folger's coffee saying that he refused to drink the "devil's brew" (Solomon 1984:1). Some consumers blamed company products for bouts of depression (Brunvand 1984:185–186). In other cases the company claims that employees were harassed and company vehicles were vandalized. The seriousness of these actions is unclear.
7. None of these libel cases were ever brought to trial; defendants signed statements deny-

ing any truth in their original allegations. The charge has been made that these legal actions were merely a public relations ploy by Procter & Gamble, and at least one target has retained an attorney and is considering suing the company for defamation.

8. Procter & Gamble sent me circulars from Arizona, Arkansas, California, Colorado, Illinois, North Carolina, Pennsylvania, and Virginia.

9. In fact, there is no connection. The late Robert Welch owned Welch's candies, a small New England candy maker.

References Cited

Allport, Gordon, and Leo G. Postman. 1947. *The Psychology of Rumor*. New York: Holt.

Bellah, Robert, and Phillip Hammond. 1980. *Varieties of Civil Religion*. New York: Harper and Row.

Bird, Donald Allport. 1979. "Rumor as Folklore: An Interpretation and Inventory." Ph.D. diss., Indiana University, Bloomington.

Bitter Beercott. 1977. *Time*, 26 December, 15.

Brunvand, Jan Harold. 1984. *The Chocking Doberman*. New York: Norton.

Cohen, Duffie. 1985. United Press International wire copy, 17 April.

Coors Beer. "What Hit Us?" 1978. *Forbes*, 16 October, 71–73.

Draper, James T. (President, Southern Baptist Convention). 1982. Personal Communication to Procter & Gamble.

Fine, Gary Alan. 1980. "The Kentucky Fried Rat: Legends and Modern Society." *Journal of the Folklore Institute* 17:222–43.

———. 1985. "The Goliath Effect: Corporate Dominance and Mercantile Legends." *Journal of American Folklore* 98:63–84.

Freund, Hugo. 1987. "Rumor and Control: A Folklorist's View of Narratives on Procter & Gamble Consorting with the Devil." Manuscript.

Goldstein, Kenneth S. 1972. "On the Application of the Concepts of Active and Inactive Traditions to the Study of Repertory." In *Toward New Perspectives in Folklore*, ed. Americo Paredes and Richard Bauman, 62–67. Austin: University of Texas Press.

Hornblower, Margot. 1985. "Rumor Bedevils Procter & Gamble." *Washington Post*, 18 April.

Madigan, Charles. 1982. "A Story of Satan that is Rated P & G." *Chicago Tribune*, 18 July.

Michelson, Peter. 1978. Coors Beer, the Union Buster. *The Nation*, 15 April.

"P & G Rumor Blitz Looks Like a Bomb." 1982. *Advertising Age*, 9 August, 1.

Salmans, Sandra. 1982. P. & G.'s Battle with Rumors." *New York Times*, 22 July.

Shook, Don. 1987. Personal communication, Coors Corporate Communication.

Simpson, Jacqueline. 1983. "Urban Legends in *The Pickwick Papers*." *Journal of American Folklore* 96:462–70.

Solomon, Julie. 1984. "Procter & Gamble Fights New Rumors of Link to Satanism." *Wall Street Journal*, 8 November.

Sussman, Pamela. 1987. Personal communication.

Turner, Patricia A. 1987. "Church's Fried Chicken and the Klan: A Rhetorical Analysis of Rumor in the Black Community." *Western Folklore* 46:294–306.

IV CORPORATE REDEMPTION

Redemption Rumors:
Mercantile Legends and Corporate Beneficence

In his letter, responding to my inquiry about stories of cigarette packages being exchanged for medical technology, William Kloepfer, Jr., the senior vice president for public relations of the Tobacco Institute, referred to these accounts as "redemption rumors." By this Kloepfer meant simply that they referred to corporate exchange of cigarette packages for medical equipment or services—such as wheelchairs, iron lungs, dialysis machines, or seeing-eye dogs—with no such corporate commitment on record. I ask his forgiveness for twisting this phrase in ways he did not intend. Specifically, I suggest these rumors provide redemption for the companies involved and for consumers, in the sense of freeing them from blame, debt, or sin.

These rumors differ from most other mercantile legends in that on their surface they paint the corporation or industry in a positive light (Fine 1985). The corporation or industry is supposedly willing to be charitable, although there is the catch that their products must be supplied in exchange for this equipment. Yet, as will become clear, such stories are a mixed blessing for the businesses involved. No one wishes to turn down a charitable request, particularly when sincere people have invested considerable time and energy. While there is no evidence that such campaigns hurt or help sales to any appreciable degree, companies believe these rumors are harmful and they occasionally attempt to squelch them.

My goal in this essay is to demonstrate how the public's attitude toward corporations and medical technology is transformed into this set of rumors. Further, I examine the social and economic conditions in which these stories originate to demonstrate their plausibility and the range of effects on this economic environment. Although these rumors have considerable power in motivating consumer action and in frustrating those stung, their flowering can be seen as the consequence of folk beliefs about American society, the moral basis of specific products, and the economic order. In this chapter I make no claims about the empirical course of particular instances of this rumor or about the specific psychodynamics of individual collectors; my concerns are with the general conditions and public attitudes that lead to these beliefs. For my data I rely primarily on accounts printed in newspapers and magazines in the United States over the past thirty years. I ask how this legend is presented in these sources.

Product Redemption Promotions

Product packaging is a relatively recent phenomenon (Goody 1982:154–61). The nineteenth century witnessed the development of numerous types of packaging culminating in the late 1800s with the development and usage of unit packaging, rather than bulk containers. By the turn of the century and into the first half of the twentieth century, packaging became more oriented toward marketing, toward getting consumers to try the products (Pope 1983). The package became an advertisement for itself and for its company. The classic instance of this was the Uneeda Biscuit, which the National Biscuit Company introduced in 1899:

> This unit package, made of paper board, had an inner protective paper wrap to hold the crackers, and a paper overwrap that displayed the brand name in large bold type. This package not only advertised the brand name by means of the printing, but actively promoted the brand because it kept the crackers in much better condition for a longer period of time than the old bulk cracker boxes, bins, and barrels could. [Raphael 1969:33]

By the early twentieth century, all of the major forms of packaging (paper, board, pottery, glass, metal, and foil), except for plastics, were in wide use (David 1967:33). With the development of self-service groceries in the 1930s the package became a crucial marketing technique, and for consumers it became an end in itself: a basis on which products were selected—a part of the ethic of consumption.

Coupons and other forms of product-redemption incentives date back to the last half of the nineteenth century. In the 1850s, Benjamin Talbot Babbitt, a soap manufacturer, decided to sell paper-wrapped laundry soap—a product that had usually been sold in a long, unwrapped bar with the grocer cutting off a piece for the homemaker. At first Babbitt's innovation failed; women wanted to buy soap, not paper. Then he offered an attractive colored lithograph for twenty-five soap wrappers, and the product became a success (Meredith and Fried 1977:11–12). In the decades that followed, cigarette and gum companies offered similar incentives (Clark 1944). By the 1890s, premium catalogs had been well established. For Arbuckle coffee coupons one could receive suspenders, clocks, or corsets (Meredith and Fried 1977:13). In the 1890s trading-stamp companies were established, and Grape Nuts cereal gave consumers a one-cent certificate for their next purchase of this health cereal, the first coupon with a monetary value (Bowman 1980:2).

In 1929 General Mills started their famous coupon-redemption promotion.[1] They provided a coupon in their bags of Gold Medal flour, which consumers could send in for a free teaspoon. General Mills was overwhelmed by the response to this promotion and expanded it to other types of silverware. This eventually expanded into the Betty Crocker Coupon Plan, which still thrives today. These promotions proved to be a great success, promoting brand loyalty and giving General Mills its reputation as a leader in consumer promotion drives. Subsequently, other major companies (such as Pillsbury, Kellogg's, and Brown and Williamson Tobacco Company) started similar programs, although none achieved the success of General Mills. In addition, corporations often have short-term promotions—such as having consumers send in a number of labels, boxtops, or seals for some desirable item. For example, R. J. Reynolds Tobacco Company once supplied cigarette lighters for Camel packages (Staunton 1968:A9). Likewise, American Brands sent five cartons of Pall Mall cigarettes for every five hundred empty packs of that brand they received (Driscoll 1971:n.p.). The stories that spread about product redemption for medical technology must be set within the context of American business practices in which such exchanges do occur.

The connections between the world of business and medical technology go even further. From 1948 to 1979, Perk Foods (owned from 1970 to 1979 by the Liggett group, which also owned Liggett & Meyers Tobacco Company) had a program in which labels of Vets Dog Food could be submitted to the Pilot Guide Dog Foundation in Chicago to be redeemed for one cent or two cents for each label—totaling over a million dollars in contributions. This money helped the foundation train seeing-eye dogs (personal communication, Cathy Dossey, C. H. B. Foods, 10 September 1984; personal communication, John J. Gray, Pilot Dogs, Inc., 25 September 1984). The H. J. Heinz Company has had a program since 1979 in which they will give to a children's hospital six cents for every baby food label redeemed. Campbell Soups maintains a program in which soup can labels can be redeemed for school equipment (personal communication, James H. Moran, Campbell Soup Company, 9 April 1984). During the mid 1970s American Brands redeemed Safari cigarette wrappers in Miami to benefit a Lions Club camp for visually impaired children (personal communication, Daniel Conforti, American Brands, 5 November 1984; Alston 1974). Some local Kidney Foundation chapters have sponsored aluminum can collections for recycling to purchase kidney machines (Bronikowski 1981).

The most extensive program of this type was run by General Mills through their Betty Crocker Coupon Program. By the 1950s the Betty Crocker redemption program had expanded so that groups could save for sets of silverware and cooking utensils. This program proved to be successful and groups asked if they could save for other items not included in the Betty Crocker catalog. General Mills decided each coupon "point" (coupons have different values) would be

worth one-half cent. A group was allowed up to eighteen months to complete a
project that had been approved by General Mills.[2] According to Walter Kost,
3,000 to 3,500 groups actively worked on projects for such diverse items as
televisions, school buses, swimming pools, a tiger for a local zoo, and hospital
beds. One Wisconsin nursing home built a wing on the home through redeeming these coupons.

In 1969 the Kidney Foundation of Ohio wrote to General Mills asking if
they might hold a coupon drive for a kidney dialysis machine (for six hundred
thousand coupon points). General Mills approved the program, and other state
Kidney Foundations, including those in Michigan and Minnesota, followed
suit, as did other medical groups (for iron lungs and heart machines). In the
words of Kost: "It went over like gangbusters."

At first General Mills was delighted with the program because they felt
here was a case of "doing well by doing good." A program such as this was
helpful for ensuring brand loyalty. However, soon after the program began,
problems developed. Although all groups were supposed to register and to follow General Mill's instructions, some did not. Originally General Mills felt
they had to honor these collections because of fear of bad publicity, but after-
ward they began turning some groups down. At the same time, some attacked
the company because they claimed the company was "trading on human mis-
ery" (*St. Paul Pioneer Press* 1970:25). So, in December 1970 General Mills
announced that they were discontinuing their program the following year.

Kost estimated about three hundred dialysis machines were purchased for a
total amount of $1 million to $1.5 million. Despite the criticism, the company
received the 1972 Trustees' Award of the National Kidney Foundation. Yet, it is
well to recall the origins and termination of the program were grounded in business considerations. While General Mills wished to be helpful, they wished to
be helpful in a way that would benefit their stockholders.

Mercantile legends about product redemption for medical technology that
are objectively untrue are set in the context of a business world in which such
promotions have occurred. The stories are not absurd delusions of naive minds.

Redemption Rumors

Redemption rumors about exchanging cigarette packages for medical technology have been reported to have occurred as far back as 1936 (Holt 1970), and by
the late 1950s they were well established. Unfortunately I have not been able to
find definitive proof of the 1936 rumor. By the late 1940s the real offer of Vet
Dog Food was already in place. However, many of the stories spread at this time
were based on little but wishful thinking.

In early 1984 I wrote to 133 companies asking if they had heard rumors from consumers that their company would supply medical technology in exchange for a number of product proof of purchases. One hundred and one companies responded; seventeen of these companies admitted to having heard such rumors about their products: Pepsi-Cola, Borden, Kellogg's, R. J. Reynolds, Hunt-Wesson Foods, Brown & Williamson, McCormick & Company, Lipton, Gerber, Philip Morris, General Foods, Martha White Kitchens, Jeno's Pizza, Wrigley's Gum, Miller Beer, General Mills, and American Brands. The actual percentage of corporations that have ever received such inquiries is likely higher. Some employees may not have been aware of such rumors if they were not a major problem for the corporations or if the employees had only worked a short time; others may not have wished to make their company "look bad" by spreading the rumor to an academic stranger. Some of those who admitted to having heard the rumor about their company reported it was very uncommon. The seventeen corporations on the list do not provide an adequate sample of what companies are most affected by this redemption rumor.

Redemption rumors are very widely spread with some companies (particularly cigarette companies) and charities (especially the National Kidney Foundation) having to respond to several calls or letters a day when the rumors are active. Between January and October 1968 (not a particularly active period), the Tobacco Institute received seventy-seven letters from twenty-eight states asking for information about the redemption rumor.

These rumors by their longevity have proven to be very adaptable. Diseases change as a function of public concern and medical technology (from seeing-eye dogs and iron lungs to dialysis machines); what is collected changes as a function of changes in packaging (viz, the emphasis on pop-can tabs). Further, they apparently have a great appeal for consumers. One incredible report claims that a department store in Syracuse saved more than two million cigarette packs before delivering them to their local hospital (Bradley 1980:7B). Other reports cite "tons" or "truckloads" of packages—part of the aesthetic of folk and media reporting, but indicating the extensiveness of the effort. From these collections a patient or hospital receives a seeing-eye dog, pints of blood, a wheelchair, an iron lung, or a kidney dialysis machine. The strength of the rumor is such that one collector after being told the rumor was false, said: "I kept on thinking, 'I have to throw these things [cigarette packages] out.' But what a waste it would be if I would throw them out and then find somebody who could use them" (Skowron n.d.).

For each product or for each pound, companies provide a certain amount of time on a dialysis machine or money to be used in purchasing one of these machines. Of course, the amounts vary dramatically. One woman in Lexington, Kentucky, apparently believed R. J. Reynolds would redeem empty cigarette packages for one dollar per package—more than the original cost of the product

(Dryden 1978). Another report said it took one thousand packages to pay for one minute on a kidney dialysis machine (Bronikowski 1981)—thus ignoring the fact that kidney dialysis machines cost only about six thousand dollars to purchase, and treatment costs under a dollar per minute (McGrath 1982). All of the stories ignore the fact that under a provision of Medicaid (passed in 1973), 80 percent of the cost of dialysis is paid by the federal government, and most insurance policies cover the rest. The stories, however, indicate the public perception and fear of medical costs and also perceived corporate generosity.

Not all redemption rumors name the victim, but those that do typically cite a young child: a two-year-old boy, a nine-year-old girl, or a seven-year-old boy are among the children being helped. In one account white Virginians avidly saved their cigarette packages for a five-year-old black girl with sickle cell anemia (Sessa 1974:G1). Sometimes collectors call the hospital where the child is supposedly being treated, discover the child doesn't exist, and then conclude that the child has died, but continue collecting for another child.

These dramatic details fit well with the story making needs of the mass media (Bird 1976; Darnton 1975). I assume that media reporters do not create these stories out of thin air—the quotations are likely genuine, the facts are provided by those involved, and many articles are accompanied by photographs of huge piles of the product involved—few reporters consciously create fiction.[3] Still, it is evidence that reporters take isolated facts and try to build a compelling narrative, based on assumptions of human behavior and belief. To the extent that reporters quote the principals, we can assume the motivations and beliefs reported are genuine, recognizing that some motivations are more likely to be reported or emphasized than others. While news reports are not the same as verbatim interviews, they are stories seen by editors as credible, genuine, and a commentary on some aspect of modern existence. Thus, press accounts can provide legitimate folkloric data when recognized for what they are (e.g., Brunvand 1981; Klintberg 1981).

Corporate Targets

In April 1984 I asked students in my Introduction to Sociology class whether they had heard of a redemption rumor about medical technology. Of the 73 students who responded, 14 (19 percent) had heard of one. Over the past three years, I have collected 36 versions of this story from undergraduate students at the University of Minnesota. Of these, 22 (61 percent) were about beer and soft drink cans and bottles—18 named can tabs, 3 mentioned bottle caps, and 1 said whole aluminum cans were needed for redemption. The only other item that was named by more than two persons was cigarette packages, which three students mentioned.[4]

Nationally it appears that collecting cigarette packages is at least as common as saving can tabs. The rumor is sufficiently prevalent that the Tobacco Institute has issued several press releases denying the story, without success in halting these collections. I have 138 accounts from newspapers (largely supplied through the Tobacco Institute's press-clipping service) that attest to the popularity and longevity of this rumor. Thirty-six states are named as settings for these collections. A third major focus of this rumor—seemingly more common in the 1960s than today—is that if one saves enough tags from the tops of teabags, the tea industry will supply medical technology.

What do these products (soft drinks, beer, cigarettes, and tea)[5] have in common? First, they come in packages that can easily be saved—whole, or in part. For example, these rumors are not spread about laundry detergents or egg cartons. One only needs to save the pull-tops of soft drink cans, not the whole can. Second, these are products one consumes in large numbers. While one might save the plastic tops from Crisco cans, Crisco is purchased so infrequently that saving them would be unprofitable. Likewise, saving labels from bags of crumpets would make little sense in a society that doesn't eat crumpets. However, these two criteria still leave considerable room for collections—after all, any can label can be saved. Saved products share a third common element: people believe consuming them may be harmful to their health. Nicotine, caffeine, and alcohol represent an "unholy trinity" in American consumer perceptions. These are the three major legal "drugs" in society. I shall not debate the actual health effects of these substances but only suggest each has been the subject of a public controversy during the second half of the twentieth century.

Collecting these packages, tops, or tags allows consumers to help others. Burns Roper, the public opinion survey expert, argues people participate as a means of "getting involved" in a society that usually doesn't provide opportunity for personal action. Roper claims, "People have strong feelings of frustration about their inability as individuals to do something. . . . Joining with friends and neighbors in a project of this sort is a way of expressing this" (Pitz 1978). Consumers find themselves in a society from which they may feel estranged or alienated. These collections indicate they have some control, even though they must operate within constraints set by corporations (Fine 1980, 1985). David Fishel, R. J. Reynolds public relations officer, calls this the "Santa Claus Syndrome" (Martin 1980), and there is no question that people do this out of compassion. As one man commented as he collected empty cigarette packages for a girl on a "cancer machine": "It's the least I figure I could do. . . . I mean people just throw them away and it means life to some little girl" (Martin 1980). Another collector, saving for a boy on a dialysis machine, commented:

"I didn't know who the boy was, but I'm softhearted. I'll try to get out and help someone who needs it if I can." Still another emphasizes the community control element: "It does go to show that if they [*sic*] was a crisis in the town, people would 'do something'" (Dryden 1978). Some people are so helpful (or so gullible) that one failure doesn't prevent them from trying again, as in the case of the Ladies Auxiliary of an Albany, New York, area American Legion post. One member commented that they

> had collected "tons and tons" of empty cigarette packs, then found out nobody wanted them. She said they had also collected tea bags and couldn't find anyone to take those either. She said the auxiliary collected a garbage bag full of cancelled stamps for the Veterans Hospital in Albany. "But when we took them down there, they looked at us as if we were crazy." [Keeney 1981:F-3]

These people are not merely collecting at random, they are collecting specific products—particularly cigarette packs. The dangers of cigarettes psychologically affect the collectors. One news article that spread the rumor had the following lead paragraph: "No matter what people say, cigarette smoking must not be all bad. At least the empty cigarette packs can be used for some good" (*Independent* 1972:3-A). Sociologist George Christie contends the rumor spreads because it provides smokers with a means of justifying their habit (Angle 1974). Mary Howland, director of community relations at Mount Vernon Hospital in Virginia, suggests a similar view:

> I've always wondered if smokers think it's justifying smoking. Like, they might say, "I know they say it's bad for me, but if my empty packages are saving someone's life, then it can't be all that bad." [Stewart 1983:A5]

One avid collector told a reporter she had three trash cans full of wrappers and "had been smoking my head off to get more" (Watson 1980:3). While I find it doubtful that many people will increase the number of cigarettes they smoke (or soda, beer, or tea they drink) in order to add to their collection, it is plausible that people will feel comforted by knowing that their habits, about which they feel ambivalent, have positive side effects. It is in this sense we can speak of these rumors as being "redemption rumors." People are morally redeemed for their perceived "sin" of ingesting nicotine (Troyer and Markle 1983), caffeine (Troyer and Markle 1984), or alcohol (Gusfield 1981). This "redemption" is perhaps most obvious in those cases in which the collection has some connection to the disease being treated: as when cigarette packages are saved for an iron lung (even though those machines do not treat lung cancer) or a vague "cancer machine," or when soft drink can tops are saved for dialysis machines.[6] In such cases, the folk aesthetic of such rumors is clear; however, the general point applies to all such stories.

Rumor Origins

Like most urban belief legends and rumors, the origin of redemption rumors recedes into history. The 1936 date of the first rumor of this type places the rumor well before any known related product promotion, although well after product redemptions began. One origin for this redemption may be based on the fact that prior to and during World War II the tinfoil paper found in cigarette packages was recycled for money (O'Toole 1971; Lipsett 1974:143; Knorr 1945); since many of the early stories dealt with saving the tinfoil from cigarette packages, this may be a point of origin. Further, real product redemption offers surely contributed to the growth of these rumors. Despite the claim that cigarette packages, tea bag tags, and can tops are worthless, this is not strictly true. Most cities have recycling programs for paper and aluminum that would permit a group to earn money from saving these artifacts—although the numbers required are so daunting as to make such projects unfeasible—yet, strictly speaking, the packages are not worthless. Likewise, the coupons on Raleigh cigarettes do have real value ($.015) and *could* be redeemed. Most of the rumors are false (and typically no evidence is provided to suggest that they are true), but they are surely *plausible,* given American business practice. Even those rumors that suggest one save all cigarette brands makes psychological sense because of the prominence of the Tobacco Institute in speaking for the cigarette industry.[7] While brands are well known by the public, companies are typically not well known, particularly as compared to other segments of the American economy.

Despite this plausibility, most industry officials, health workers, and newspeople dismiss the rumor with the formulaic expression that it is "a cruel hoax." This phrase appears in a 1957 article on the rumor (the earliest article I have seen), and is regularly repeated, particularly once the Tobacco Institute picked up that characterization (Ziemer 1957). Although an internal memorandum by the staff of the Tobacco Institute (Cahill 1968) explains it is "just the usual rumor pattern," and the Tobacco Institute is careful not to denigrate any of their good-hearted consumers (Saad 1974), the common depictions of the rumor origin are that it is a vicious hoax, sick joke, or a fraud.[8] The idea that it could be a transformation of fact is rarely mentioned in the popular press.

When one recognizes that this rumor really does very little direct harm (and possibly some good, as shall be discussed later), the remarks of officials are startling: Bob Renwick, the head of the Better Business Bureau for the Central Alabama area calls these rumors "the most vicious of all he's known" (Atkinson 1971). Ed Campbell, administrator at the Oklahoma Children's Memorial Hospital commented, "It's just a cruel hoax. . . . I'd like to find the cave where someone who starts this kind of story must live" (Watson 1980). The actress

Joan Crawford speaking for the American Foundation for the Blind called these rumors "a cruel hoax" resulting in "heartbreak and anger" (Tobacco Institute, press release, 24 May 1974). The American Kidney Fund reports: "Someone has played a cruel joke on these people, and even more so on the poor kidney victim who is waiting to be helped. Saving all these things will not enable one helpless victim to receive even one minute of dialysis" (Gold 1978:DC8).

The vehemence of these remarks is quite remarkable considering no one is defrauded, and in few of these cases is an actual patient expecting aid. In most cases the victim is as imaginary as the offer. Yet, the existence of these rumors has the potential for underlining the belief that large corporations do not help the average citizen, and therefore they may emphasize the moral bankruptcy (to some) of free-market capitalism. Nowhere is this possibility more true than in these product areas in which products are claimed to harm their consumers. The threat to the moral legitimacy of these companies is real, even though it is implicit and, as I shall argue, in fact politically impotent. Yet, the existence of these stories does *in principle* undermine the smooth relations between consumers and corporations.

Effects of Redemption Rumors

Despite claims that these rumors have devastating effects, their economic effects seem to be mild. To be sure some of those who have been taken in and collected huge numbers of products feel foolish or embarrassed for having spent so much time and for having asked their relatives, friends, and neighbors to participate. As one pull-tab collector commented: "It makes you look like a jackass" (Gordon 1984:1). Yet, these effects seem transitory. If someone smoked or drank more in response to such rumors, this might be a social cost, but such an effect doesn't seem common. Indeed, it is reasonable that the psychological and social benefits during the collection, such as increasing one's self-esteem, sense of altruism, and social network, may outweigh the effects of the aftermath. To be sure, some persons may be more cautious in blindly helping in the future, but it is not certain this caution is harmful.

The effects on the community are similarly mild. Although there may be a letdown after discovering the rumor was not valid, and there may have been some inconvenience while the collection occurred, this may be balanced by the fact that the community demonstrated it could work together for a noble cause. People were shown to be kind, if naive. Further, such a collection may significantly reduce trash in the community. As a colonel at Pope Air Force Base near Fayetteville, North Carolina, wrote his sergeant who organized such a collection: "You've probably done a big job in making our base cleaner by collecting cigarette packs before they became litter" (*Raleigh News and Observer* 1970; see also Opie and Opie 1959:307).

Companies sometimes see themselves as the real victims of this "hoax." Bill Toohey, director of media relations of the Tobacco Institute, speculates the rumor might be designed to discredit someone (presumably them) (Bronikowski 1981), and William Kloepfer, Jr., senior vice president of the Tobacco Institute, worries that consumers might think they are "cold-hearted in respect to medical problems" (*St. Petersburg Times* 1976). They also are concerned that some consumers may think the Institute started the rumor in the hopes of increasing sales—a public relations stunt (Stewart 1983:A5; Bradley 1980:7-B). While I find it hard to believe companies would spread such rumors or people would consciously choose to smoke more because of this collection, it certainly gives smokers a reason to continue and a sense of satisfaction from their habit. I know of no evidence suggesting that after these stories are discredited, cigarette sales decrease, nor is there substantial bitterness toward the cigarette companies—at least not on the part of smokers themselves. One must suspect the rumors affect sales and credibility little and possibly create slight benefits of support for smoking as a legitimate enterprise and positive feelings toward the tobacco industry during the collection itself. As Walter Kost of General Mills indicated, legitimate redemptions, and perhaps those redemption rumors that name a specific brand, may increase product loyalty, as in the case of the one smoker who switched brands from Kool to Marlboro when he believed that the brand was having a product redemption offer (Tobacco Institute, internal memo, R. J. O'Rourke, 31 May 1974).

Finally, what about the medical victims? First, as I noted, few of these rumors have flesh-and-blood victims. Few individuals suffer directly, although occasionally this may happen (Morgan 1971:1A). More often when there is a real victim, the response is similar to that of the mother of a two-year-old girl who needed a heart operation: "Mother was dubious . . . she said . . . that she had never placed her hopes on the collection because it did not seem to make sense to her that cigarette companies would redeem empty packs" (Carmody 1972:M27). However, the uncovering of several of these rumors has had positive effects. Often money is collected for the victim. On other occasions someone will supply the machine in question for the victims. In 1963, for example, residents of Springfield, Illinois, saved empty cigarette packages for wheelchairs, only to learn later the collection had no value: "W. Clement Stone, president of the Combined Insurance Co. of America in Chicago, read of the hoax and decided to provide up to 50 wheelchairs 'as a redemption of good faith'" (*National Observer* 1963). Similar conclusions have occurred around the country. Well-publicized collections may achieve their goals, although in an indirect fashion. And although direct contributions and volunteering would be more efficient, medical benefits do sometimes result from some collections.

Citizens should not be encouraged to go out and start collections of tags, packages, or can tops, but the outrage of media, industry, and health officials at redemption rumors seems excessive. Certainly people have spent their time doing worse things.

Redemption and Corporate Beneficence

I have previously argued that mercantile legends express important values the public holds about its social environment. In describing the legends about the Kentucky Fried Rat, narrators indirectly express the view that the organizational changes in modern society are harmful. As America has moved from a personalized economy to a bureaucratized, mass-consumption economy, the products that are available are seen as less desirable and more dangerous (Fine 1980). These mercantile legends attach themselves to the largest corporation in a market, perhaps as a means of protesting the conglomeration of the American economy (Fine 1985).

The rumors about corporate beneficence examined in this essay seem at first glance to present a strikingly different point of view. In these rumors (at least during the time they are believed and acted upon) the corporation or industry is the hero. The corporation or industry will supply the money or technology necessary for saving a child or helping a community. In their time of need citizens turn to the large corporation to provide services.

Yet, the picture is not so simple. First, these redemption rumors recognize by their existence and popularity that only large corporations or industries have the capital necessary for such give-aways. The community cannot by itself raise the money necessary—even when by objective fact they could do so, and sometimes do so when the rumors prove false. Corporations are perceived as having resources local communities do not. Consumers believe medical costs have inflated to the point where no individual can afford them. The public has simultaneously become enamoured of the "magical" curative power of medical technology—a view that doctors and hospitals have done little to curb. The belief in the need for sophisticated medical machinery combined with the belief about their cost constitute a favorable environment for rumors about corporate charity.

Second, the implication of all of these stories is that the corporation or industry will not provide the medical resources out of the goodness of its heart. These corporations require consumers to collect their products in order to reap the benefit. Thus, community service and profit are intimately linked. As Walter Kost emphasized, General Mills would not have engaged in this promotion if it had not made economic sense to do so. Related is the belief among some consumers that the companies are making these offers out of a desire for un-deserved public relations benefits, much as Henry Ford IV gave to Jewish causes to offset damage caused by earlier anti-Semitic remarks (personal com-munication, Simon Bronner, 4 February 1985).

Even though the rumors have no basis in fact, the public perception of the justifications remains grounded in economic concerns. This extends to those members of the public who suspect the corporation is involved in spreading the rumors. Such a view, implausible to many, makes sense to some who empha-size the economic benefits that companies derive from the increased sales of their products. Even while relying on corporations, consumers are reported to feel that, indirectly or directly, economics is involved. They rarely respond with bitterness, but still they recognize that business altruism is mingled with self-interest. Although in some sense people feel they are getting something for nothing, because otherwise they would merely discard the packages, tops, and tags, it is not truly for nothing, and some explicitly decide the beneficent cor-poration should receive their business, as a small economic token of thanks.

I have called these rumors "redemption rumors" because they express con-sumers' needs to justify their own behavior. They are redeemed from their eco-nomic roles by the existence of these collections. With the decline of com-munity, neighbors are no longer so likely to help each other. We do not raise barns, harvest together, or hold quilting bees—or at least not as part of our ex-pected routine. Modern life has become more insulated and isolated. Further, with the decline of the extended family, we are on our own. We are less likely to help our kinfolks. These product collections seem, in some measure, to be at-tempts to recapture the romance of our image of a folk community. For a time, the community works together—redeems itself—on an important project. Peo-ple prove they are a moral community, despite the isolation these individuals might otherwise feel. In making this claim, I am not arguing that consumers are consciously aware of these issues—they simply believe they are helping an-other. Yet, conscious motivation must be understood in its web of social con-straints. Why this rumor—when any rumor might be possible? When the be-havior of individuals points in a clear direction we can postulate an explanation, even when it is an explanation not consciously attested to (viz, Dundes 1971:22–26).

Finally, as I noted, only certain products are collected. While there may be some good pragmatic reasons for not saving other products, the range of possi-ble collections is quite large. The products that are the focus of these rumors are products of "sin," products that are outside a narrowly defined religious or moral pale: tea, soft drinks, beer, and cigarettes. I suggest it is more than just chance that rumors focus on these products. Each product is surrounded by con-troversy, and consumption may provoke guilt, at least in some consumers. By doing something good with the containers, consumers are expiating their misgivings about using these products. The harm they do to themselves is justified by the good they do for others, and perhaps in the process they have avoided self-blame. The "evil" corporations also, through their beneficence, expiate their own guilt. This underlines the fact that when we examine any corpus of mercantile legends we must explicitly consider the social and psychological meanings of the products for the consumers. Products and industries are not interchangeable, but each carries with it a set of themes, implications, nuances, and values. The fact that these redemption rumors are about a small set of products provides the key to uncovering their meaning, just as stories about prestigious products provide a key for their meanings (Fine 1985). Urban belief legends are set within both a social-psychological and an economic web of public understanding.

While my conclusions are not definitive, they have the virtue of explaining the corpus of such rumors and provide, if not a true explanation, at least a plausible one. Clearly we need other studies grounded in specific cases of this rumor—sites at which individuals are actually collecting these products—in order to bolster the large number of cases presented here with one examined ethnographically. I suggest these rumors are not malicious, but have a moral basis in a society filled with threats from the economic and the chemical environment.

Notes

This is a revision and extension of a paper presented to the Annual Meeting of the American Folklore Society, San Diego, California, October 1984. I wish to thank Walter Kost of General Mills and William Kloepfer, Jr., of the Tobacco Institute for their help in the preparation of this essay. Jan Brunvand and Simon Bronner provided helpful comments on a previous draft.

1. The material about General Mills derives from an interview with Walter Kost, retired Director of Consumer Protection Services, 2 May 1984.
2. This allowed General Mills to screen out organizations that might cause corporate embarrassment. One such group was a motorcycle gang that wished to purchase black leather jackets.
3. Since researching this article I have come across two collections of pop-can tabs—one at the University of Chicago Social Psychology Laboratory and the other at the University of Minnesota Hospital.
4. Simon Bronner reports 6 of 30 students (20%) questioned at Pennsylvania State University-Capitol Campus were aware of the rumor. Three heard it about cigarette packs, one about pop tabs, and one about beer labels.
5. Other items are occasionally mentioned in the same vein, such as Universal Product Code markings, used postage stamps, or bus tickets (Opie and Opie 1959:306–309). These rumors do not seem particularly common in the American context and do not involve corporate responsibility, so I will not discuss them in this paper. My argument

does not assume that every rumor spread will deal with a product of "sin," only that the preponderance of them do.

6. Soft drinks are also often condemned for their sugar or artificial sweeteners, and generally are thought of as "poor" sources of nutrition.

7. This is less true for soft drinks where specific companies are well known. Yet, since the tops look very similar, this belief that all can be collected makes sense as well. Sometimes it is said that the charity comes from the metal companies, such as the Aluminum Association.

8. The rumor is so plausible that some National Kidney Foundation workers are taken in. In January 1984, the executive director of the Central Washington Kidney Foundation, no doubt responding to assurance of the rumor's truth, wrote to Alcoa Aluminum asking if they would finance one hour of dialysis for each aluminum pull-tab collected.

References Cited

Alston, John A. 18 April 1974. "Officials Confirm Wrappers Worthless." *Charleston News and Courier.*

Angle, Adlee. 9 June 1974. "Cigarette Pack Hoax." *Syracuse Herald American.*

Atkinson, Clettus. 18 February 1971. "People and Things." *Birmingham Post-Herald.*

Bird, Donald A. 1976. "A Theory of Folklore in the Mass Media: Traditional Patterns in the Mass Media." *Southern Folklore Quarterly* 40:285–305.

Bowman, Russell. 1980. *Couponing and Rebates: Profit on the Dotted Line.* New York: Leibhar-Friedman Books.

Bradley, Barry. 6 January 1980. "It's Been 20 Years, But Myth Just Won't Go Away." *St. Petersburg Times.* Pp. 1-B, 7-B.

Bronikowski, Lynn. 10 April 1981. "Cigarette Pack Hoax Is Back." *Fort Walton Beach Playground News.*

Brunvand, Jan Harold. 1981. *The Vanishing Hitchhiker: American Urban Legends and Their Meanings.* New York: Norton.

Cahill, T. K. 31 October 1968. Inter-Office Memorandum. Tobacco Institute. P. 4.

Carmody, Deirdre. 20 May 1972. "A Million Cigarette Packs Collected for Sick Girl." *New York Times.* P. M27.

Clark, Thomas D. 1944. *Pills, Petticoats, and Plows.* Indianapolis: Bobbs-Merrill.

Darnton, Robert. 1975. "Writing News and Telling Stories." *Daedalus* 104:175–94.

Davis, Alec. 1967. *Package and Print: The Development of Container and Label Design.* London: Faber and Faber.

Driscoll, Thomas F. 17 October 1971. "Are You Collecting Cigarette Wrappers?" *Parade.*

Dryden, Steven. 2 March 1978. "Cigarette Packs Won't Help 'Miracle Child.'" *Lexington Dispatch.* N.C.

Dundes, Alen. 1971. "On the Psychology of Legend." In *American Folk Legend,* ed. Wayland D. Hand, 21–36. Berkeley: University of California Press.

Fine, Gary Alan. 1980. "The Kentucky Fried Rat: Legends and Modern Society." *Journal of the Folklore Institute* 17:222–43.

———. 1985. "The Goliath Effect: Mercantile Legends and Corporate Dominance." *Journal of American Folklore* 98:63–84.

Gold, Bill. 23 February 1978. "The District Line." *The Washington Post.* P. DC8. Washington, D.C.

Goody, Jack. 1982. *Culture, Cuisine and Class*. Cambridge: Cambridge University Press.

Gordon, Richard E. 6 December 1984. "Redemption Rumors: Cruel Hoax or Guilt?" *Richmond Times-Dispatch*. Pp. 1, 4.

Gusfield, Joseph. 1981. *The Culture of Public Problems*. Chicago: University of Chicago Press.

Holt, David. 31 December 1970. "Hopes as Empty as Cigarette Packs." *Louisville Courier-Journal*. P. 1.

Independent. 2 April 1972. "Hoax—One of Hundreds." P. 3-A. Kannapolis, N.C.

Kenney, Irene Gardner. 8 February 1981. "Lots of Empties: All Worthless." *Albany Times Union*. Pp. F-1, F-3. N.Y.

Klintberg, Bengt af. 1981. "Modern Migratory Legends in Oral Tradition and Daily Papers." *Scandinavian Yearbook of Folklore* 37:153–60.

Knorr, K. E. 1945. *Tin Under Control*. Stanford, Calif.: Food Research Institute.

Lipsett, Charles H. 1974. *A Hundred Years of Recycling History*. New York: Atlas.

McGrath, Mary. 1982. *Omaha World-Herald*.

Martin, Terry. 13 June 1980. "When Smoke Clears, Where's Santa?" *Monroe Enquirer Journal*. N.C.

Meredith, George and Robert P. Fried. 1977. *Incentives in Marketing*. Union, N.J.: National Premium Sales Executives Education Fund.

Morgan, Philip. 8 June 1971. "Golons Dump 100,000 Empty Packs." *Lakeland Ledger*. Pp. 1A, 7A. Fla.

National Observer. 15 April 1963. "Man of Compassion Puts a Stop to Hoax."

Opie, Iona, and Peter Opie. 1959. *The Lore and Language of Schoolchildren*. London: Oxford University Press.

O'Toole, Kathy. 12 January 1971. "Old Myth 'Burns' Altruists." *Rochester Democrat & Chronicle*. Pp. 1B, 3B. N.Y.

Pitz, Marylynne. 17 July 1978. "Boxtop Savers Discover They're Rumor Victims." *White Plains Reporter Dispatch*. N.Y.

Pope, Daniel. 1983. *The Making of Modern Advertising*. New York: Basic.

Raleigh News and Observer. 26 June 1970. "Pack Collection Found to Be Useless."

Raphael, Harold J. 1969. *Packaging: A Scientific Marketing Tool*. East Lansing: Michigan State University Book Store.

Saad, Chuck. 12 July 1974. "Empty Packages Won't Help Sick Child." *Colorado Springs Sun*.

Sessa, Cammy. 6 January 1974. "Empty Wrappers Hold Empty Hope for Medical Help." *Virginia-Pilot*. P. G1.

Skowron, Sandra. n.d. "Unlucky Strike: Cigarette Wrapper Rumor Hits Again." *Owensboro Messenger-Inquirer*. Ky.

Staunton, Evie. 30 October 1968. "Anyone Need 20,000 Wrappers?" *Sanford Herald*. P. A9. N.C.

Stewart, Sally Ann. 19 August 1983. "Sick Girl Story Just a Hoax." *Arlington Journal*. Pp. A-1, A-5. Va.

St. Paul Pioneer Press. 18 December 1970. "General Mills Quits Dialysis." P. 25.

St. Petersburg Times. 30 May 1976. "A Rumor Wrapped in Tragedy is Explained."

Troyer, Ronald J., and Gerald E. Markle. 1983. *Cigarettes: The Battle Over Smoking*. New Brunswick, N.J.: Rutgers University Press.

———. 1984. "Coffee Drinking: An Emerging Social Problem?" *Social Problems* 31 (April):403–16.

Watson, Ervin. 26 March 1980. "'Cruel Hoax' Resurfaces." *Oklahoma City Times*. P. 3.

Ziemer, Gregor. 21 April 1957. "The Ghost with the Red Band." *The New York State Lion*.

II

Redemption Rumors and the Power of Ostension

On picking my children up from school one afternoon, I noticed a container partially filled with pop-can tabs. Having previously written about this instance of contemporary folklore (Fine 1986), I was startled. While a steady stream of popular articles has continued to debunk this hardy rumor, I was amused at what people continue to believe without any grounding.

Upon questioning the teacher organizing this collection, I was assured that they were saving the tabs for the Ronald McDonald House in Minneapolis—a home for families whose children are being treated for cancer. My scoffing could not convince her that the enterprise was a fraud, a fake, "mere folklore." I promised to return with my article in the *Journal of American Folklore*—the proof of my claims—and she promised to check with the Ronald McDonald House. The next day this teacher informed me that the Ronald McDonald House was, indeed, collecting pop-can tabs, and I was given the name of the organizer of the project, Cheryl Blair, a St. Paul nurse.[1]

Here was an instance of "ostension" in action. *Ostension* refers to the process by which people act out themes or events found within folk narratives (Dégh and Vázsonyi 1983). Dégh and Vázsonyi suggest that some of the legends linked to Halloween were acted out by those who see in these narratives models of possible action. In their words, "not only can facts be turned into narratives but narratives can also be turned into facts." For instance, Ellis (1989a) contends that at least some "cult" murders may actually involve killers attempting to hide their routine homicides and misdirect police by making it appear that the victim died in an esoteric, satanic ritual. Likewise, Halloween poisonings are most likely the result of parents or other kin attempting to make it appear that strangers did the dirty work; letting folk villains take the blame for their deeds (Grider 1984). Some product tampering, such as the mouse deliberately placed in a Coors beer can, is based on people attempting to replicate the rumors that they have heard (Preston 1989). The phenomenon of "copy-cat" crimes is based on the same dynamics of ostension in which a person borrows an idea from a narrated text and then acts upon it—either claiming credit for the action or attempting to direct blame to others.

The dilemma in dealing with criminal ostension is that the actors have a well-founded justification for denying that they translated legend to behavior. By examining ostension in the context of a positive legend, a legend about corporate beneficence in redeeming pop-can tabs, I present a definitive and acknowledged instance of ostension.

Ostension and Pop-Can Tabs

In 1987 Cheryl Blair was asked to serve as the Cancer Chairman of her local Veterans of Foreign Wars post in South St. Paul. Each year this individual is supposed to organize some project to raise money in the first against cancer. Blair was employed at the time as a nurse for the University of Minnesota Hospitals and had worked with young cancer patients.

In the hospital someone had been collecting pop-can tabs, a project that she termed a "farce." No one knew who was to get the tabs and what was to be done with the money. She had heard about such projects but never their outcomes. This was the classic redemption rumor scenario. Blair decided that she would do the project correctly. She called the Minneapolis Ronald McDonald House and offered to raise money for them by recycling aluminum can tabs.[2] They agreed to assist her. The original goal was to raise a few hundred dollars, simply by collecting tabs through her contacts at the VFW.

The project ballooned beyond Blair's wildest dreams. A brochure distributed by the Ronald McDonald House in the fall of 1989 claimed that "Over 22 tons (51,246 pounds) of tabs have been collected. That's 39,100,698 tabs! Those tiny pieces of aluminum have generated $28,302.53 for the Ronald McDonald House program." When I interviewed Blair in March 1990, they had raised over $30,000—$20,000 was raised in 1989 alone. The project currently relies on fifteen volunteers.

Her project caught the attention of Minnesotans and others from neighboring states. The brochure notes: "The tabs have captured the imagination and interest of thousands of collectors. . . . It's an easy and fun task for young and old, and a great way for people across the nation to lend support to children and their families during a time of crisis in their lives." The existence of the pop-can tab legend, and the desire of people not to waste tabs that would otherwise be of no value, made it easy for the project to generate support, just as it is easy for the rumor to be believed. Blair acted out the rumor. The psychological dimension of collecting packaging from products that are perceived as harmful (Fine 1986; Mechling and Mechling 1983) is as valid in this instance of ostension as in the rumor itself. As I have previously argued, people are motivated to deny the harmful consequences of their behavior. By "doing good" with products that they recognize "do harm," consumers justify their purchases. While smokers who attempt to redeem tobacco packages for medical equipment are most overt about this, recycling pop-can tops reveals the same theme.

Just as the project played off beliefs about the rumors, Blair had to fight the skepticism of those who "knew" that the rumors were false, perhaps relying on information cited in the local newspaper from this author. Several people expressed skepticism to Blair about her collection, feeling that it was a waste of her time.[3] Indeed, she had to construct a means of translating her project to reality—building a shed in her backyard to hold the tabs until they were recycled, negotiating with companies to contribute sturdy bags, and then negotiating a suitable price for recycling (currently she receives $.48 per pound, down from $.70 per pound).[4] Perhaps the major problem with the project, aside from its increasing scale is the fact that at $.48 per pound it may cost more to process the tabs than they are worth. Those good citizens who ship her tabs, pay UPS more than $.48 per pound. It would be more economically rational to send a check, but this defeats the *emotional* context of the rumor—to do good work by participating in a community of concern. The standard claim of the rumor that the soft drink or beer companies will pay remains false, and the money is given as a general contribution to the Ronald McDonald House, not for kidney dialysis machines for particular individuals.

The success of this project demonstrates the vigor and emotional resonance of this rumor, and it further reminds us of some of the special qualities of rumors and contemporary legends that lend themselves to ostensive action. Because these narratives depict nonmagical, possible actions that are presented as topics for belief, it is relatively simply to translate them from story to action. Unlike supernatural legends or rumors, people *can* perform the actions depicted with little cost. In the case of rumors with positive themes, such as redemption rumors, there is a strong psychological motivation to do so. While few may avail themselves of this opportunity, the fact that there are people in the world like Cheryl Blair means that reality is potentially a stepchild of a rumor.

Ostension pays heed to the ability of people to model behavior on texts that have been presented to them. Not all texts will be the subject of ostensive action, but those that are deemed possible, those that fit in with cultural and personal themes, and those that engage the self-identity of a member of the folk community can be so used. Just as behavior can be the impetus for a rumor, rumor can spark a creative response that may in some way shape the world.

Notes

I wish to thank Simon Bronner, Jan Brunvand, Bill Ellis, and Molly Kleven for their help in the preparation of this manuscript.

1.   Jan Brunvand (personal communication, 1990) also confirmed that the Ronald McDonald House organizes such a program.

2. Apparently the National Kidney Foundation now encourages aluminum recycling and asks that individuals donate the proceeds to them (Ross 1990:B2), giving in to the longevity and strength of the rumor. Blair tells me that one American Legion Junior unit also attempts to raise money for the organization through pop tabs. The Hemodialysis Patients' Association of Northeastern Pennsylvania has a similar fund-raising project for dialysis patients (Ellis 1989b:10).
3. The Ronald McDonald House has a similar problem in dealing with skeptical inquiries (Brunvand, personal communication, 1990).
4. Blair receives no support from the aluminum industry or from the soft drink manufacturers, the usual benefactors in the story.

References Cited

Dégh, Linda, and Andrew Vázsonyi. 1983. "Does the Word Dog Bite? Ostensive Action: A Means of Legend-Telling." *Journal of Folklore Research* 20:5–34.
Ellis, Bill. 1989a. "Death by Folklore: Ostension, Contemporary Legend, and Murder." *Western Folklore* 48:201–20.
———. 1989b. "Redeemed After All." *FOAFtale News* 16 (December):10.
Fine, Gary Alan. 1986. "Redemption Rumors: Mercantile Legends and Corporate Beneficence." *Journal of American Folklore* 99:208–22.
Grider, Sylvia. 1984. "The Razor Blades in the Apples Syndrome." In *Perspectives on Contemporary Legend*, ed. Paul Smith, 128–40. Sheffield: Centre for English Cultural Tradition and Language.
Mechling, Elizabeth Walker, and Jay Mechling. 1983. "Sweet Talk: The Moral Rhetoric Against Sugar." *Central States Speech Journal* 34:19–32.
Preston, Michael. 1989. "The Mouse in the Coors Beer Can: Goliath Strikes Back." *FOAFtale News* 14 (June):1–3.
Ross, Robert, 1990. "It's Called a Myth That Will Not Die." *Harrisburg Patriot-News* (7 February):B1–B2.

Index